A Rich
A Poor Man's Fight

THE LIBRARY OF ALABAMA CLASSICS

A Rich Man's War, A Poor Man's Fight

DESERTION OF ALABAMA TROOPS
FROM THE CONFEDERATE ARMY

BESSIE MARTIN

With an Introduction by Mark A. Weitz

THE UNIVERSITY OF ALABAMA PRESS
Tuscaloosa and London

Copyright © 2003 University of Alabama Press
University of Alabama
Tuscaloosa, Alabama 35487-0380

Originally published 1932 by Columbia University Press

Typeface: ACaslon

Manufactured in the United States of America

∞

The paper on which this book is printed meets the minimum requirements
of American National Standard for Information Science–Permanence of
Paper for Printed Library Materials, ANSI Z39.48-1984.

Library of Congress Cataloging-in-Publication Data

Martin, Bessie, 1891–1959.
[Desertion of Alabama troops from the Confederate Army]
A rich man's war, a poor man's fight : desertion of Alabama troops
from the Confederate Army / Bessie Martin ; with an
introduction by Mark A. Weitz.

p. cm.—(The library of Alabama classics)
Originally published under title: Desertion of Alabama troops from the
Confederate Army. New York : Columbia University Press, 1932.

ISBN 0-8173-5010-1 (pbk. : alk. paper)
1. Alabama—History—Civil War, 1861–1865. 2. Desertion, Military—
Confederate States of America. 3. Confederate States of America—
History, Military. I. Weitz, Mark A., 1957– II. Title. III. Series

E551 .M25 2003
973.7'461—dc21
2002043550

British Library Cataloguing-in-Publication Data available

INTRODUCTION

Mark A. Weitz

In the years following the American Civil War, the war became one of the most written about and analyzed periods in American history. The participants wrote feverishly about their experiences, and much of their work has survived, both in diaries and in letters. It is difficult to find an aspect of the conflict that has not been thoroughly plowed, yet even within this massive body of scholarship it is possible to find neglected areas. Perhaps the most conspicuous example is military desertion.

The topic of desertion has been relegated to the back pages of history, often appearing without detail in general works. More than seventy years ago, two women devoted themselves to this topic deemed unmentionable among mainstream historians and lost-cause apologists. Even though these books came out within four years of each other, most academics, and even some among the large popular audience that consumes books on the Civil War, are aware only of Ella Lonn's 1928 work, *Desertion during the Civil War*. Few people remember, or are even aware of, Bessie Martin's study that came out in 1932. Columbia University published *Desertion of Alabama Troops from the Confederate Army: A Study in Sectionalism* (which was based on Martin's dissertation), but it languished in almost complete obscurity until 1966, when AMS reprinted it. Still, few people embraced the work, and today Lonn's work, not Martin's, is remembered.

Superlatives like *glory, duty, honor,* and *devotion* are used to describe the men and deeds of the war. The writers of Martin's day remembered the Civil War in terms of glory and self-sacrifice. Southern men confronted with overwhelming odds remained true to the sunny South until Robert E. Lee, himself virtually deified, could no longer justify the sacrifice of so many of the South's brave sons. It was a war in which those at home, despite their suffering, supported their brothers, sons, and husbands with unerring fortitude. It was not a period in which people wanted to accept either that the South broke or that the Confederacy did not enjoy total loyalty and that men did desert.

Perhaps Martin's work has been ignored because she herself was somewhat obscure. We know little about the woman who was born in Marion, Alabama, in 1891 and who wrote the only Alabama-based study of Confederate desertion. We know virtually nothing of her parents except her mother's name, Minnie Gordon Martin. Martin attended college at a time when many southern women did not, graduating from Judson College in Marion in 1911 with an A.B. She went on to receive both her M.A. and Ph.D. from Columbia University. From 1913 to 1940, Martin taught intermittently at Judson College, taking time to earn her doctorate. In 1940 she left Judson and became the librarian at Thomasville High School in Thomasville, Alabama, a position she held for nineteen years. After retiring in 1959, Judson honored her by naming a portion of its library collection the Bessie Martin Memorial Collection. The best hope of discovering more of this woman died in a 1944 fire that consumed most of Judson's alumni records.

By drawing on courts martial records, Martin arrived at a simple definition of desertion as leaving military duty with the intent not to return. She explained how this definition could give way to a large gray area that in many cases obscured what should have been obvious. Temporary absence plagued the Confederate army. Men left briefly to go home and then returned, creating definition problems. Sometimes they simply straggled. Did they desert? Intent mattered here. Deserting to the enemy was clear, but going home was less so. As the war progressed, the government and military tried to define desertion more clearly, sometimes circumventing the intent element. Joining another unit was desertion, and, regardless of why a soldier left, returning to the service did not mitigate the crime. Martin ultimately concluded that the haziness of the intent element actually increased desertion because it provided soldiers with a defense in the event they were caught or their conduct was otherwise called into question.

From definition, Martin moved into an area she called "distribution." Desertion was classified by time period, total numbers, county of deserter, and social class of deserter. Using newspapers, letters, and governors' correspondence, and the *Official Records of the Union and Confederate Armies in the War of the Rebellion,* Martin identified three "waves" of Alabama deserters and surmised that the majority of deserters came from north Alabama's mountains and the southeastern pine barrens.[1] She found desertion to be the practice of poor soldiers, and the lower socioeconomic regions of Alabama were the mountains and the pine barrens.

Having defined the problem and its statistical parameters in Alabama, Martin addressed causation. She divided cause into military/political and social/economic. Chief among the military/political causes was the unlimited duration of enlistment, altered early in the war from twelve months to the duration of the conflict. The volunteer nature of enlistment also created problems, because soldiers who were dissatisfied with service believed they had the option to quit. A related problem stemmed from the ability of individuals to choose their command. Martin argued that the combining of depleted commands, the change in officers leading a unit, and the dissolution of units were perceived as a breach of the original agreement these men made when they joined, a breach that justified their departure. Elected officers also created a military problem. Many were incompetent and unable to effectively lead their commands or deal with desertion. Martin also addressed a seldom discussed aspect of desertion—desertion directly into the Union lines and subsequent allegiance to the United States—and concluded that fewer men did this than went directly home.

Basic problems of poor food, forced conscription, inadequate supplies, and the difficulty of obtaining furloughs also contributed to desertion. Martin claimed that the government's imposition of a tax in-kind further encouraged desertion. The tax fell particularly hard on poor soldiers and their families, because soldiers had nothing to spare. The pay they received—when they were paid—was woefully inadequate to compensate for crops or livestock paid in tax. Martin also looked at the peace movement in Alabama as a political cause of desertion.

The men at war were directly affected by home-front social and economic issues. The concept "a rich man's war, a poor man's fight" figures prominently in this argument, and Martin delved deeply into it. She examined the records of the relief funds set up by the state of Alabama and administered by the counties for soldiers' families. Martin demonstrated how quickly the inhabitants of certain counties became indigent. The lack of crops and livestock left many households desperate. The lack of surplus, combined with the loss of the male labor population proved devastating. This crisis did not escape the attention of newspapers or politicians. Alabama's leadership appreciated the disastrous effect of home-front suffering on the fighting spirit of the soldiers but seemed powerless to improve the situation. Men were driven to desert by pleas from home, fear that their families would starve, and by their recognition of the government's inability to protect their homes from Unionists and federal troops.

Martin addressed Confederate efforts to control desertion and concluded that the Confederate army was unable to effectively prevent it. The most significant deterrent was giving aid to help soldiers' families, but the conspicuous failure of these efforts made it virtually impossible to prevent desertion. Punishment proved the only other course of action, but prevention was difficult due to the leniency demonstrated early in the war. It was not that desertion did not go unpunished but that, according to Robert E. Lee and others, punishment short of death was ineffective. Efforts to bring men back proved even more difficult. Laws designed to punish civilians for harboring or aiding deserters were passed, yet they also proved futile.

It is an unfortunate quirk of history that we know so little about Martin. It would be fascinating to know why she approached the topic of desertion. Aside from being a southerner, Martin was a woman, and in the old southern perception of male honor, she would have been the keeper of her husband's honor during the Civil War. Her efforts would have been expected to encourage him to fulfill his obligations to her and his country, the two in many ways being inseparable. Further, when she received her undergraduate degree in 1911, a considerable number of veterans were still living. The new South had embraced Jim Crow, and the Civil War had become a unifying symbol for a defeated people, providing an element of cohesion that did not exist during the war years. By 1915 the second Ku Klux Klan would rise (eventually growing to more than two million nationwide) and would not decline until the second world war. In bringing desertion out of the shadows, Martin certainly did not endear herself to people who saw the conflict as the American soldiers' finest hour. It was probably no accident that she wrote the book in New York, at Columbia University. There, her professors and mentors saw the topic for its historical value, stripped of the emotional baggage that attended the subject in the South.

Unfortunately, few people gave Martin's work a chance. Poor circulation attended the publication by Columbia and virtually guaranteed that the book would fall into obscurity. Had Martin's contemporaries taken the time to read this well-crafted and vigorously researched study, they would have learned of the connectedness between home and battlefield, an aspect of the war that was not being discussed at the time. For Martin, desertion was not an act of cowardice. She did not characterize deserters as traitors to country and cause. Martin recognized that desertion did occur, not by men from "another" state or county, but by Alabama soldiers—men who in another era would have been her neighbors or family. She recognized that men who deserted did so based on a rational decision predicated on several factors, the least of which was fear of dying in battle. Martin recognized that the boredom and reality of camp, the place where soldiers on both sides spent most of their time, provided the breeding ground for desertion. Martin also recognized that desertion might have been connected to wealth. "A rich man's war, a poor man's fight" always applied to the inequities of serving. Martin makes a compelling argument that it also dictated who deserted.

In many ways, Martin's work is superior to Lonn's more recognized study. Even though Lonn's study stands as an isolated monument to the study of Civil War desertion, its broad coverage of both the North and South and its emphasis on sources limit its use. The main source for Lonn's study came from the then-untapped *Official Records of the Union and Confederate Armies in the War of the Rebellion*.[2] These military records provide excellent groundwork for studying desertion, but they limited Lonn's conclusions.

Martin's work stepped beyond Lonn's in at least three important areas. First, Martin approached desertion in a regional sense. She explored the premise that where soldiers were from influenced why and when they deserted. She focused her research on Alabama, and within the study of that state she sought deeper answers to the problem of desertion. Her dissertation's subtitle, "A Study in Sectionalism," recognizes not only that "South" was not a cohesive, homogeneous entity but also that within the South's eleven states, each state possessed stark regional, cultural, and economic differences. In other words, Martin acknowledged that there was more than one "South" and more than one "Alabama," two concepts that present-day scholars put to use.

The second difference between Martin's study and Lonn's is that Martin's sources go beyond the *Official Records*. In an effort to uncover the nature of desertion among Alabama Confederate soldiers, Martin makes generous use of state and Confederate government papers, soldiers' diaries and letters, newspapers, official Alabama state records on indigent families, court records, and Union army records. One of her most striking recoveries was the report of Colonel William Fowler (commissioned by the Alabama legislature in 1863 and assembled in 1864–65) in which he tried to list, by regiment, the conduct of each Alabama soldier during the war. Unfortunately, only one part of Fowler's report survived the war: the data on the Army of Northern Virginia. The report on the Army of Tennessee, in which most Alabama soldiers served, was lost when the Confederate government fled Montgomery in the latter stages of the war. However, Martin used a variety of other sources to provide some insight into a portion of the record that was lost.

With a narrower focus and expanded sources, Martin tried to define at least a portion of the desertion problem by tying incidents of desertion to particular soldiers from particular parts of the state over specific periods of the war. In order to do this, Martin's study takes on aspects of quantitative history, a field virtually unknown at the time she published her work—a fact that might be at least partially responsible for the obscurity of her book. Writing history with the aid of statistics is an accepted and legitimate part of current scholarship, but it lacked professional recognition in the 1930s. Quantitative history is sometimes still perceived as dry and uninteresting recitation of information, lacking the storytelling attributes of narrative.

While Martin's effort never received the attention it deserved, this historian owes her a deep debt of gratitude. As a graduate student in 1995, I seized on desertion as my dissertation topic. The absence of any significant literature in this area made it an appealing choice; however, the lack of sources made it an equally difficult subject to tackle. In the course of reviewing secondary materials I came across Martin's book. As I searched through her bibliography, I discovered that between 1863 and 1865 the

Union army compiled a written record of all Confederate soldiers who deserted into Union lines, swore the oath of allegiance, and then returned home. It took me almost six months to find the present-day repository, the *Register of Confederate Deserters,* but the discovery was worth the effort.[3] This Union record provided the basis for my study of desertion among Georgia soldiers.[4] Equally important, Martin's bibliography served as a guide for the types of sources that could unlock answers to my questions on desertion. Desertion remains virtually unexplored, and Martin's efforts from seventy years ago still provide invaluable assistance to contemporary historians.

No book is perfect, and Martin's is certainly no exception. But its shortcomings do not deter from its usefulness both as history and as a tool for further study. The most glaring shortcoming is probably her attempt to identify exact numbers. While Martin's analysis of the periods when desertion was most prevalent is specific to Alabama soldiers, her data on the total number of deserters are less specific to Alabama and tend to be broad army numbers or total Confederacy figures. To arrive at numbers for Alabama, she attempted to extrapolate. Martin's efforts reveal how difficult it is to precisely define the numerical extent of Confederate desertion. Standard figures, derived from congressional documents at the close of the war, put Alabama desertion at almost 1,600. Those same numbers indicate that more than 5,500 men deserted and returned.[5] Martin starts with 104,000, the standard number for all the Confederate armies and then uses estimates of what fraction of the army was listed as "absent," estimates of the number who returned, contemporary observations, and the numbers in Fowler's report of the Army of Northern Virginia. Using this methodology allowed Martin to conclude that 10,000 to 20,000 Alabama deserters went directly home. However, even she had to admit hard numbers were tough to come by, and she could only safely say, "To the total number of deserters, whatever it was, contributions were made from every county."

Using estimates and contemporary observations is an obvious problem. Observers could not generally gauge numbers, just
size or impact. In the process of trying to arrive at a number,
Martin says something very important about the issue of specific
figures: range may be all that is important. The real questions
become Did desertion damage the Confederacy? and If so, how?
She hinted at the harm it caused, but neither she nor anyone
else has ever squarely addressed this question. Broader works
on the war certainly suggest that desertion was a problem, but
there has been no real attempt to say why. Statistics or numbers
do not in and of themselves illuminate this issue. If we assume
that the desertion figure of 104,000 is correct, then roughly 12
percent of the 850,000 men who served in the Confederate army
deserted.[6] Given the South's lack of resources—human and otherwise—it could be debated that the loss of men at any level
hurt the war effort. However, what Martin's book implies is
that regardless of the precise numbers, the problem did hurt the
Confederacy. It remains for contemporary historians to answer
the question as to what effect desertion had on the ability of the
Confederacy to wage war. Was it just a nuisance, or did it cripple
the southern war effort? As scholars probe an area still fraught
with social and cultural stigma, they can take comfort in not
having to wander in the wilderness. Seventy years ago Bessie
Martin helped carve out a narrow but discernable trail for those
who would one day follow. I know, I walked it.

NOTES

1. Bessie Martin, *Desertion of Alabama Troops from the Confederate
Army: A Study in Sectionalism* (New York: Columbia University Press,
1932; reprint, New York: AMS, 1966), 26–27. Martin claims Alabama troop desertion increased steadily over the course of the war.
The first wave was from February 1862 to February 1863, the second
from June 1863 to April 1864, and the third from August 1864 to
April 1865.

2. Ella Lonn, *Desertion during the Civil War* (Gloucester, Mass.: American Historical Association, 1928; reprint, Lincoln: University of Nebraska Press, 1998), xiii, 237.

3. *Register of Confederate Deserters, 1863–65,* Books 1 and 2, Microfilm Group M598, Roll 8, NARA. This record was compiled by the Union army as part of its policy to encourage Confederate desertion. It lists deserters by name, rank, unit, state, county, the date they took the oath of allegiance, and the place they were released from service. In limited instances the record lists the date and place of desertion. Unlike the War Department Collection of Confederate Records (NARA RG 109) in which, over the course of one thousand rolls of microfilm, men are listed sometimes as deserters and sometimes as AWOL and in which when dates are given they are sometimes contradictory, the *Register of Confederate Deserters* provides a concise collection of men whose intent was unmistakable. It contains more than 30,000 names, almost one-third of the 104,000 generally accepted as the Confederate desertion number.

4. Mark A. Weitz, *A Higher Duty: Desertion among Georgia Troops during the Civil War* (Lincoln: University of Nebraska Press, 2000).

5. See Lonn, *Desertion during the Civil War,* 231–32.

6. James McPherson, *Ordeal by Fire: The Civil War and Reconstruction,* 2nd ed. (New York: McGraw Hill, 1992), 184. McPherson conceded that exact numbers for the Confederate army are not known. Confederate records were lost or poorly kept, and Union records counted enlistments, which may not have accounted for the reenlistment of the same man. Thus many of the problems that impede an accurate count of Confederate deserters also hinder efforts to determine how many men actually fought in the war.

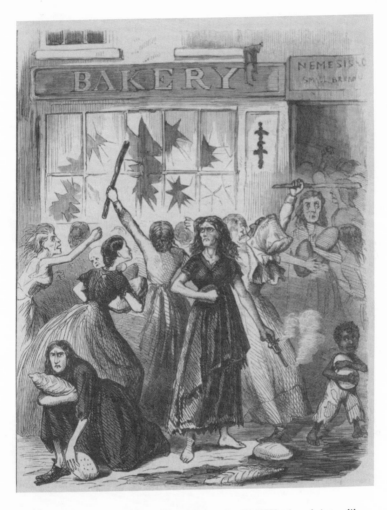

As civilian poverty became prevalent during the Civil War, bread riots—like the Virginia bread riot depicted above—erupted in Alabama. (*Frank Leslie's Illustrated Newspaper,* May 23, 1863)

DESERTION OF ALABAMA TROOPS FROM THE CONFEDERATE ARMY

A STUDY IN SECTIONALISM

BY

BESSIE MARTIN, Ph.D.

Professor of History in Judson College
Marion, Alabama

To

My Mother

MINNIE GORDON MARTIN

PREFACE

THIS study presents a phase of war which cannot be glorified, though it has its heroic aspects, and emphasizes a topic of military history which has been generally ignored. Desertion of Alabama troops in the Civil War was a manifestation of sectionalism in the state, due largely to the prevalence of poverty. Since similar conditions existed in the other parts of the South, desertion persisted as a dangerous weakness of the Confederate States and was one of the factors in the failure of their "war for independence."

In the preparation of this work, I have found a course on the social and economic bearings of the Civil War given by Professor William E. Dodd of Chicago University a helpful background. For the use of materials and for other courtesies, special thanks are due the publishers of the Mobile *Register* and of the Montgomery *Advertiser,* the Adjutant-General of the War Department and officials of the Confederate Section of the Old Records Division, and the authorities and staffs of the Mobile Public Library, of the Library of Congress, of the Library of Columbia University, and of the Alabama State Department of Archives and History. I am under obligation to Dr. C. P. Denman, former Professor of History in Baylor College, for the loan of the outline map, which was made from Colton's *Alabama, 1859* (Library of Congress), and to Mr. Peter A. Brannon, Curator of the Alabama State Department of Archives and History, for critical suggestions about the materials and the subject-matter of Alabama history.

Among those whose interest in this study I shall remember with appreciation are Dr. Thomas P. Martin, Acting-Chief of the Manuscripts Division of the Library of Congress, and Miss Mabel Bower, Associate-Professor of Philosophy in Judson College.

Above all, I am under deepest obligations to Professor David Saville Muzzey of Columbia University, under whose direction this study has been made. His standards of thoroughness; accuracy and fairness, his inspiring interest and stimulating criticism have been invaluable.

BESSIE MARTIN.

JUDSON COLLEGE, 1932.

CONTENTS

9

MAPS

11

CHAPTER I

DEFINITION OF DESERTION

DESERTION was denounced by Confederate authorities as one of the highest military crimes, a combination of perjury, cowardice and treachery.[1] By desertion the soldier violated the oath which he had taken upon enlistment, promising faithful service to the Confederate States and obedience to its officers according to the *Rules and Articles of War*.[2] He abandoned the flag of his country. He betrayed his comrades in arms, imposing increased hardships upon them by his refusal to do his duty toward the common cause. Under military law, desertion was punishable by death.[3] Although military authorities frequently described the gravity of the crime, they seldom made any statements approaching a definition of it. From the practice of courts-martial, desertion may be defined as the crime of leaving the military service without permission and without intention to return to it.[4] Thus, the elements of desertion were the act, leaving the military service without permission, and

[1] Mobile *Register and Advertiser*, June 26, 1863, quoting General Polk; *The Governor's Letter Book*, July 21, 1863, p. 172, to Brigadier-General Forney; *General Orders* no. 55, April 9, 1863, Department and Army of Northern Virginia; *General Orders* no. 33, April 13, 1864, Headquarters of the Army of Tennessee.

[2] *The Statutes at Large of the Confederate States of America* (Richmond, 1864), vol. i, p. 62, sec. vi; *Rules and Articles of War for the Government of the Army of the Confederate States of America* (Atlanta, 1861), art. x.

[3] *Rules and Articles of War*, art. xx.

[4] *General Orders* no. 35, March 2, 1863, Headquarters of the Department of South Carolina, Georgia and Florida, by Beauregard; *General Orders* no. 16, February 12, 1864, Department and Army of Northern Virginia, by Lee.

13

the motive, the intention not to return to it. Military service included work to which soldiers were detailed in arsenals and other factories producing supplies for the army
as well as service in the field.[5] The act of leaving such
service with the intention to return to it was the offense of
absence without leave.[6] The act of desertion and the act
of absence without leave were identical. The distinguishing
difference between them lay in the motives, *animus manendi*
and *animus revertendi*.[7]

It was difficult to determine the motives for absence except in cases of desertion to the enemy. Going to the enemy
was an overt act which established proof of the intention
not to return.[8] But a majority of those who left the army
did not go to the enemy; they went home.[9] Going home
was not an act which established proof of the intention not
to return to the army. Most of the absentees, it was generally believed, intended to return after they had enjoyed a
visit or attended to some business at home.[10] Some ab-

[5] Selma *Daily Reporter*, September 21, 1863; *Official Record of the
War of the Rebellion* (Washington, 1880-1901), ser. iv, vol. ii, p. 78;
E. F. Falconnet, enrolling officer, to Governor Watts, August 22, 1864;
Montgomery *Weekly Advertiser*, September 23, 1863, and Selma *Reporter*,
October 23, 1863, advertisements; *G. O.* no. 75, January 1, 1863, Dept.
of S. C., Ga. and Fla.

[6] *G. O.* no. 60, April 21, 1863, Dept. of S. C., Ga. and Fla.

[7] *G. O.* no. 16, February 12, 1864, Dept. and Army of Nor. Va.; *G. O.*
no. 60, April 21, 1863, Dept. of S. C., Ga. and Fla.; Memphis *Daily
Appeal*, April 21, 1864, a letter from a judge advocate of a military court;
Richmond *Examiner*, September 11, 1863.

[8] *The Governor's Letter Book*, July 21, 1862, p. 172; *Records of
Alabama Commands*, compiled by company officers under the direction
of Colonel Fowler, Superintendent of Army Records for the State of
Alabama, *passim*. Cited later as *Fowler Reports*.

[9] *O. R.*, ser. i, vol. xlvi, pt. ii, p. 1265; pt. iii, pp. 1353-1356.

[10] *Clarke County Journal*, October 13, 1864, Proclamation by Governor
Watts; *O. R.*, ser. iv, vol. ii, p. 688, Proclamation by President Davis;
Richmond *Examiner*, November 25, 1864, quotation of a speech made in
Congress by Mr. Miles of South Carolina.

sentees were doubtless uncertain about their own intentions. In order to relieve the military courts of some of the difficulty of determining motives, a bill was introduced into the Congress of the Confederate States in 1865 proposing to declare reputation *prima facie* evidence of desertion but the bill failed to pass.[11] Uusally, soldiers, charged by courts-martial with desertion, plead guilty of absence without leave — not desertion — and produced evidence designed to prove their intention to return to their commands. Examples of this kind of evidence were declarations made by the accused before or during absence of his intention to return; credentials of his reliable character; statements of conditions which required his presence at home, the most urgent of which were the necessity of providing support for his family and the need of aiding them in sickness or death; and affidavits of his voluntary return to his command.[12] Although General Lee insisted that voluntary return was no test of desertion, the courts usually accepted it as proof of the intention not to desert, and, on the other hand, regarded arrest as a presumption in favor of guilt though not a proof of it.[13] As it was usually very difficult for soldiers to secure furloughs,[14] the courts recognized " extenuating or mitigat-

[11] Richmond *Examiner,* February 3, 1865. Introduced by Mr. Semmes of the Judiciary Committee of the Senate, January 30, 1865.

[12] *G. O.* no. 98, 1862, Dept. and Army of Nor. Va.; *Proceedings of Courts-martial,* Headquarters of the District of Mississippi and East Louisiana, January 4, March 20 and 24, and June 15, 1864, in cases of Alabama soldiers.

[13] *G. O.* no. 137, 1862; *G. O.* no. 28, February 27, 1863; *G. O.* no. 3, January 8, 1864, Department and Army of Northern Virginia; Memphis *Appeal,* April 21, 1864. See the *Fowler Reports* for the same view held by company commanders.

[14] *General Orders* no. 1, January 1, 1862 and no. 16, March 24, 1862; *General Orders* no. 135, October 15 1863, Adjutant and Inspector-General's Office; J. B. Gordon, *Reminiscences of the Civil War* (New York, 1903), p. 384; W. H. Taylor, *Four Years with General Lee* (New York, 1878), p. 145; Mobile *Register,* November 27, 1863.

ing circumstances " causing absence which made the soldier not guilty of desertion, but guilty of absence without leave.[15]

There was no relation between the length of absence and the motive of absence. Proposals were made by newspaper editors for legislation defining desertion in terms of a certain number of days of absence without leave,[16] but probably such difficulties as variation in distance between the residences of soldiers and their commands and difference in facilities of transportation made such a definition impracticable. However, an approach to a definition of desertion in terms of length of absence was made by military authorities in orders to absentees from their commands to return "immediately" or within a specified number of days— from four to twenty—or else be accounted deserters. Such orders were issued to various Alabama commands on an average of one every other month.[17] The only one of them which attempted to fix a general rule of action was an order

[15] *General Orders* no. 69, no. 98 and no. 120, 1862; *G. O.* no. 19, no. 62, no. 66 and no. 100, 1863; *G. O.* no. 16, 1864, Department and Army of Northern Virginia; *G. O.* no. 19, 1862; *G. O.* no. 29, no. 50 and no. 190, 1863; *G. O.* no. 6, no. 7, no. 8, no. 12 and no. 42, 1864, Headquarters of the Army of Tennessee; *G. O.* no. 114 and no. 123, 1863, Department of South Carolina, Georgia and Florida. For an exception, see *G. O.* no. 71, 1863, Hdqrs. of Army of Tenn. For examples of promotion after return, see *Fowler Reports*, 15th Regiment, Company 1 and 4th Regiment, Company D.

[16]Mobile *Register*, January 12, 1864. See also Richmond *Examiner*, September 4, 1863.

[17] *O. R.*, ser. iv, vol. i, p. 1120; Selma *Reporter*, February 22 and August 16, 1862; *O. R.*, ser. iv, vol. ii, pp. 214-215; Mobile *Register*, December 11, 1862; Montgomery *Daily Advertiser*, December 14, 1862; *Clarke County Journal*, February 5, 1863; Selma *Reporter*, January 27, 1863; Montgomery *Daily Advertiser*, March 8, 1863; Jacksonville *Republican*, March 12, 1863; Montgomery *Weekly Advertiser*, July 29, 1863; *Democratic Watchtower*, September 30, 1863; Jacksonville *Republican*, January 30, 1864; *Democratic Watchtower*, February 3, 1864; Montgomery *Daily Mail*, September 1, 1864; *Democratic Watchtower*, October 11, 1864.

of General Bragg issued January 28, 1863, declaring that from that time on any soldier who failed to give within seven days satisfactory explanation of his absence would be considered a deserter.[18] But this order had no more effect than the others. It is probable that these orders, which may have seemed at times to originate in the caprice of an officer, tended to obscure the meaning of desertion. The proceedings of courts-martial also show no relation between length of absence and motive of absence. Five soldiers from Alabama after an absence of three days were convicted of desertion and sentenced to death; another soldier from Alabama after an absence of eighteen months was acquitted of desertion, convicted of absence without leave and sentenced to undergo a trifling penalty.[19] Between these extremes, many other cases show that the courts acted upon other evidence than length of absence.[20] Beauregard, Bragg and Lee declared that absence during a whole campaign should be regarded by the courts as proof of intention to desert,[21] but the courts did not adopt their view.

[18] *General Orders* no. 13, January 28, 1863, Headquarters of the Army of Tennessee.

[19] *General Orders* no. 28, April 2, 1864, Hdqrs. of the Army of Tenn. In this case, General Johnston appealed to President Davis for remission of the death penalty because of the meritorious service of four brothers of one of the condemned men and of one brother of another of the condemned men. *General Orders* no. 3, January 8, 1864, Department and Army of Northern Virginia. In this case, the general commanding protested against the light sentence.

[20] *General Orders*, Department and Army of Northern Virginia, Headquarters of the Army of Tennessee, and Department of South Carolina, Georgia and Florida, *passim*. For examples, see *General Orders* no. 98 and no. 137, 1862; no. 28, 1863; no. 1 and no. 2, 1865, Dept. and Army of Nor. Va.; G. O. no. 94, 1863, Hdqrs. of the Army of Tenn.

[21] G. O. no. 75, June 1, 1863, Dept. of S. C., Ga. and Fla., by Beauregard; G. O. no. 50, Hdqrs. of A. of Tenn., Mar. 9, 1863, by Bragg; G. O. no. 64, May 18, 1863 and G. O. no. 3, January 8, 1864, Dept. and Army of Nor. Va., by Lee.

Company records showed no uniformity of practice by officers in determining the length of time which should elapse before absence without leave should be marked desertion.[22] Sometimes absentees were "dropped" by order of the officer commanding the brigade or by order of the War Department and reckoned with deserters, but usually it was left to the discretion of regimental and company officers to determine the time when absence became desertion. Regimental and company officers were reluctant to make this decision, because, aside from a desire for good standing of their commands, they were uncertain as to the motives back of absence. Knowing that sickness, wounds, occupation of territory by the enemy, or other causes prevented the return of some absentees,[23] they usually gave the benefit of doubt to all. The result was leniency. Some Alabama deserters were carried on the rolls marked " absent without leave " from eighteen to thirty months and then not dropped as deserters.[24] Since the motive, not the act, determined desertion, military authorities could use no general objective test of the crime, but had to make an examination into motives of each individual accused of desertion. It was natural that the public should be less discriminating in applying subjective tests than military authorities and, conse-

[22] *Fowler Reports* and miscellaneous records of Alabama commands, *passim.*

[23] Johnson Hagood, *Memoirs of the War of Secession* (Columbia, 1910), p. 318; D. S. Freeman, *Lee's Dispatches* (New York, 1915), no. 84, p. 157.

[24] *Fowler Reports*, Ninth Regiment, Company C, Company E, Company F and Company K; Forty-fourth Regiment, Company H, Company I and Company K; Forty-eighth Regiment, Company C, Company D, Company E and Company I. An example of extreme caution was the marking of several soldiers absent without leave and lying out in the woods for over two years.—*Fowler Reports,* Forty-fourth Regiment, Company K. On the other hand, some absentees may have been marked deserters who were only technically deserters.

quently, should feel some uncertainty about what constituted desertion.

This uncertainty was increased by certain conflicting interpretations of the connotation of desertion. According to the *Articles of War*, a soldier's enlisting in a company without discharge from his former company was "reputed" desertion.[25] But military authorities did not agree on the meaning of this statement. One said that this kind of desertion had had pernicious effects on the army; another said that the practice was almost as injurious as the crime of desertion.[26] Orders by command of General Lee bore the following conflicting opinions: (1) "Joining another command is the crime of desertion as defined by the 22nd Article of War" and (2) "This though a crime of such gravity that the same penalty is affixed to it as desertion is not desertion, but abandonment of the service of the Confederate States."[27] Although directions for judge advocates of military courts, approved by the Secretary of War, classified this act as desertion, the courts sometimes preferred two charges, "Desertion" and "Enlisting in another command without a proper discharge from his former command," and usually imposed lighter sentences upon soldiers convicted of enlisting in a command without a proper discharge.[28] The company officers of commands of Alabama infantry quite uniformly marked this act deser-

[25] *Rules and Articles of War*, art. xxii. See also *O. R.*, ser. iv, vol. ii, p. 401.

[26] *G. O.* no. 17, February 18, 1864, Headquarters of the Army of Tennessee, by Johnston; *O. R.*, ser. i, vol. xlvi, pt. ii, pp. 1230-1231, by Lee.

[27] *G. O.* no. 16, February 12, 1864 and *G. O.* no. 71, June 14, 1863, Department and Army of Northern Virginia.

[28] *G. O.* no. 42, April 26, 1864, Hdqrs. of Army of Tenn.; *G. O.* no. 7, January 19, 1864 and *G. O.* no. 16, February 12, 1864, Dept. and Army of Nor. Va.; *G. O.* no. 51, March 31, 1863 and *G. O.* no. 109, December 26, 1863, Dept. of S. C., Ga. and Fla.

tion, but some officers, although forbidden under heavy penalty to do so, received soldiers from other commands and even actively recruited them.[29]   On the whole, military authorities considered enlisting in another command without a discharge from a former one desertion. It is doubtful whether the public did. Many civilians and soldiers believed that the act was not desertion nor any other crime.[30]

Another act which might be included under desertion was evasion of military service by those liable to conscription. According to law, military orders, and executive proclamation, this act was desertion. In the conscription act of April 16, 1862, Congress declared that conscripts enrolled in the reserves who refused to obey the call to service should be considered deserters.[31]   In a call issued in July of the next year, extending the age limits of conscription, the President declared that those who refused to obey the call to service should be considered deserters.[32]   By General Orders no. 82, September, 1862, the War Department went a step further, stating that conscripts who failed " to repair to the place of rendezvous for enrollment " should be considered deserters.[33]   These orders were repeated in Alabama

[29] *Fowler Reports* and other records of Alabama commands, *passim*; Freeman, *Lee's Dispatches*, no. 73, pp. 131-132; J. S. Mosby, *Mosby's War Reminiscences* (New York, 1898), pp. 98-100; *O. R.*, ser. iv, vol. iii, p. 255.

[30] Mobile *Register*, November 8, 1862; *G. O.* no. 17, February 18, 1864, Hdqrs. of the Army of Tenn.; *O. R.*, ser. iv, vol. ii, pp. 774-776.

[31] *O. R.*, ser. iv, vol. i, p. 1096.

[32] *O. R.*, ser. iv. vol. ii, p. 635.

[33] *O. R.*, ser. iv, vol. ii, p. 168, *G. O.* no. 82, sec. xiii. " Mr. Wigfall said that by the passage of the conscription act, every male in the Confederacy between the ages of 18 and 45 was *ipso facto, eo instante*, a soldier, and when now found traveling about, the presumption was fair that he was a deserter." (August 27, 1862)—*Southern Historical Society Papers*, vol. vii, " Proceedings of the Congress of the Confederate States of America, First Congress, Second Session," p. 252. The conscription

in 1863 and 1864.[34] But, according to a decision of the Confederate States district court in south Alabama rendered in 1864, a conscript before enrollment, or enlistment, was not a soldier subject to the *Rules and Articles of War*, and so could not be a deserter.[35] Of more significance than this decision was the treatment accorded by military authorities to conscripts after arrest. Conscripts were placed immediately in military service; they were not turned over to courts for trial and punishment.[36] In their correspondence, military authorities implied a distinction between the two classes by usually employing both terms, " deserters " and " conscripts." [37] In popular parlance, conscripts who evaded service—most often by hiding in the woods—were called " moss-backs." [38] In law, then, conscripts who evaded service were usually considered deserters, but in practice, they were treated as a separate class.

A similar condition existed in the case of abandonment

act of February 17, 1864 appeared at first to be subject to even more drastic construction.—*O. R.,* ser. iv. vol. iii, pp. 178-181; D. Appleton and Company, *Annual Cyclopedia,* 1864 (New York, 1865), p. 231.

[34] Jacksonville *Republican,* August 15, 1863, orders to conscripts; *Democratic Watchtower,* May 18, 1864, orders to conscripts.

[35] Montgomery *Weekly Advertiser,* July 27, 1864, direct quotation of the decision. For a similar decision by a Georgia court, see the Mobile *Register,* June 7, 1863. In 1864, the Supreme Court of Alabama declared that every man liable to military service under the conscription laws was "constructively in the army as a conscript."—39 *Alabama Reports,* 1864, p. 459. February 26, 1864, General Grant stated that in his opinion no wholesale conscription act could cover as deserters persons who escaped into Union lines before they had been sworn into the Confederate Army.—*O. R.,* ser. ii, vol. vi, p. 991.

[36] Montgomery *Weekly Advertiser,* August 12, 1863, instructions from General Pillow.

[37] *O. R.,* ser. i, vol. xxxviii, pt. iv, p. 657; *O. R.,* ser. iv, vol. ii, pp. 675-678, pp. 680, 754, 805, 819-820.

[38] W. L. Fleming, *Civil War and Reconstruction in Alabama* (Cleveland, 1911), p. 113.

of military service by an officer. According to the *Articles of War*, "All officers and soldiers who have received pay, or have been duly enlisted in the service of the Confederate States and shall be convicted of having deserted the same shall suffer death or other such punishment as by sentence of court-martial shall be inflicted." [39] However a military officer declared that there was no such offence known to the *Articles of War* as desertion by an officer. [40] For the most part, military courts concurred in his opinion and charged officers who had left the service with absence without leave or with conduct to the prejudice of good order and military discipline. [41] The board to relieve the army of incompetent officers could recommend after investigation that an officer for absence without leave be "dropped by order of the War Department." [42] Officers who were "dropped" for absence without leave were sometimes included with deserters in reports of Alabama commands. [43] Officers who went home were usually called absentees; those who went to the enemy were regularly called deserters.

The term "desertion" was popularly used to cover any one, or all three, of the offences against military discipline known as "absence without leave," "straggling," and "skulking." [44] A newspaper editor after a climactic enumeration of the offenders, "absentees without leave, stragglers, deserters, and skulkers," said, "What is the due of

[39] Article xx.

[40] *G. O.* no. 141, June 24, 1863, Hdqrs. of the Army of Tenn.

[41] *G. O.* no. 7, January 21, 1863 and *G. O.* no. 48, March 26, 1863, Dept. and Army of Nor. Va.; *G. O.* no. 44, April 28, 1864 and *G. O.* no. 6, March 27, 1865, Hdqrs. of the Army of Tenn.

[42] *O. R.*, ser. iv, vol. ii, pp. 205-206, Oct. 13, 1862.

[43] *Fowler Reports, passim.*

[44] Richmond *Examiner*, February 13, 1863 and September 11, 1863; *Southern Punch*, September 19, 1863; Montgomery *Daily Advertiser*, February 24, 1864; *Fowler Reports*, Fourth Regiment, Company D.

those wretches who straggle to rob and beg, who are visible here, there and everywhere except in their companies when the roll is called? . . . Their name is deserter." [45] " Absence without leave " or " absenteeism " and " straggling " were polite terms, found even in military correspondence, for desertion.[46] " Absence without leave " and " straggling " were usually interchangeable terms.[47] However, in strict usage, " straggling " meant falling out of line on a march or in battle without intention of leaving the service.[48] It is probable that a certain soldier expressed the opinion of many when he rather cynically explained that the difference between absence without leave, straggling and desertion lay in the humor of the officer when the soldier without a pass was presented under arrest to him.[49] Skulking was avoiding military service by fraud.[50] It was practiced both by soldiers and by evaders of the conscription laws. The most frequently used methods were securing forged papers of paroles, furloughs, exemptions and contracts; collusion with medical boards for exemption or with subordinate military officers for assignment to easy details; and pretending disability after expiration of a furlough or

[45] Richmond *Examiner*, August 7, 1863.

[46] E. A. Pollard, *Southern History of the War* (New York, 1866), vol. ii, p. 516; *O. R.*, ser. iv. vol. ii, pp. 798 and 830; *O. R.*, ser. iv, vol. iii, p. 224; Montgomery *Daily Mail*, March 4, 1863 (General Pillow).

[47] *O. R.*, ser. i, vol. xxxiii, pt. iii, pp. 824-825; ser. iv, vol. ii, pp. 963-964.

[48] *G. O.* no. 100, November 20, 1863 and *G. O.* no. 105, December 7, 1863, Dept. and Army of Nor. Va.; *G. O.* no. 19, December 19, 1862, Hdqrs. of the Army of Tenn.; *Muster Roll*, Twenty-second Regiment, Company H, June 30–December 31, 1862; *Orderly Book*, Forty-first Regiment, Company A; Mobile *Register*, May 31, 1863.

[49] Union Springs *Times*, June 20, 1866, Major R. H. Powell, "The Third Alabama Infantry."

[50] Mobile *Register*, January 3, 1864; *O. R.*, ser. i, vol. xvii, pt. ii, pp. 791-792; ser. iv, vol. iii, p. 977.

just before a battle.[51]   A rarely used method was self-mutilation.[52]   A colloquial term used in Alabama for desertion was "outlying," coined to indicate the habit of deserters of hiding in the woods.[53]

Desertion was used often to include toryism, but was not identical with it.   While both might be technically called treason, desertion was primarily a military crime and toryism was primarily a political crime.   Toryism has been defined as rebellion against the authority of the Confederate States.   Some tories were conscripts who evaded service or who, if pressed into service, became deserters; others were deserters and conscripts who became tories after they were liable to conscription.   But some tories were not liable to conscription and many deserters wished that the Confederate States would win the war—without their help.[54]

Thus, distinctions between desertion and enlisting in another company without discharge from a former company, evasion of conscription, abandonment of military service by an officer, absence without leave, straggling, skulking and toryism were not generally agreed upon in Alabama.

[51] Hagood, *Memoirs*, p. 318; Memphis *Daily Appeal,* October 12, 1864, a letter from B. H. Hill, Senator from Georgia.

[52] *Fowler Reports*, Thirteenth Regiment, Company K; Fifteenth Regiment, Company A; Forty-sixth Regiment, Company A; *G. O.* no. 92, October 7, 1863, Department and Army of Northern Virginia; K. Cumming, *A Journal of Hospital Life* (New Orleans, 1866), p. 137; Hagood, *Memoirs*, pp. 286-287.

[53] E. B. Smith to Governor Watts, April 18, 1864; Jos. D. McCain to Governor Watts, August 20, 1864; Nancy Twilbey to Governor Watts, November 7, 1864; Josiah Jones to Governor Watts, March 20, 1865.

[54] Fleming, *Civil War and Reconstruction in Alabama*, pp. 113-114; A. T. Goodloe, *Confederate Echoes* (Nashville, 1907), p. 345; Memphis *Daily Appeal*, October 25, 1864.   In popular speech, "deserter" and "tory" were often used interchangeably.   For example, see Thos. Armstrong to Gov. Shorter, July 2, 1863 and Montgomery *Weekly Advertiser,* May 25, 1864.

In this study of desertion of Alabama troops from the Confederate army, the use of the word "desertion" reflects the varied interpretations placed upon it during the war. The uncertainty of the meaning of desertion had the effect of encouraging desertion. It was a protection against ill-will of the public and against severe treatment by military authorities. The fact that desertion was distinguished from absence without leave, a comparatively minor offence, only by the motive gave to deserters the benefit of doubt as to their status and, further, offered a good chance of escape from conviction for crime.

Deserters from Alabama troops were divided into two classes: (1) deserters who went home or to some other place in the Confederate States and (2) deserters who went to the enemy. The first class was much larger than the second.[55] The following chapters on distribution of deserters, causes for desertion, and efforts to check desertion deal chiefly with deserters who went home; the seventh chapter deals with deserters who went to the enemy; and the concluding chapter with both classes of deserters.

[55] *O. R.*, ser. i, vol. xlvi, pt. ii, p. 596, "Their testimony is that many more go to their own homes than come within our lines."—General Grant; *O. R.*, ser. i, vol. xlvi, pt. ii, p. 1265, "Most of these men are supposed to have gone to their homes, but a number have deserted to the enemy." —General Lee. *Cf. infra*, p. 41.

CHAPTER II

DISTRIBUTION OF DESERTERS

DISTRIBUTION of deserters may be studied by time, by number, by counties, and by classes of soldiers.

Desertions of Alabama troops occurred from the beginning to the end of the war in increasing volume. They occurred in three great waves, each higher than the preceding. These waves covered the following periods of time:

(1) February, 1862 – February, 1863 [1]
(2) June, 1863 – April, 1864 [2]
(3) August, 1864 – April, 1865. [3]

[1] O. R., ser. i, vol. xix, pt. ii, pp. 597-598, 622-623, 639; vol. xvii, pt. ii, p. 622; vol. xx, pt. ii, p. 407; Advertisements in Alabama newspapers for deserters each month of this period except February and October, 1862; Dunbar Rowland, *Jefferson Davis, Constitutionalist* (Jackson, 1923), vol. v, pp. 377, 378; Colonel James W. Jackson (47th Alabama) to his wife, September 21, 1862; Captain J. E. Hall (59th Alabama) to his sister, December 6, 1862; Montgomery *Weekly Mail*, July 11, 1862; Selma *Reporter*, August 25, 1862, quoting the Lynchburg *Republican;* Mobile *Register and Advertiser*, October 19, November 21, 1862; Selma *Reporter*, January 27, February 5, 1863; W. L. Fleming, *Civil War and Reconstruction in Alabama*, p. 98; William Polk, *Leonidas Polk, Bishop and General* (Boston, 1915), vol. ii, p. 117; E. A. Pollard, *Life of Jefferson Davis* (Atlanta, 1869), p. 210.

[2] O. R., ser. i, vol. xxix, pp. 806-807; vol. lii, pt. ii, p. 496; ser. iv. vol. ii, p. 618; ser. iv, vol. iii, pp. 68, 69; Advertisements in Alabama newspapers for deserters; Crenshaw Hall to his father, June 4, 1863; Bolling Hall to his sister, June 3, 1863; Mobile *Register*, June 26, 1863; Richmond *Daily Examiner*, August 8, 1863, quoting the Columbus *Sun;* Polk, *Leonidas Polk*, vol. ii, p. 228; Pollard, *Life of Jefferson Davis*, pp. 325-326; *Democratic Watchtower*, September 16, 1863.

[3] O. R., ser. i, vol. xlii, pp. 1175-1176, 1182-1183, 1213; U. S. Grant, *Personal Memoirs of U. S. Grant* (New York, 1885-1886), vol. ii, pp. 426,

The troughs covered: (1) 1861 – January, 1862,[4] (2) March, April and May, 1863,[5] and (3) May, June and July, 1864.[6] The first wave reached its highest crest in July, 1862 or in the fall of 1862;[7] the second, in July and August, 1863.[8] The third wave mounted steadily from August, 1864 to the end of the war with a slight subsidence in February.[9] The upward movement of these waves of de-

480; U. S. Grant, *Letters to a Friend* (New York, 1897), p. 38; *Letter Book of the Commandant of Conscripts of the State of Alabama*, p. 333; J. B. Jones, *A Rebel War Clerk's Diary* (Philadelphia, 1866), vol. ii, p. 302; Memphis *Daily Appeal*, September 28, 1864; Selma *Reporter*, September 14, 1864; J. B. Hood, *Advance and Retreat* (New Orleans, 1880), pp. 71-72; Pollard, *Life of Jefferson Davis*, p. 384; J. F. Rhodes, *A History of the United States since the Compromise of 1850* (New York, 1928), vol. v, p. 78. For additional references for these periods of desertion, see *infra*, pp. 29-37.

[4] Mobile *Register*, March 20, 1863. The absence of references in the contemporary records is the best reference for this statement. For example, there were no advertisements for deserters in Alabama newspapers and no correspondence in the *Official Records* on the subject of desertion during this period.

[5] Mobile *Register*, April 23 and 25, 1863; Montgomery *Daily Advertiser*, February 3, 1864. During these three months, comparatively few references to desertion are found in contemporary records.

[6] *O. R.*, ser. iv. vol. iii, pp. 326-327; *MS Returns of General Johnston's Army*, December 10, 1863, April 30, 1864; J. E. Hall to his sister, June 5, 1864; Polk, *Leonidas Polk*, vol. ii, pp. 365, 366; Montgomery *Weekly Advertiser*, February 28 and August 7, 1864; Mobile *Register*, March 24 and March 29, 1864; Rhodes, *History of the United States*, vol. v, p. 384.

[7] *Governor's Letter Book*, July, 1862, p. 174; *O. R.*, ser. iv, vol. ii, p. 7; Grant, *Memoirs*, vol. i, p. 317; *O. R.*, ser. i, vol. xix, pt. ii, pp. 597-598; vol. xvii, pt. ii, p. 622; vol. xx, pt. ii, p. 407; J. E. Hall to his sister, December 6, 1862; Advertisements in Alabama newspapers for deserters.

[8] *O. R.*, ser. iv, vol. ii, pp. 636-639, pp. 722-723, 786; ser. i, vol. xxix, pt. ii, pp. 649, 651; Advertisements in Alabama newspapers for deserters.

[9] *O. R.*, ser. i, vol, xlii, pt. ii, pp. 1175-1176, 1182-1183; pt. iii, p. 1213; vol. xlv, pt. ii, p. 775; J. E. Hall to his father, February 8, 1865, Hagood, *Memoirs*, pp. 365-367. It may have been no accident that desertions in-

sertion may be seen in the field returns of the absent from the army in spite of the fact that these returns include both the absent with leave and the absent without leave:

Date	Aggregate number present and absent	Percentage absent
December 31, 1861	326,768	28
June 30, 1862	328,049	31
December 31, 1862	449,439	32
April 30, 1863	498,169	27
June 30, 1863	473,058	35
December 31, 1863	464,646	40
June 30, 1864	315,847	38
December 31, 1864	400,787	51
Latest, 1865	358,692	44 [10]

The difficulties in determining the number of deserters from Alabama troops are great. First, Confederate records are incomplete. In the confusion at the end of the war, some records were lost through accident, like part of the archives of the Army of Northern Virginia, which was burned; others were lost through the efforts of officials or other persons to hide them safely.[11] During the war, some records were not fully kept. For example, the Bureau of Conscription complained that for the last six months of 1863 they received no reports of the conscription service in

creased during summer, because the soldiers knew that at that season they could travel homeward with greater ease and security and that at that season, if they stayed in the army, they would have to take part in harder campaigns.

[10] *O. R.*, ser. iv, vol. i, p. 822; vol. i, p. 1176; vol. ii, p. 278; vol. ii, p. 530; vol. ii, p. 615; vol. ii, p. 1073; vol. iii, p. 520; vol. iii, p. 989; vol. iii, p. 1182. These periods of desertion reflect the operation of the causes for desertion analyzed in Chapters III and IV.

[11] *Southern Historical Society Papers*, vol. vi, G. L. Christian, "General Lee's Headquarters Records and Papers." For example, *The Letter Book of the Commandant of Conscripts of the State of Alabama*, 1864, was recently received by the Alabama Archives from private hands. I have not been able to find out the fate of the *Alabama Deserter Book*.

Alabama, which was engaged in the business of catching deserters, and during 1864, the commandant of conscripts in Alabama was continually urging his subordinates to send in reports of absentees and deserters.[12] Other records were made in such a way as to give little information about the total number of soldiers absent, both with leave, including absent sick, wounded, furloughed and detailed, and without leave, including absent captured and absent at home.[13] Again, the estimates of the number of deserters may be exaggerated as they were usually made by citizens who feared depredations of deserters or who advocated the return of deserters instead of further extension of conscription or by officials who accompanied their reports with requests for larger forces to deal with deserters. Finally, references to the number of deserters reflect the variations in interpretation of the meaning of desertion. At one time, estimates may be made of the number of deserters and absentees; at another, of the number of deserters and tory conscripts or of the number of men evading service. In view of these difficulties, quotations will be the most effective, as well as the safest, method to suggest the number of deserters during each period of desertion and during the whole war.

In June, 1862, the Secretary of War wrote a circular letter to the governors asking for help in dealing with desertion and saying, " Our armies are so much weakened by desertion and by absence of officers and men without leave that we are unable to reap the fruits of victory and invade the territory of the enemy." [14] In reply to this letter, the Governor of Alabama asserted, " The evil com-

---

[12] *O. R.*, ser. iv, vol. iii, p. 100; *Letter Book of the Commandant of Conscripts*, pp. 140-145, 147-148, 178, 181. See also *O. R.*, ser. iv. vol. ii, p. 1059 (neglect and accidents of war).

[13] For example, see *O. R.*, ser. i, vol. xxxiii, p. 1173.

[14] *O. R.*, ser. iv, vol. ii, p. 7.

plained of is dangerous and growing more widespread continually." [15]   In the fall of that year President Davis sent
a similar circular letter to the governors, asking their cooperation in dealing with desertion.[16]   In the fall, the commanders of both of the great armies complained of straggling.   Bragg announced " with pain the shameful fact that
numerous officers and soldiers are absent from the army
without leave or sanction " and reported to the War Department, " Our armies are gradually but certainly melting
away whilst we are getting no reinforcements, no recruits
and cannot see a source from which they are to come.
Some of my regiments are down to 100 privates for
duty." [17]   Lee wrote to President Davis that the main cause
for his retreat from Maryland was the fact that the army
was greatly decreased by desertion and straggling and to
Secretary Randolph that the absent were scattered broadcast over the land.[18]   During 1862 and during January
and February, 1863, several hundred deserters from Alabama commands were advertised for in various newspapers
of the state.   The largest number advertised for in any one
month was about 200.[19]

[15] *Governor's Letter Book*, July 23, 1862, p. 174.

[16] Rowland, *Jefferson Davis, Constitutionalist,* vol. v. pp. 377-388.

[17] *O. R.*, ser. i, vol. xx, pt. ii, pp. 407, 386 (November 3, 1862).

[18] *O. R.*, ser. i, vol. xix, pt. ii, pp. 622-623; vol. xvii, pt. ii, p. 622
(September 23, 1862).   See also: *O. R.*, ser. i, vol. xix, pt. i, p. 1413;
pt. ii, pp. 633, 640, 597-598, 624-625.

[19] December, 1862.   Mobile *Register and Advertiser,* February 10, April
1, May 7, June 12, June 26, July 6, August 29, September 7, November 7,
21, 29, December 2, 10, 12, 28, 1862; January 3, 11, 14, 25, 28, February 21,
1863; Jacksonville *Republican,* February 19, 26, 1863; Selma *Reporter,*
June 2, 1862; February 6, 1862; *Democratic Watchtower,* January 6, 13,
1863; Montgomery *Daily Advertiser,* January 14, February 18, 1863;
Clarke County Journal, February 5, 1863.   These advertisements do not
include a singular general advertisement, headed " Brand them Deep, Dye
them Black " and signed " Captain and Provost-marshal Army of the
West, Tupelo, Miss." for 12 car loads of deserters (480) who left Tupelo
on September 11.—Mobile *Register and Advertiser,* September 17, 1862.

According to field returns, the Confederate army reached its maximum strength in the spring of 1863, having then the largest enrollment and the smallest percentage of absentees.[20] But in June, the Acting-Chief of the Bureau of Conscription declared that desertion was " on the increase." [21] And, in July, the Assistant Secretary of War spoke of " the crime of desertion, if so general a habit can be called a crime," and estimated the number of men evading service at from 50,000 to 100,000, of whom from 40,000 to 50,000 were absent without leave.[22] At the same time General Pillow, who was in charge of conscription in Alabama, Mississippi and Tennessee, reported to the War Department that there were " from 8,000 to 10,000 deserters and tory conscripts in the mountains of north Alabama, many of whom had deserted the second, third, and fourth (some of them) time." [23] After a few weeks' campaign against these deserters and tories, he reported the number to be from 6,000 to 8,000, " so many that shooting them appears to be out of the question." [24] In his report of November, 1863, the Secretary of War stated that the effective force of the army was generally a little over a half but never two-thirds of the enrollment and that it might be safely assumed that " one-third of our army on an average are absent from their posts and may with due efforts be

[20] *O. R.,* ser. iv. vol. ii, p. 530, April 30, 1863.

[21] *O. R.,* ser. iv, vol. ii, pp. 607-608, June 24. See also *O. R.,* ser. iv, vol. ii, p. 618.

[22] *O. R.,* ser. iv, vol. ii, p. 674. The Secretary of War wrote December 31, 1863, " The arrest and return of all absentees and deserters without leave from this army amounting this day to so frightful a percentage that it may not be prudent to express a conjecture . . . "—*O. R.,* ser. iv, vol. ii, p. 1070.

[23] *O. R.,* ser. iv, vol. ii, pp. 680-681, 741-743, July 28 and August .23. See also *ibid.,* p. 639.

[24] *O. R.,* ser. iv, vol. ii, pp. 819-820, September 21, pp. 853-854, October 5.

returned." [25]   In a letter to the War Department, Pillow
said that one-half of the Armies of Mississippi and of
Tennessee were absentees and deserters, and added that he
spoke from the field returns of those armies and therefore
accurately.[26]   The field returns from the Army of Tennessee dated December 10, 1863 showed that the effective
total present was 44% of the enrollment.[27]   The statement
of the Secretary of War was widely quoted and commented
upon.   Smith of North Carolina said in Congress that of
the 400,000 men on the muster rolls, probably 200,000 were
absent.[28]   Senator Hill of Georgia in a speech at Macon
said that about 60% of Bragg's army were absent and
almost as many of Lee's; " they are wearing the uniform
and receiving the pay, but they are spending their time on
railroad trains, at hotels, at the houses of unsuspecting
kindness in the country and taking pleasure rides and walks
with thoughtless women." [29]   The Charleston *Mercury* estimated the number of absentees, deserters, and soldiers detailed to catch deserters and to do other work at 200,000.[30]
The newspapers of Alabama stated that 200,000 soldiers
were absentees and deserters.[31]   The Jacksonville *Repub-*

[25] *O. R.*, ser. iv, vol. ii, p. 995, November 26.

[26] *O. R.*, ser. iv, vol. ii, p. 820, September 21.

[27] *Field Returns.*

[28] Appleton, *Annual Cyclopedia*, 1863, p. 18.

[29] Jacksonville *Republican*, December 19, 1863, quoting the Macon
Telegraph, November 30.   The Macon *Telegraph* pointed out Senator
Hill's omission of officers who left the army in order to shine in legis-
lative halls.—Mobile *Register*, December 9, 1863.

[30] Montgomery *Daily Mail*, January 13, 1864; *Alabama Beacon*, January 22, 1864.

[31] Montgomery *Weekly Mail*, January 6, 1864; Montgomery *Daily Mail*,
January 3, January 7, 1864.   See also: Montgomery *Daily Mail*, September 2, 1863; *Alabama Beacon*, January 22, 1864; Selma *Reporter*, January 27, 1864; Mobile *Register*, December 2, 1863; January 3, January 5,

lican, referring to Senator Hill's charge, said that it was confidently asserted and not contradicted that 60% of Bragg's army were absent.[32] The Mobile *Register and Advertiser* printed a letter from a correspondent, stating that 200,000 men had evaded military service by fraud and that he would give the names of 300 of them living in Mobile.[33] The Greensboro *Alabama Beacon* quoted a correspondent of a Georgia paper, " We venture to say that there are more men able to bear arms traveling today on the railroad from Montgomery to Augusta than on any corresponding day in 1860." [34] The editor of the Mobile *Register and Advertiser* quoted the opinion of a traveler in the Confederacy that there were as many soldiers out of camps as in them and concluded, " this statement agrees with reports from all quarters and from the Secretary of War." [35] Although these statements of the number of deserters and absentees made no distinction between absence with leave and absence without leave, they indicated agreement with President Davis's statement that desertion was " a frightful evil." [36] The number of deserters and absentees in north Mississippi and north Alabama was considered so large by Confederate authorities that in April, 1864, General Polk directed a campaign against them and returned several thousand soldiers to the army.[37] However, three officers engaged in the campaign in northwest Alabama re-

January 7, 1864. " . . . the Richmond *Enquirer's* declaration of one-half absent may be dismissed as a wild newspaper guess."—E. Lonn, *Desertion during the Civil War* (New York, 1928), pp. 29-30.

[32] Jacksonville *Republican,* January 9, 1864.

[33] Mobile *Register,* January 9, 1864.

[34] *Alabama Beacon,* July 31, 1863.

[35] Mobile *Register,* January 13, 1864.

[36] *O. R.,* ser. iv, vol. iii, p. 369, February 4, 1864.

[37] *O. R.,* ser. i, vol. xxxii, pt. iii, pp. 855-856, 824-825.

ported to General Polk that the force of tories and deserters there had been exaggerated.[38]

Because of this campaign and because of other reasons, desertions of Alabama troops decreased for a few months, but they increased again in a general swell of desertions of Confederate troops, beginning the latter part of July and lasting to the end of the war. In August, 1864, General Grant wrote to a friend that the Confederate army was losing, aside from the toll of battles, at least a regiment a day by desertion and other causes.[39] This estimate included both classes of deserters and probably was made in terms of Confederate regiments, which had been reduced by the casualties of war to a small fraction of their original size.[40] However, Confederate sources give evidence of the fact that the number of desertions during the third period was large. It was reported in Richmond that about 72,000 soldiers had deserted from the armies east of the Mississippi river from October 1, 1864 to February 4, 1865.[41] During this period, General Lee wrote frequently to the War Department of " the alarming number " of desertions and expressed "painful apprehensions about the future." [42] The Chief of the Bureau of Conscription reported March 4,

[38] *O. R.*, ser. i, vol. xxxii, pt. iii, pp. 853, 859, 860.

[39] Grant, *Letters to a Friend* (E. B. Washburne), August 16, p. 38.

[40] W. C. Oates, *The War between the Union and the Confederacy* (New York, 1905), p. 429. For example, on March 23, 1864, the 18th Alabama regiment numbered 92, present and absent.—Report of troops reënlisted, March 23, 1864. The returns of General Johnston's army for January, 1865 showed that the 19th, 22nd, 25th, 39th and 50th regiments each mustered from 119 to 194 men.

[41] Appleton, *Annual Cyclopedia*, 1865, p. 188.

[42] *O. R.*, ser. i, vol. xlvi, pt. ii, p. 1143 (January 27, 1865), p. 1254 (February 24, 1865), p. 1258; vol. xlii, pt. ii, pp. 1175-1176 (August 14, 1864), pt. iii, p. 1213 (November 14, 1864) ; vol. xlvi, pt. iii, pp. 1353-1356 (March 27, 1865).

1865, over 100,000 deserters and absentees scattered over the Confederacy.[43] The Assistant Secretary of War thought that this estimate was too high but acknowledged on March 5, 1865 that desertions had been frequent during the whole season and that the morale of the army was "somewhat impaired."[44] The Secretary of the Navy on April 24, 1865 cited as evidence of the apathy of the people "the vast army of deserters and absentees from our military service during the past twelve months."[45] On November 30, 1864, the commandant of conscripts for Alabama reported that there had been recorded in the "Deserter Book" in the office at Montgomery since April the names of 7,994 deserters and absentees from Alabama regiments in the Army of Tennessee and the Army of Northern Virginia. He reported that 4,323 of these had been returned, leaving 3,671 still absent in the state. He stated that since returns from the Army of Tennessee had not been received for two months and since reports of increase in desertion came from all sides, it could be safely said that there were 6,000 deserters and absentees then out in the state.[46] January 15, 1865, a judge from southeast Alabama wrote to the Attorney-General of Alabama that the number of deserters in that section of the state, including those on the Florida line, was about 2,000.[47]

On a trip to the lower South in the fall of 1864, President Davis urged the necessity of the return of absentees to the army. According to newspaper reports, he said in a speech at Macon on September 30, "Two-thirds of our

[43] *O. R.*, ser. iv, vol. ii, p. 674.

[44] J. A. Campbell, *Reminiscences and Documents relating to the Civil War in 1865* (Baltimore, 1887), pp. 27-30.

[45] Rowland, *Jefferson Davis, Constitutionalist*, vol. vi, p. 574.

[46] *O. R.*, ser. iv, vol. iii, pp. 880-881 (H. C. Lockhart).

[47] *O. R.*, ser. iv, vol. iii, p. 1044 (Judge Yelverton).

army are absent, some sick, some wounded, but most of them absent without leave," and added that if one-half of the absentees from Hood's army would return to the field, Sherman would be driven from Georgia.[48]   This speech aroused a storm of criticism. The Montgomery *Mail* called it " a harangue."[49]   The Richmond correspondent of the Memphis *Appeal* wrote that the Richmond *Enquirer*, which usually supported the President, considered his admission about absentees worth an army to the enemy.[50]   The *Appeal* accepted the statements as authoritative but called the utterance that if one-half of the absentees from General Hood's army would return, Sherman would be driven from Georgia " the foulest stigma cast upon Confederate soldiery."[51] Senator Orr of South Carolina attacked the speech in the Senate and Senator Hill of Georgia replied that the President had not been correctly quoted, that he had said that two-thirds of the Army of Tennessee were absent, many without leave. But Senator Orr said that the people had understood the President to mean that a majority of the absentees were without leave and that no matter which he had said, the speech was the most unfortunate ever made by a public man.[52]   Such criticism probably reflected more hostility to the President than doubt of the truth of his statements.   However, in other addresses made at Montgomery, Columbus, Augusta and Columbia, President Davis

[48] Memphis *Appeal*, September 26, 1864, quoting the Macon *Daily Telegraph*; Rowland, *Jefferson Davis, Constitutionalist*, vol. vi, pp. 341-344, quoting the *Daily Enquirer*, September 29, 1864.

[49] Montgomery *Daily Mail*, September 27, 1864.

[50] Memphis *Appeal*, September 26, 1864; October 7, 1864. The Richmond correspondent added his opinion that the President should keep his temper.

[51] Memphis *Appeal*, October 7, 1864.

[52] Richmond *Examiner*, February 4, 1865. See also: Appleton, *Annual Cyclopedia*, 1864, p. 206; Montgomery *Daily Advertiser*, October 3, 1864.

did not repeat the statement that one-third of the army was absent without leave, though in each of these addresses he said that if one-half of the absentees from Hood's army would return, Sherman could be driven out of Georgia.[53] Probably, if he did not make the statement at Macon that one-third of the army was absent without leave, he thought denial of it unnecessary, or if he did make it, he thought repetition of it indiscreet. It was probably accurate in the case of the Army of Tennessee, if not of the whole army. The field returns of the Army of Tennessee dated July 10, 1864 showed that the effective force was about 40% of the enrollment and that the absentees without leave, exclusive of prisoners of war, were about one-third of the total number of absentees.[54] The field returns of the armies dated December 31, 1864 showed that the effective force of the Army of Tennessee was 25% of the enrollment and that the effective force of the whole army was 38% of the enrollment.[55]

After Lee's surrender, Johnston's army, as its commander said, " melted like snow before the sun." [56] The other armies, in spite of the efforts of officers to prevent them, did likewise.[57] Since the war was really, if not technically,

[53] Memphis *Appeal*, September 30, 1864 (Montgomery) ; Montgomery *Daily Mail*, October 4, 1864, quoting the Columbus *Enquirer*; Memphis *Appeal*, October 7, 1864, quoting the *Constitutionalist* (Augusta) ; Rowland, *Jefferson Davis, Constitutionalist*, vol. vi, p. 349, quoting the Charleston *Daily Courier* (Columbia).

[54] MS returns.

[55] *O. R.*, ser. iv, vol. iii, p. 989.

[56] F. H. Alfriend, *The Life of Jefferson Davis* (Richmond, 1868), p. 624.

[57] Hagood, *Memoirs*, pp. 370-372; L. C. Daniel, *Confederate Scrap Book* (Richmond, 1893), p. 3, Magruder's Address, May 25, 1865; p. 5, E. K. Smith's Farewell, May 30, 1865.

ended on April 9, soldiers who left the service after that date have not been included in this study of desertion.

The total number of Alabama soldiers who left the army and went home may be suggested in four ways: (1) by estimates of the fraction of the army absent, (2) by partial reports of the number of deserters returned from the state to the army, (3) by estimates made by observers of the total number of Alabama soldiers absent at various times, and (4) by records of Alabama commands in the Army of Northern Virginia made by Colonel Fowler. The estimates of the fraction of the army which was absent without leave vary with sources and with time but in the absence of other information about an average rate, they are suggestive. In 1901 Colonel Oates of the Twenty-sixth Alabama Regiment expressed the opinion, which he later considered too conservative, that from 5% to 10% of the Confederate soldiers were absent without leave when the war closed.[58] On July 10, 1864, the field returns of the Army of Tennessee showed that about one-sixth of that army was absent without leave.[59] One-tenth and one-sixth of the total number of troops furnished by Alabama to the Confederate army, at least 90,000,[60] represent estimates of the total number of absentees, respectively, 9,000 and 15,000.

Reports of the number of deserters returned from Alabama, though definite, covered only 14 months and counted the deserter each time he was returned. The reports were: October, 1863, 511; January, 1864, 853; February, 1864 to February, 1865, 5,055;[61] total, 6,419. The report for

[58] Oates, *The War between the Union and the Confederacy*, p. 430.

[59] MS Field Returns.

[60] *O. R.*, ser. iv. vol. iii, p. 102; MS Report of the Adjutant-General to the Governor, October 31, 1864; Fleming, *Civil War and Reconstruction*, pp. 78-80.

[61] *O. R.*, ser. iv, vol. ii, pp. 963-964; vol. iii, p. 362, p. 1109.

October, 1863 also gave the number of absentees and stragglers returned, 4,461. Thus, the total number of deserters and absentees reported returned from Alabama was 10,899. But they were only part of the absentees. According to Colonel Livermore, [62] muster rolls of " a considerable portion of Confederate regiments," including 1 battalion and 20 regiments from Alabama, averaging about two years, record 104,428 deserters, of whom 21,056, or about one-fifth, were returned. General Pillow sent about one-third of the deserters and tory conscripts in north Alabama to the army and Colonel Lockhart about two-fifths of the deserters and absentees in 1864. If one-third of the deserters from Alabama were returned, or about 4,461, the total number of deserters was about 19,000.

Estimates of the number of absentees in the state made by observers at various times often overlap or fail to meet each other. The chief official estimates are those of General Pillow in the summer of 1863 and Colonel Lockhart in the fall of 1864. General Pillow's estimate of 8,000 to 10,000 deserters and tory conscripts in north Alabama included some deserters from other states but the number from other states in Alabama was probably balanced by the number from Alabama in Mississippi and Florida.[63] Of the deserters reported by General Pillow, about 3,000 were returned from north Alabama before Colonel Lockhart's report for April 1 – November 30, 1864.[64] According to his report,[65] the number of Alabama soldiers who had left

[62] T. L. Livermore, *Numbers and Losses in the Civil War* (Boston, 1901), pp. 5, 7.

[63] *O. R.*, ser. iv, vol. ii, pp. 741-743; Montgomery *Daily Advertiser*, November 11, 1863; Macon *Beacon*, May 18, 1864; Mobile *Register*, March 22, 1864; Fleming, *Civil War and Reconstruction*, p. 117.

[64] *O. R.*, ser. iv. vol. ii, pp. 741-743, 819-820, 963-964; vol. iii, p. 362; Montgomery *Daily Advertiser*, November 11, 1863.

[65] *O. R.*, ser. iv, vol. iii, pp. 880-881.

their commands during this period was 7,994, of whom
4,323 had been returned to the army, and the number who
were still out in the state was at least 6,000, a total of over
10,000. If the rate of leaving the army for the eight
months preceding November 30, about 1,000 a month, continued till the close of the war, the total number of absentees
and deserters was about 14,000. However, it is probable
that during the last four months of the war some of the
4,000 absentees who were returned under Lockhart's administration deserted again. But it is possible that some of
the 3,000 deserters who were returned under Pillow's administration remained in the army, and it is practically
certain that the rate of leaving the army was higher after
than before November 30.[66] In view of these considera-
tions, the total number may remain 14,000 or 15,000. By
a synthesis of about fifty estimates made during the war by
officials and observers and later by other persons familiar
with conditions at that time, Professor Fleming has made
estimates of the total number of deserters, tories and " conscripts " in southeast Alabama as 2,000 or 2,500, and in
north Alabama as 8,000 or 10,000, and characterized his
estimates as " rather too small than too large." [67]

Colonel Fowler, Superintendent of Army Records for
Alabama, reported from the records made under his supervision by company and regimental officers in the field that
the total number of " permanent " deserters from Alabama
troops in the Army of Northern Virginia from the beginning of the war to January 1, 1865 was a little over 1,800,
or 6% of the aggregate enrollment.[68] If the rate were the

[66] *Supra*, pp. 34-37.

[67] Fleming, *Civil War and Reconstruction*, pp. 128-129.

[68] *Publications of the Alabama Historical Society Transactions*, 1897-
1898, vol. ii, pp. 190-191, " Recapitulation of Alabama Troops in the

same for all Alabama troops, the total number was 5,400. Colonel Fowler's report of deserters included both deserters who went home and deserters who went to the enemy. It did not include absentees without leave, but was accompanied by a report of "absent captured" and of "absent otherwise." As part of the records upon which Colonel Fowler based his recapitulation of Alabama troops in the Army of Northern Virginia has been lost, it is impossible to determine exactly the number in each class of deserters and the number in each class of "absent otherwise." However, estimates may be made from a little over one-third of his records of Alabama troops in the Army of Northern Virginia, complete in manuscript form of the Fourth, Ninth, Tenth, Eleventh, Thirteenth, Forty-fourth, Forty-eighth, Sixtieth and Sixty-first regiments of Alabama infantry from the date of organization of each regiment to January 1, 1865.[69] According to these records, the number of "permanent" deserters and absentees without leave from these regiments was 9% of their aggregate enrollment and the number of deserters who went to the enemy was 15% of the deserters and absentees without leave. If the rates were the same for all Alabama troops, the total number of deserters and absentees without leave was 8,100, of whom 6,900 went home and 1,215 went to the enemy. It is probable, however, that the rate of desertion from Alabama troops as a whole for the entire war was higher than 6% or 9%. The rate of desertion in the Army of Northern Virginia was probably lower than the rate of desertion in other armies because its morale remained relatively higher. The rate of desertion in the Army of Northern Virginia

Army of Northern Virginia, February 1, 1865." The date should be January 1, 1865, according to the manuscript records collected in the Archives at Montgomery.

[69] *Fowler Reports.*

DESERTERS, 1861 - 1865......▨
Mountain counties............................x
Black belt counties...........................+
(includes 4 partly in belt)

itself increased after the Fowler records closed, January 1, 1865.[70] The number of deserters to the enemy thus estimated from the Fowler records was much smaller than the number reported in Federal records for the war.[71] Thus 6,900 " permanent " deserters and absentees is a very conservative estimate of the total number of deserters and absentees who went home.

The most probable number lies somewhere between 10,-000 and 20,000.

To the total number of deserters, whatever it was, contributions were made by every county in the state but these contributions were not made evenly. Distribution by counties of deserters who returned to their homes showed concentration in two sections of the state, the northern and the southeastern. The northern section in which deserters collected lay between the Tennessee valley and the black belt and embraced parts of six counties and all of eighteen counties, thus forming an area not far from half the size of the state. This section is hilly and mountainous. The Appalachian range extends from Georgia westward over at least nine of the counties of 1860, and slopes to the Tennessee valley on the north, to the state of Mississippi on the west and more gradually to the black belt on the south. For convenience, it may be divided into two parts, (1) the hill and mountain counties lying south of the Tennessee valley and (2) the hill counties lying between the mountain counties and the black belt. The former part was described by Governor Shorter as a "mountain country sparsely populated and difficult of communication." [72] In 1863 this country was said by the Governor to be full of deserters from the Army of Tennessee and by General Pillow to

[70] *Supra*, pp. 34-37.

[71] *Infra*, pp. 236-237.

[72] *Governor's Letter Book*, July 28, 1863, p. 56.

shelter securely thousands of deserters and tory conscripts in its mountain fastnesses.[73]   In 1864, six counties in the northwest were the objective of a special expedition against deserters.[74]   According to reports of officers of this expedition, Franklin county, which lies south of the Tennessee river and next to Mississippi, contained numerous deserters in its poor southern hills; Marion county, which lies south of Franklin, numerous deserters in its mountains; and Fayette county, which lies south of Marion, about 250 or 300 deserters hiding in the woods in small squads.[75]   According to reports of officers of this expedition, Winston and Walker were favorite resorts of deserters, who found security in the mountain fastnesses, containing " cliffs so abrupt that nothing but a mountain deer or a goat would attempt to scale them "; and Jefferson, which adjoins Walker, was a shelter for numerous squads of deserters concealed in mountains almost inaccessible to cavalry.[76]   According to popular reports in 1863, Winston contained 200 deserters and Walker, 250 to 300.[77]   Five of these counties, Franklin, Marion,

---

[73] *Ibid.*; *O. R.*, ser. i, vol. lii, pt. ii, p. 496.   See also: *Governor's Letter Book*, June 26, 1863, p. 40; *O. R.*, ser. iv. vol. ii, pp. 636-639, 680-681, 741-743, 819-820.

[74] *O. R.*, ser. i, vol. xxxii, pt. iii, pp. 666-667, 855-856.

[75] *O. R.*, ser. i, vol. xxxii, pt. iii, pp. 683-684, 859, 864, 860.   It was reported that deserters were hidden in the caves as well as in the hills and mountains of Franklin county.—Montgomery *Daily Advertiser*, May 25, 1864.

[76] *O. R.*, ser. i, vol. xxxii, pt. iii, pp. 853, 859.

[77] Nelson Fennell to Governor Shorter, June 28, 1863.   Captain Fennell of the Morgan county rangers reported that he had been driven from the mountains of Winston before superior numbers of deserters who had every advantage in position and who were wild and wary from living in the woods.   Montgomery *Weekly Advertiser*, September 2, 1863, quoting the Fayette *Sentinel*.   A candidate who canvassed Walker county was told by a party of deserters that the county contained this number of deserters and that they feared no danger whatever.

Fayette, Winston and Walker, and three other counties, Lawrence and Morgan, hill counties south of the Tennessee river, and Blount, a mountain county south of Morgan, were called by General Roddey in a letter to the state legislature, " harborers of the disaffected, tories, and deserters." [78] The mountain counties in the northeast were harborers of the same groups and furnished as safe hiding places for them as the northwestern counties.[79] In 1863 Marshall, DeKalb, Cherokee and St. Clair were named by Governor Shorter as the counties in north Alabama most in need of a cavalry force to arrest deserters in the mountains and at the same time St. Clair and "adjoining counties" were said by General Clayton to contain large numbers of deserters banded together.[80] According to various estimates, St. Clair county contained from 200 to 400 deserters and tories, who were audacious outlaws.[81] Calhoun county, which is south of Cherokee and also next to Georgia, contained a good many deserters but very few tories lying

[78] P. D. Roddey to Messrs. Sykes and Clark, October 10, 1863. For the statement that parts of Winston, Walker, Marion, Franklin and Lawrence were filled with Lincolnites and were being impoverished by cavalry pretending to catch deserters, see David Hubbard to Governor Watts, December 19, 1863.

[79] J. W. Jones to Governor Shorter, February 4, 1863; *Governor's Letter Book*, July 24, 1863, p. 55; Col. Bush Jones (9th Ala. Battn.) to Governor Shorter, July 16, 1863.

[80] *Governor's Letter Book*, June 23, 1863, p. 37; H. D. Clayton to Governor Watts, July 16, 1863; For Cherokee, see also *Governor's Letter Book*, June 9, 1863, p. 31.

[81] *Governor's Letter Book*, May 18, 1863, p. 7; Capt. Thos. E. Barr to Governor Shorter, Jan. 10, 1863; Col. Bush Jones to Governor Shorter, July 16, 1863; E. J. Kirksey to Governor Shorter, July —, 1863; *Governor's Letter Book*, July 24, 1863, p. 55; Montgomery *Weekly Mail*, September 23, 1863, quoting the Asheville *Vidette;* *Southwestern Baptist*, March 30, 1865.

quietly in its mountains.[82]   The counties of Alabama in which deserters and tories offered most serious resistance to military service were named in 1864 by the commandant of conscripts from west to east, thus: Monroe (Marion?), Walker, Fayette, Winston, Lawrence, Blount, Marshall, DeKalb, Cherokee, and St. Clair.[83]

South of the mountain counties, two rows of counties,— from east to west, Randolph, Talladega, Shelby, Bibb and Tuscaloosa and, from west to east, northwest Perry, north Autauga, Coosa, Tallapoosa and north Chambers, — contained deserters in their hills.   In 1862, Randolph county so alarmed Confederate authorities by threats of resistance to compulsory military service that at Governor Shorter's request a battalion of cavalry was ordered by the Secretary of War to the county to suppress disaffection, enforce the conscription law, and arrest deserters.[84]   In 1863, according to a newspaper report, the number of deserters in the county had reached 400 and the next year, according to reports from a militia officer, the number was increasing rapidly.[85] Talladega county contained a good many deserters in its hills, which in places were so high that they were like mountains and everywhere so densely wooded that after deserters got warning of the approach of cavalry, in the words

[82] Jacksonville *Republican*, December 19, 1863; William Bean to Governor Watts, March 25, 1864; Meade H. Jackson to Governor Watts, March 24, 1865; Fleming, *Civil War and Reconstruction*, p. 110.

[83] *Letter Book of the Commandant of Conscripts*, p. 344, to Major Duffield, A. A. G., B. of C.

[84] *O. R.,* ser. iv. vol. ii, p. 258.

[85] Montgomery *Weekly Mail*, October 21, 1863, quoting the Columbus *Times*; Jefferson Faulkner to Adj.-Gen. H. P. Watson, November 1, 1864. Captain Faulkner also said that a squad of fifteen deserters who had just arrived in the county told him that the woods would soon be full of deserters and that they did not intend to be taken. But Captain Faulkner thought that with his five companies of militia he would give a good account of some of them.

of a militia officer, "you would as soon catch a flea." [86]
In September, 1864, Shelby county contained in the north
deserters, from whom a private at home on furlough requested permission from the Governor to raise a company
of 100 or 200, and in the south deserters, 75 or 100 of
whom a militia officer reported to be banded together.[87]
An indication of the number of deserters in the county was
the report of the militia dated March 4, 1865, "notwith-
standing within the last three weeks we have got in from
the woods over 100 deserters, still there is more." [88] The
hills near the black belt contained fewer deserters than the
hills near the mountains. From Bibb county, the deputy
sheriff reported an organization of over 50 deserters who
defied the civil authority of the county.[89] From Tuscaloosa
county, some citizens petitioned the Governor for help, saying that tories and deserters were very troublesome in that
county.[90] From Perry county, some citizens reported to the
Governor that the northwest corner of Perry and the territory in Bibb, Tuscaloosa and Greene adjoining it contained

[86] Joseph D. McCain to Governor Watts, August 13 and 20, 1864,
and January 6, 1865. The commandant of militia of Randolph also
reported that it was very difficult to get deserters out of the thick woods
in that county.—E. B. Smith to Adj.-Gen. H. P. Watson, April 18, 1864.

[87] M. Freeman to Governor Watts, September 18, 1864; John P. West
to Governor Watts, September 9, 1864.

[88] John P. West to Governor Watts, March 4, 1865.

[89] C. J. Rotenberry to Governor Shorter, September 3, 1863. See also:
F. M. Eiland to Governor Watts, January 5, 1865; O. C. C. Brown to
Governor Watts, January 12, 1865; A. B. Moore to Governor Watts,
October 23, 1864; J. M. Shelton to Governor Watts, December 28, 1864.

[90] John M. Marcum and 13 others, October 20, 1864. See also: Petition
of John D. Rather and others to Governor Watts, February 7, 1864;
Confederate Veteran, vol. ii, pp. 71-72, "Last Days of the Confederacy.
Letters from Jefferson Davis." North of the city of Tuscaloosa, deserters found hiding places in caves on the hill sides.—Unwritten reminiscences of a citizen of the county.

deserters.[91] The northwest corner of Perry, which was described as "a very illiterate section," was said by Judge Brooks, ex-chairman of the secession convention, to abound in tories and deserters.[92] There a military company was organized to aid Federal troops in case of raids, but through the efforts of an inhabitant of the section, "the den of traitors and deserters" was broken up by the arrest of 25 deserters and 10 tories.[93] Upper Autauga contained deserters, of whom 41 were arrested by the reserves and returned to their commands by February 1, 1865.[94] Coosa and Tallapoosa contained deserters, especially in their northern hills. In these two counties and in Talladega and Randolph, Governor Shorter reported October 24, 1863 to the War Department in a request for permission for Colonel Loomis to raise a battalion to arrest absentees "there are now large numbers of deserters and conscripts whom there is great difficulty in reaching."[95] From Coosa, in the summer of 1863, a candidate for office who had canvassed the county wrote to the Governor that the number of deserters, especially in the northern part, was so alarming that steps to arrest them should be taken and that a small force of cavalry would be entirely useless.[96] From Tallapoosa, in October, 1864, an officer reported to the Governor that the militia had captured 75 or 100 deserters, and a disabled soldier informed him that 51 able-bodied young men of the county

[91] Burrell Johnston to Governor Watts, September 5, 1864.

[92] A. Q. Bradley to Adj.-Gen. Watson, September 7, 1864; William Brooks to Governor Watts, March 29, 1864.

[93] Porter King to Governor Watts, May 3, 1864.

[94] Thomas A. Davis, commandant of reserves to Governor Watts, September 4, 1864; Thomas A. Davis to General Watson, February 19, 1865.

[95] *Governor's Letter Book*, October 24, 1863, p. 85.

[96] John Clisby to Governor Shorter, July 22, 1863.

had secured exemption from military service "through whiskey, money and intrigue." [97]   In upper Chambers, deserters, of whom the county commandant of militia reported on August 30, 1864 the capture of 30, were in hiding in swamps.[98]

The section in southeast Alabama where deserters collected was comparatively small. It was roughly a right triangle, having as its long arm the boundary between Alabama and Florida and as it short arm the valley of the Chattahoochee river from lower Henry into south Barbour. Thus it included south Conecuh,[99] south Covington,[100] south Coffee,[101] Dale,[102] Henry,[103] south Barbour,[104] south Pike,[105]

[97] John Oden to Governor Watts, October 19, 1864; Croom Green to Governor Watts, August 3, 1864. Another citizen, who said he was in favor of carrying the war into Africa, informed the Governor that croakers and deserters were thick in all Tallapoosa county, March 18, 1865.

[98] W. S. Jackson to Governor Watts, April 22, April 28, April 29, 1864; May 27, 1864; August 30, 1864; Montgomery *Daily Mail*, October 18, 1864, quoting the *Chambers County Tribune* of the 13th.

[99] Fleming, *Civil War and Reconstruction*, p. 110; Wilson Ashley to Governor Watts, August 15, 1864.

[100] Selma *Reporter*, March 10, 1864, quoting the Mobile *Tribune*; Andrew Jay to Governor Watts, December 29, 1864; Wilson Ashley to Governor Watts, August 15, 1864; Mobile *Register*, October 27, 1863.

[101] Mobile *Register*, October 27, 1863; B. W. Starke to Governor Shorter, July 30, 1863; John R. Ard to Governor Watts, March 25, 1865; Montgomery *Daily Advertiser*, September 14, 1864; Petition of some citizens of Coffee county to Governor Watts (January, 1865).

[102] Joseph Hough to Governor Watts, March 20, 1865; William Bush to Governor Shorter, January 23, 1863; Telegram from Eli Shorter to Governor Shorter, September 20 (1863?); *Governor's Letter Book*, September 4, 1863, p. 67; Petition of some citizens of Henry county to Governor Watts, March 23 (1865).

[103] *Governor's Letter Book*, September 4, 1863, p. 67; August 4, 1863, p. 60; William Wood to Governor Shorter, September 11, 1863; Col. J. N. Lightfoot to Governor Watts, October 18, 1864; Petition of some citizens from Henry county to Governor Watts, March 23 (1865); George W.

and south Butler.[106] In Florida, contiguous to this section lay another right triangle of about the same size, having the same long arm and having the southernmost course of the same river, the Apalachicola, as its short arm. This section of Florida and Alabama is level and is intersected by numerous rivers flowing into the Gulf of Mexico. In the dense swamps of these rivers deserters found secure hiding places.[107] Deserters from Henry county frequented the swamps of the Chipola and its tributaries; those from Dale and Coffee, south Barbour and south Pike, the Choctaw-hatchee and its tributaries, especially the Pea river; those from Covington, the Yellow-water; and those from Cone-cuh and south Butler, the Conecuh river.[108] Besides swamps, the region contained caves and dense thickets or brushes, sometimes called " tight-eyes," where deserters might hide

Culver to H. P. Watson, December 19, 1864; G. W. Williams to Governor Shorter, September 17, 1863.

[104] D. M. Seales to Governor Watts, January 5, 1865; Seth Mabry to Governor Watts, March 15, 1865.

[105] E. B. Wilkerson to Governor Watts, January 11, 1865; N. W. Murphey to Governor Watts, January 9, 1865; B. A. Hill to Governor Watts, January 1, 1865; G. W. Wicker to Governor Watts, December 20, 1864.

[106] Fleming, *Civil War and Reconstruction*, p. 110; Unwritten reminiscences of a citizen of the county.

[107] *Governor's Letter Book*, August 4, 1863, p. 60; January 6, 1863, p. 299; January 14, 1863, p. 307; William Wood to Governor Shorter, September 16, 1863; Governor Milton to Governor Shorter, December 30, 1862 (telegram); Governor Milton to Secretary Mallory, May 23, 1864; Petition from captains of the Fifty-seventh Alabama to Governor Watts, November 7, 1864; *O. R.*, ser. i, vol. xiv, p. 716.

[108] M. Tuomey, *Geology of Alabama* (Montgomery, 1858), frontispiece, Colton, " Geological Map of Alabama "; *Governor's Letter Book*, August 4, 1863, p. 60; Joseph Hough to Governor Watts, January 9, 1865; Petition from B. W. Starke, Judge of Probate of Coffee county, and 25 others, ———; B. W. Starke to Governor Shorter, July 30, 1863; *Governor's Letter Book*, July 6, 1863, p. 46.

safely.[109] Moreover, the region was generally poor and sparsely populated.[110] Altogether, it offered such good facilities for concealment that it was a favorite resort of runaway slaves, deserters, tories and conscripts from 1862 when Governor Shorter declared that there were hundreds of deserters and conscripts in this region to 1865 when Judge Yelverton reported that the total number of deserters there was about 2,000.[111] As west Florida was much more thinly settled than southeast Alabama, it offered a safer place for deserters and attracted them not only from Florida and Alabama, but also from Mississippi, Tennessee and Georgia.[112] Many Alabama deserters preferred to stay on the Florida side of the boundary line, where they were still not far from home, and where they could conveniently make raids into populous sections of Alabama or trade by way of the rivers with the enemy on the Florida coast.[113] Moreover, they felt safer on Florida soil from Alabama militia, although Governor Milton not only gave Governor Shorter permission to arrest the numerous deserters and fugitives from conscription who claimed to be citizens of Alabama and who were hiding in west Florida, but also offered any

[109] Fleming, *Civil War and Reconstruction*, p. 123; Thomas Armstrong to Governor Shorter, July 2, 1863.

[110] *Governor's Letter Book*, January 10, 1863, p. 303; September 3, 1863, p. 67.

[111] *Governor's Letter Book*, December 31, 1862, p. 294; *O. R.*, ser. iv, vol. iii, p. 1044.

[112] *Governor's Letter Book*, January 14, 1863, p. 307; Judge G. W. Williams to Governor Shorter, September 17, 1863; William Wood to Governor Shorter, September 16, 1863.

[113] Joseph Hough to Governor Watts, March 22, 1865; January 9, 1865; Mobile *Register*, October 27, 1863, quoting the *Southern Christian Advocate*; *Governor's Letter Book*, January 6, 1863, p. 299; Memphis *Appeal*, September 8, 1864, quoting the Richmond *Whig*.

assistance in his power.[114] However, Governor Shorter said that a large force in persistent pursuit was necessary to get deserters out of west Florida and southeast Alabama.[115] Since he was seldom able to command such a force, the Florida line remained, in the words of the captain of an Alabama company trying to catch deserters, "one of the Graitest Dens for Tories and deserters from our Army in the World." [116]

The other counties of the state contained very few deserters. The four counties north of the Tennessee river, in spite of the fact that they are cut off by the valley, are part of the hilly and mountainous section of north Alabama, but since they were under occupation by Federal troops during the war,[117] they were not safe places for the collection of deserters who wished to go home but not to join the enemy. The counties of the black belt and of southwest Alabama, which together may be called south Alabama, composed a large section in which few deserters were found.

There were differences between the two sections in which deserters collected and the section in which they did not collect. South Alabama was unified by the longest navigable waterway in the state, the Alabama-Tombigbee system, at the mouth of which was located the seaport of the state, Mobile. This section contained a proportionately larger area of rich, cultivatable soil than either of the other

[114] Governor Milton to Governor Shorter, February 2, 1863; William Bush to Governor Shorter, January 23, 1863.

[115] *Governor's Letter Book*, September 4, 1863, p. 67.

[116] Captain William Bush to Governor Shorter, January 23, 1863. See also: John Ard to Governor Watts, March 25, 1865; *Letter Book of the Commandant of Conscripts*, p. 334.

[117] Willis Brewer, *Alabama, Her History, Resources, War Record and Public Men from 1540 to 1872* (Montgomery, 1872), pp. 347, 283, 295, 318, 65.

sections. The black belt, which covered all, or a good part
of thirteen counties and a little part of three others, was a
generally level region, covered with fertile, black soil of
cretaceous formation.[118] The three counties of southwest
Alabama bordering on the black belt contained numerous
river valleys with fertile, alluvial soil. The other three
counties of southwest Alabama, although they had a light
soil and, exclusive of the city of Mobile, were sparsely
populated, contained the oldest settlements in the state because of their location on the lower course of the Alabama-
Tombigbee river system. The black-belt country merged
gradually into the levels of southeast Alabama and into the
uplands of north Alabama. Southeast Alabama had for the
most part a light, sandy soil, which was poor, and north
Alabama contained rugged hills and mountains which were
not adapted to agriculture. In both of these sections there
were fertile river valleys which resembled the black belt as
a whole, and in south Alabama there were poor lands which
resembled southeast Alabama or the mountain region as a
whole. In spite of indistinct boundaries between sections
and in spite of some sectionalism within sections, south
Alabama was distinguished from north Alabama and from
southeast Alabama by the possession of superior natural
facilities for transportation and for agriculture.[119]

This physical difference was the basis of economic and
social differences. In 1860, the chief business of the state
was agriculture. The counties of the black belt and of the
Tennessee valley contained more than the average percent-

[118] M. Tuomey, *Geology of Alabama*, frontispiece, Colton, "Geological
Map of Alabama"; Fleming, *Civil War and Reconstruction*, p. 359;
Edmund Ruffin, *Notes on the Canebrake* (Richmond, 1860), p. 4;
Brewer, *Alabama*, counties in alphabetical order.

[119] M. Tuomey, *Geology of Alabama*, frontispiece, Colton, "Geological
Map of Alabama"; Brewer, *Alabama*, pp. 105-585, counties in alphabetical order.

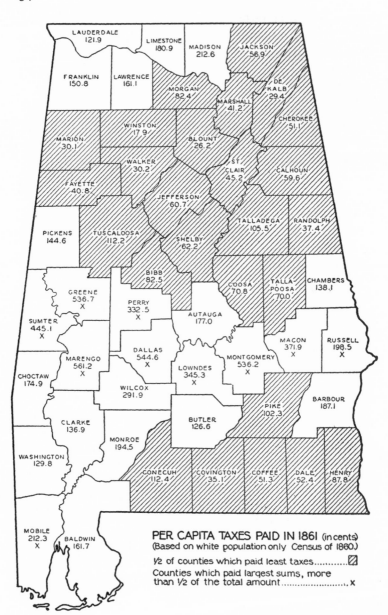

LAUDERDALE
121.9

LIMESTONE
180.9

MADISON
212.6

JACKSON
56.9

FRANKLIN
150.8

LAWRENCE
161.1

MORGAN
82.4

DE
KALB
29.4

MARSHALL
41.2

WINSTON
17.9

MARION
30.1

BLOUNT
26.2

CHEROKEE
51.1

WALKER
30.2

ST.
CLAIR
45.2

CALHOUN
59.6

FAYETTE
40.8

JEFFERSON
60.7

PICKENS
144.6

TUSCALOOSA
112.2

SHELBY
62.2

TALLADEGA
105.5

RANDOLPH
37.4

BIBB
82.5

COOSA
70.8

TALLA-
POOSA
70.0

CHAMBERS
138.1

GREENE
536.7
X

PERRY
332.5
X

AUTAUGA
177.0

SUMTER
445.1
X

DALLAS
544.6
X

MACON
371.9
X

RUSSELL
198.5
X

MARENGO
561.2
X

MONTGOMERY
536.2
X

CHOCTAW
174.9

LOWNDES
345.3
X

WILCOX
291.9

BARBOUR
187.1

CLARKE
136.9

BUTLER
126.6

PIKE
102.3

MONROE
194.5

WASHINGTON
129.8

CONECUH
112.4

COVINGTON
35.1

COFFEE
51.3

DALE
52.4

HENRY
87.8

MOBILE
212.3
X

BALDWIN
161.7

PER CAPITA TAXES PAID IN 1861 (in cents)
(Based on white population only Census of 1860.)

½ of counties which paid least taxes............ ▨
Counties which paid largest sums, more
than ½ of the total amount....................... x

age of improved farms of the state (33); the counties of southeast and southwest Alabama and most of the counties of north Alabama contained less.[120] The chief money crop of the state was cotton, which every county raised, from Winston with 353 bales to Marengo with 63,428 bales in 1860, but the production of cotton was concentrated in southern Alabama.[121] A secondary business was manufacturing. The value of the factory products was greatest as a whole in the counties of south Alabama and of the hill section of north Alabama bordering on the black belt, but the value of home manufactures was greatest in the counties of southeast Alabama and of the mountain section.[122] The per-capita value of property, which varied from $168 in Winston to $6,431 in Dallas, was greater in the counties of south Alabama.[123] Map B,[124] the distribution of taxes in 1861, shows this economic sectionalism. A large part of the wealth of the state was invested in slaves, which were considered the most profitable labor for cotton plantations.[125] Map C,[126] the distribution of slaveholders, sug-

[120] For statistics upon which this computation is based see *Statistics of the United States in 1860 Compiled from the Original Returns and Being the Final Exhibit of the Eighth Census* (Washington, 1866), *Agriculture*, pp. 2-5.

[121] *Eighth Census of the United States, Agriculture*, pp. 2-5.

[122] For statistics upon which this computation is based, see: *Eighth Census of the United States, Manufactures*, pp. 13, 5; *Population*, p. 8.

[123] For statistics upon which this computation is based, see: *Eighth Census of the United States, Population*, p. 8; *Mortality and Miscellaneous Statistics*, p. 296.

[124] For statistics upon which this computation is based, see: *Eighth Census of the United States, Population*, p. 8; *Annual Report of the State Comptroller of Public Accounts to the General Assembly, 1861-1866* (Montgomery, 1861-1866), November, 1862, statement no. 8, p. 71.

[125] *Eighth Census, Mortality and Miscellaneous Statistics*, p. 296.

[126] For statistics upon which this computation is based, see: *Eighth Census, Mortality and Miscellaneous Statistics*, p. 340; *Agriculture*, p. 223.

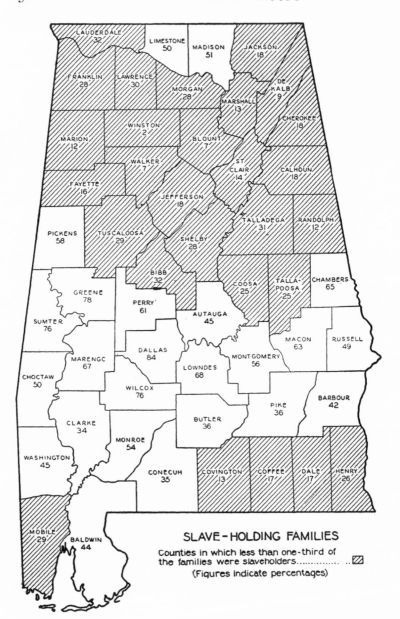

SLAVE-HOLDING FAMILIES

Counties in which less than one-third of
the families were slaveholders............... ..▨
(Figures indicate percentages)

gests economic and social differences between south Alabama and north and southeast Alabama. The concentration of wealth in certain counties doubtless produced other social differences for which statistics are not available.[127] Intercourse between the sections was not easy in 1860. There was no railroad in southeast Alabama and the common roads from that section into the black belt were impassable during part of the year. There was no railroad connecting the counties north of the mountains with south Alabama and a journey from Huntsville to Mobile required at least three days.[128] There was only one railroad connecting the black belt counties with the hill counties south of the mountains.[129] Economic and social differences produced political differences. From the admission of the state to the union in 1819 to the opening of the civil war, sectionalism between north and south, partly from conflicting interests, partly from habit, was a factor in the political life of Alabama.[130]

The distribution by counties of deserters who went home indicated that sectionalism, which was as old as the state, was making a new manifestation of itself, desertion.[131]

Distribution of deserters by classes of soldiers showed concentration in one class. According to method of enlist-

[127] Statistics from the original returns of the eighth census show that the percentage of children in southeast Alabama who attended school was smaller than the percentage in several of the black-belt counties. However, the social statistics from the original returns of the eighth census are incomplete.

[128] M. Tuomey, *Geology of Alabama*, frontispiece, Colton, "Geological Map of Alabama"; Montgomery *Daily Mail*, December 31, 1862; Fleming, *Civil War and Reconstruction*, p. 109.

[129] W. E. Dodd, *The Cotton Kingdom* (New Haven, 1921), p. 4 (map).

[130] T. H. Jack, *Sectionalism and Party Politics in Alabama, 1819-1842* (Wenasha, 1919); Fleming, *Civil War and Reconstruction*, pp. 53-54, 109-110.

[131] See Map A.

ment, Confederate soldiers were grouped into three classes—volunteers, conscripts and substitutes. Volunteers formed by far the largest class but included many who, though technically serving from choice, had joined the army to avoid conscription.[132] Conscripts, decreased in number on one side by men who were forced to volunteer and on the other side by men who evaded service, formed a small class. Of Alabama troops, 14,875 were classed by conscription officials as conscripts, but as much of this enrollment was only nominal, the number of real conscripts was only a few hundred.[133] It was generally believed that the percentage of volunteers who deserted was smaller than the percentage of conscripts who deserted.[134]

Substitutes, men who for pay undertook military service for " principals," who were or were not liable to conscription, formed the smallest class of soldiers. The total number of substitutes in the Confederate army was not definitely known and was estimated at from 30,000 to 150,000.[135] In November, 1863, the Secretary of War reported that from the best computation possible with incomplete statistics the number was at least 50,000.[136] Substitutes were the

---

[132] Fleming, *Civil War and Reconstruction*, pp. 98-99.

[133] *O. R.*, ser. iv. vol. iii, pp. 110-111; Fleming, *Civil War and Reconstruction*, pp. 106-107.

[134] *Governor's Letter Book*, August 4, 1863, p. 60; Gordon, *Reminiscences*, pp. 398-399; A. B. Moore, *Conscription and Conflict in the Confederacy* (New York, 1924), p. 359; Appleton, *Annual Cyclopedia*, 1862, p. 245; *Bulletin of the University of Georgia*, Brooks, R. P., " Conscription in the Confederate States of America " (reprinted from the *Military Historian and Economist*, vol. i, no. 4), p. 441. Cf. *infra*, pp. 75-77.

[135] *O. R.*, ser. iv, vol. ii, p. 1059; 30,000, by the Chairman of the Military Committee of the House.—Richmond *Examiner*, December 23, 1863; Montgomery *Weekly Mail*, January 6, 1864; 150,000 by General Bragg and fourteen of his officers.—*O. R.*, ser. iv, vol. ii, pp. 670-671.

[136] *O. R.*, ser. iv, vol. ii, p. 997.

least reliable class of soldiers. Since they were usually men over the age of conscription, many of them had to be discharged or sent to hospitals on account of disability.[137] And substitutes were notorious for desertion.[138] According to statistics said to be furnished to the Richmond *Examiner* by a medical officer, the number of substitutes received into the second corps of Stonewall Jackson's army was 2,376, of whom 23% were discharged or sent to hospitals and 38% deserted.[139] General Bragg and fourteen officers of his army, including three from Alabama, stated in a petition to Congress that in their opinion not one substitute in a hundred was still in the army, and the assistant adjutant-general of the Confederate army reported to the Secretary of War on November 11, 1863 that of 50,000 substitutes not more than 3,000 or 4,000 above the age of conscription were actually in the field.[140] Judge Campbell stated that over two-thirds of the 50,000 substitutes had deserted.[141]

The frequency of desertions among substitutes was increased by the practice of professional substitutes. During 1862 and 1863, a regular business in the procuration of substitutes developed and flourished.[142] In July, 1863, three brokers advertised in the Mobile *Register* their services in procuring substitutes who would go to any part of the Con-

---

137 *O. R.*, ser. iv, vol. ii, pp. 45, 670-671.

138 *O. R.*, ser. iv, vol. ii, p. 1041 (Pres. Davis).

139 Richmond *Examiner*, February 23, 1863; Montgomery *Daily Mail*, March 4, 1863.

140 *O. R.*, ser. iv, vol. ii, pp. 670-671, p. 947.

141 *O. R.*, ser. iv, vol. ii, p. 656. Mr. Miles of S. C. said that substitutes formed nine-tenths of the deserters and Mr. Sparrow of Virginia said that 100 substitutes deserted for every one volunteer or conscript.— Montgomery *Weekly Advertiser*, December 30, 1863; February 5, 1863.

142 *O. R.*, ser. iv, vol. ii, p. 45; Montgomery *Weekly Advertiser*, December 23, 1863.

federacy.[143] Often substitutes procured by brokers deserted as soon as they reached the army and, as the Secretary of War said, again made "sale of themselves with a view to like shameful evasion." [144] Professional substitutes and brokers who forged the necessary papers were sometimes in collusion with military officers who received a share of the principal's money.[145] In 1863, such an organization in Mississippi and Alabama was detected by General Pillow through the complaint of a principal of Mobile that he had been swindled by a broker, an officer, and a substitute who looked like "a lusty son of Mars" but turned out to be a professional deserter.[146] General Jackson was quoted as saying that 90 out of 100 substitutes deserted within the first week of their army service.[147] Frequently substitutes deserted on the same day on which they were received in camp and sometimes left the army on the train with the principals.[148] Foreigners and Baltimoreans were said to be especially apt at this business.[149] The following advertisement for a deserter from an Alabama command suggests a professional substitute:

[143] Mobile *Register*, June 7, 1863. Only two of these stated that substitutes secured by them would go to any part of the Confederacy.

[144] *O. R.*, ser. iv, vol. ii, p. 996; Mobile *Register*, November 29, 1862.

[145] *O. R.*, ser. iv, vol. ii, pp. 582-583; vol. iii, pp. 24-25. The Superintendent of the Bureau of Conscription deplored the immunity which guilty officers enjoyed in this nefarious business.—*O. R.*, ser. iv, vol. ii, pp. 582-583.

[146] Mobile *Register*, October 30, 1863.

[147] Montgomery *Weekly Advertiser*, December 23, 1863.

[148] *Fowler Reports, passim*; Richmond *Examiner*, December 23, 1863, quoting Mr. Hilton of Florida.

[149] *O. R.*, ser. iv, vol. ii, p. 45; Mobile *Register*, May 20, 1863. See also: *O. R.*, ser. iv, vol. ii, pp. 1054, 2; Rhodes, *History of the United States*, vol. v, p. 483.

$30 Reward

Deserted from Ft. Morgan, April 25.

—————— ——————, a substitute, at $2500, Age, 26. Mechanic. Native of Virginia. Exhibited a discharge by way of having furnished a substitute. Sprightly and handsome and a sharp one.

E. M. Campbell, Captain Company E,

First Artillery of Alabama.

Ft. Morgan
June 5, 1863.[150]

It is possible that both the impression of the inferiority of conscripts as soldiers and the estimates of the percentage of desertion among substitutes were affected by the strong popular prejudice against conscripts and substitutes. Statistics of a cross-section of Alabama soldiers in the Army of Northern Virginia are suggestive. On December 31, 1864, the aggregate enrollment of the Eighth, Ninth, Tenth, Eleventh, Thirteenth, Fifteenth, Forty-third, Forty-fourth, Forty-eighth, and Sixty-first regiments of Alabama infantry was 12,523, distributed among the three classes of soldiers as follows: volunteers, 12,153; conscripts, 225; substitutes, 145. From the date of organization of each regiment to January 1, 1865, 6% of the volunteers, 2% of the conscripts and 17% of the substitutes deserted.[151] According to these figures, the rate of desertion was highest among substitutes, but the absolute number of desertions was highest among volunteers.

[150] Mobile *Register*, May 17, 1863.

[151] *Fowler Reports*. For a favorable opinion of conscripts as soldiers, see Moore, *Conscription and Conflict in the Confederacy*, pp. 359-360.

CHAPTER III

MILITARY AND POLITICAL CAUSES OF DESERTION

CERTAIN features of the organization and maintenance of Alabama troops in the Confederate army were causes of desertion. The primary feature of the organization of Alabama troops was voluntary service. It was seen best in the number of early volunteers. Before enforcement of the compulsory military service law, the state had contributed to the Confederate army about 60,000 men. These early volunteers formed about two-thirds of all the Alabama troops in the Confederate army.[1] Many of the early volunteers enlisted under misapprehension as to the length and nature of the military service which would be necessary. Before Lincoln's call for troops, the people as a whole in Alabama, influenced by the opinions of the press and political leaders, both North and South, believed that secession would be a peaceful achievement.[2] In a mass meeting in Montgomery after the election of Lincoln, William L. Yancey, who was one of the leaders of the secession party and who had just returned from a tour of the North, expressed this opinion in the following words: " I have good reason to believe that the action of any state will be peaceable—will not be resisted—under the present, or any probable prospective condition of Federal affairs." [3]   Leroy

---

[1] *O. R.*, ser. iv, vol. i, p. 1131; Brewer, *Alabama*, pp. 589-662 (history of regiments); *Confederate States Almanac, 1864* (Mobile, 1863), p. 56; Selma *Reporter*, May 31, 1861.

[2] Joseph Hodgson, *The Cradle of the Confederacy* (Mobile, 1876), chap. xvii; Richmond *Examiner*, July 28, 1863.

[3] Hodgson, *The Cradle of the Confederacy*, p. 466.

Pope Walker, who had not belonged to the secession party before the election of Lincoln and who became the first Secretary of War of the Confederate States, expressed it as he traveled up and down the state advising the people to secede and promising to wipe up with his pocket handkerchief all the blood that would be spilled.[4] The delusion that secession would be a peaceful achievement was dispelled by Lincoln's call for volunteers on April 15, 1861. The people of Alabama with remarkable unanimity accepted the war as a war of self-defense and undertook it in a white heat of patriotism.[5] In the outburst of enthusiasm, they did not foresee a war of long duration and great hardship. They thought that the war would be short and the victory easy. They thought that the period of twelve months fixed by Davis in his call for volunteers in contrast with the period of three months fixed by Lincoln in his call for volunteers was a sign of overcaution on Davis' part. They thought that it would not take more than two or three months to whip the Yankees.[6] Some orators with an effervescent though probably sincere patriotism helped to heighten this illusion by disguising the character of war and by disparaging the ability of the enemy. By such statements as that one Southerner could whip ten Yankees, that if Lincoln and his men invaded the South they could be driven

[4] Pierce Butler, *Judah P. Benjamin* (Philadelphia, 1907), pp. 234-235.

[5] Hodgson, *The Cradle of the Confederacy*, pp. 477, 511, 515, 469-470; W. G. Brown, *A History of Alabama* (New York, 1900), pp. 234, 235; L. D. Miller, *History of Alabama* (Birmingham, 1901), pp. 155-156; Brewer, *Alabama*, pp. 64-65; Appleton, *Annual Cyclopedia*, 1861, p. 146; Robert Tansill, *A Free and Impartial Exposition of the Causes Which Led to the Failure of the Confederate States to Establish Their Independence* (Washington, 1865), p. 5.

[6] T. C. DeLeon, *Four Years in Rebel Capitals* (Mobile, 1890), pp. 27, 75; Appleton, *Annual Cyclopedia*, 1862, p. 203; Moore, *Conscription and Conflict in the Confederacy*, pp. 4-5; Fleming, *Civil War and Reconstruction*, p. 138; Butler, *Judah P. Benjamin*, p. 235.

back by old women armed with broomsticks, and that hunting Yankees was more fun than hunting squirrels, they made war with the Yankees seem a holiday pastime.[7] Some men with a view to raising commands in which they should hold offices used high-pressure methods in recruiting volunteers, making promises about equipment, furloughs and the like which they could not keep and giving rise to complaints that they "allured" men into enlistment.[8] Two examples may illustrate the popular misapprehension as to the length and the nature of the military service to be required. A company of poor men from the northern part of Sumter county volunteered under the belief received from placards calling for recruits and from the caption of the muster roll which they signed that they would not be called into service unless absolutely necessary and that they would not be compelled to serve outside the county nor in arsenals and forts.[9] Equally ignorant of the nature of the service to be required were the wealthy young privates who went by boat from Montgomery to Mobile with body servants and three trunks apiece.[10]

[7] Fleming, *Civil War and Reconstruction*, p. 98; F. Moore, *Rebellion Record* (New York, 1862-1868), vol. viii (Incidents), p. 45; *Confederate Veteran*, vol. xxxi, p. 382, I. G. Bradwell, "Memories of 1860"; Goodloe, *Confederate Echoes*, pp. 156-157; *O. R.*, ser. iv, vol. i, p. 305.

[8] *Confederate Veteran*, vol. xxiv, p. 21, I. G. Bradwell, "Life in the Confederate Army"; Unwritten reminiscences of a Confederate soldier; *Proceedings of courts-martial*, in cases of a few privates from Alabama commands; Ephraim Parker to Jefferson Davis, March 13, 1861; William S. Chapman to Governor Moore, April 5, 1861. See also Jere Clemens, *Tobias Wilson* (Philadelphia, 1865), p. 85. Mr. Gentry of Tennessee raised a laugh in Congress by the statement that his efforts to raise volunteer companies had cost him a good deal of labor and a good deal of whiskey (September 8, 1862).—*Southern Historical Society Papers*, vol. viii, p. 35, "Proceedings of Congress."

[9] J. C. Kendall, W. I. Vandegraff and others to Governor Moore, August 6, 1861.

[10] J. M. Morgan, *Recollections of a Rebel Reefer* (Boston, 1917), p. 40.

Many volunteers knew as little of military organization as they did of the nature of military service. Some of the early companies were very loose organizations. Volunteers occasionally stipulated conditions upon which they would join organizations.[11] Many thought that since joining a company was voluntary, leaving it should also be voluntary. A group stated to the Governor that their company understood that a principle of voluntary organization was the right of the majority to accept the resignation of any member who offered an acceptable reason for his resignation.[12] Several privates offered their resignations, stating that they were dissatisfied.[13] Some volunteers ignored marching orders when the time came to leave home; others treated their officers, often old friends, with easy familiarity; others declined to carry passes, which reminded them of slaves' passes.[14] Not only privates but also some new officers were ignorant of military organization. For example, one captain asked the Governor if he could compel twelve stout, vigorous men who had backed out to go with his company, and another asked if he could " let off " a man who wanted to " get off " from his company.[15]

[11] M. R. Boyd to Governor Shorter, April 22, 1862; John D. Burns to Governor Moore, June 10, 1861.

[12] J. C. Kendall, W. I. Vandegraff and others to Governor Moore, August 6, 1861.

[13] W. T. Ayres to Governor Moore, July 25, 1861; R. H. Locke and John Watt to Governor Moore, August 3, 1861; J. C. Kendall, W. I. Vandegraff and others to Governor Moore, August 6, 1861; Robert Stiles, *Four Years under Marse Robert* (New York, 1903), pp. 46-47.

[14] D. M. Richards, October 10, 1861; Thomas Hollis, November 1, 1861; G. C. Eggleston, *A Rebel's Recollections* (New York, 1874), pp. 35-36; Morgan, *Recollections of a Rebel Reefer*, p. 45; Union Springs *Times,* June 20, 1866, Powell, " The Third Alabama Infantry."

[15] William C. Allen to Governor Moore, September 24, 1861; W. M. Stone to Governor Moore, August 7, 1861. See also: Robert P. Blount

So convinced were the early volunteers that they would easily win the war that many were impatient to fight and bring it to a victorious close. One captain reported to the Governor that his company would disband unless they soon received marching orders; another captain, that his men had all joined another company which had the prospect of going sooner to fight.[16] The captain of a Mobile company wrote to the *Register* from Pensacola that many soldiers from Mississippi, Florida and Alabama were deserting in disgust at doing garrison duty after they had volunteered to fight.[17] The colonel of the Second Alabama Regiment at the same place wrote to the Governor that he had only 500 men left because the others had gone home, disappointed in " the inactive and defensive policy " of the commanding officer.[18] Thus the earliest cause of desertion was disappointment at not being allowed to fight.[19] After the volunteers had an opportunity to fight at the battle of Manassas, many of them were convinced that the war was won by this victory which they had anticipated a long time. Thousands went home.[20] But they were assured by the passage of the conscription act that the war was not over and by their own experience that it was not easy. Reaction followed. Depression took the place of enthusiasm. Many of the volunteers, in spite of loss of enthusiasm, in the spring of 1862 returned to the army, but others, unable or unwilling to

to Governor Moore, January 8, 1861; D. M. Richards to Governor Moore, October 10, 1861; Thomas Hollis to Governor Moore, November 1, 1861.

[16] L. B. Haughey, June 18, 1861; C. J. Cunningham, July 21, 1861.

[17] Mobile *Register*, January 24, January 26, February 2, 1861.

[18] T. Lomax, February 7, 1861.

[19] See also Edward Channing, *History of the United States* (New York, 1925), vol. vi, p. 414.

[20] Fleming, *Civil War and Reconstruction*, p. 98.

adjust themselves to the change from the glamorous picture of war to the harsh reality, deserted.[21]

Under the system of voluntary service which obtained in the Confederate army, a volunteer was allowed to choose the command to which he wished to belong. The choice of command was a privilege highly prized by soldiers because it promised them service under an officer whom they trusted and among friends and acquaintances, thus insuring them against injustice and loneliness. It was one of the chief means of stimulating volunteering and formed an important distinction between volunteers and conscripts. This privilege was recognized by Confederate authorities as such an effective method of securing morale, that it was extended in a limited way to conscripts.[22] However, certain abuses of this privilege caused desertion. The right of original choice of a command was interpreted by certain volunteers to include the right of transfer from one command to another in which service appeared desirable. Thus numerous members of the veteran Ninth Alabama Regiment, feeling that injustice had been done in the dismissal of a favorite officer, went home in the summer of 1864 to join cavalry commands being organized in north Alabama.[23] Men from General Bragg's and General Johnston's armies were said to be constantly " sloughing off," going home and, after staying there a few days, joining the cavalry, and at least

[21] A. J. L. Freemantle, *Three Months in the Southern States* (New York, 1864), p. 123; G. F. R. Henderson, *Stonewall Jackson and the American Civil War* (Bombay, 1906) vol. ii, p. 204, p. 350; *O. R.*, ser. iv, vol. ii, p. 280; Memphis *Appeal*, October 25, 1864; *Applications for Amnesty and Pardon*, vol. i, p. 174, no. 518.

[22] Rowland, *Jefferson Davis, Constitutionalist*, vol. v, pp. 362-363, 139-140.

[23] *O. R.*, ser. i, vol. xlii, pt. ii, p. 1175; *Letter Book of the Commandant of Conscripts*, p. 371; *Proceedings of the Board of Examiners and Report upon the Case of Colonel Sam Henry*, February 13, 1863.

two-thirds of Roddey's and Chalmers' cavalry commands were said to be composed of deserters from the infantry.[24] Unauthorized transfers, especially from infantry to cavalry and from Confederate to state organizations, were so frequent that they constituted a menace to the army. The practice was aggravated by illegal recruiting, which persisted from 1862 to 1865. Since recruiting officers were usually chosen company officers, authority to raise companies was coveted and when it could not be obtained was often assumed.[25] As the object of officers and men of illegal companies was to avoid service, some of the companies simply remained in the process of formation; others went through the motions of rendering service. For example, in 1864, several cavalry companies composed largely or wholly of deserters were formed in Calhoun, St. Clair and DeKalb counties with the ostensible object of protection against invasion of the enemy and against depredations of deserters.[26] General Lee said that the immunity which lawless organizations afforded was a great cause of desertion and General Longstreet said that most of the desertions in his corps could be traced to such causes.[27]

The right to select commands was extended in a limited way to conscripts by general orders from the War Department directing officers whenever they could to assign conscripts to commands recruited from their respective re-

---

[24] *O.R.*, ser. iv, vol. ii, p. 775 (report by General Pillow). One advantage offered by cavalry service was the practice of allowing men furloughs to secure horses. It was much abused.—*O. R.*, ser. iv, vol. iii, p. 796.

[25] *Statutes at Large,* vol. i, pp. 248-249; *O.R.*, ser. iv, vol. ii, p. 775, p. 783; vol. iii, pp. 1353-1356, 694; ser. i, vol. xlii, pt. ii, pp. 1176, 1182-1183; vol. xlviii, pp. 1394-1395; Meade H. Jackson to Governor Watts, March 24, 1865.

[26] *Letter Book of the Commandant of Conscripts*, p. 371.

[27] *O.R.*, ser. i, vol. xlvii, pp. 1353-1354; vol. xlvi, pt. iii, p. 1356.

gions.[28]   But complaint was made by the Governor of Alabama to the War Department that officers violated these instructions.[29]   The assignment to commands of strangers was alleged as one of the chief causes for desertions of soldiers from southeast Alabama.   These soldiers were said to be ardent secessionists and loyal Confederates, but because they lacked means to support their families, they had not volunteered but had been conscribed.   Under the circumstances, they considered denial of choice of regiments an injustice which excused desertion and they refused to return to the army unless they could choose their commands.[30]   For a similar reason, the majority of conscripts in north Alabama, according to a statement made in 1864 by the state commandant of conscripts, deserted on the way to the camps of instruction to which they had been assigned and joined organizations of their own choosing, usually cavalry.[31]

Another feature of the organization of volunteers which tended to cause absence without leave and desertion was election of officers.   The fifty-odd regiments of infantry and the other units organized in Alabama before the conscription act went into effect elected their company and regimental officers and, to the end of the war, volunteers who formed organizations exercised the privilege of electing certain officers.   Vacancies occurring in certain higher offices after organization were filled by appointment through promotion, but the lowest commissioned company officers were always elective.[32]   Election of officers made the rela-

28 *O. R.*, ser. iv, vol. i, p. 1097, *G. O.* no. 30, 1862.

29 *O. R.*, ser. iv, vol. ii, pp. 911-912.

30 *O. R.*, ser. iv, vol. iii, pp. 1042-1044.

31 *Letter Book of the Commandant of Conscripts*, pp. 371-372.   See also the *Clarke County Journal*, February 5, 1863.

32 *Statutes at Large*, vol. i, pp. 223, 248-249; vol. ii, pp. 29-32; Moore, *Conscription and Conflict*, p. 3.

tionship between men and officers close.   It fixed a sort of
popular government in the army.   Officers as the chosen
representatives of the men had to be governed to a certain
extent by their wishes and were dependent for success in
their positions and for promotion to higher offices largely
upon popular approval.   It helped to prevent development
of a sharp distinction between officers and men.   As a rule,
company officers and men were not separated by differences
in social position or in military training, and as they had
been neighbors and friends before volunteering, they maintained during the war an easy comradeship.[33]   This method
of selecting officers permitted the game of politics to be
played in the army.   Occasionally, rival candidates split
commands into factions; frequently, ambitious officers used
their positions to develop a devoted constituency of soldiers
which would insure a later political career.[34]

Officers who were elected under such circumstances could
not enforce strict discipline.   To secure obedience to regulations, they had to exercise tact rather than authority and
to depend upon goodwill rather than compulsion.   Officers
understood that volunteers as a whole considered strict
discipline neither pleasant nor necessary and that consequently they wished to be free from it.   As some officers
shared the men's view of discipline and as all officers were
compelled to show a certain amount of consideration for
their wishes in regard to it, generally lax discipline prevailed in the army.[35]   In the opinion of the Secretary of

[33] Henderson, *Stonewall Jackson*, vol. i, p. 254; Beauregard to his
wife, March 11, 1861; Moore, *Rebellion Record*, vol. iii (Diary of
Events), p. 96; Rowland, *Jefferson Davis, Constitutionalist*, vol. v, pp.
139-140.

[34] Freemantle, *Three Months in the Southern States*, p. 122; Tansill,
Free and Impartial Exposition, p. 20.

[35] Henderson, *Stonewall Jackson*, vol. ii, p. 350; J. B. Beall, *In Bar-*

War, the regimental and company officers who were elected in the spring of 1862 in the reorganization of the army were generally inferior to their predecessors.[36] According to the Richmond *Examiner*, officers who had attempted to enforce strict discipline were replaced in 1862 to such an extent by officers who promised leniency that discipline was cashiered and drummed out of the army.[37] It was true that some elected officers who were utterly incompetent or who were very ambitious for political advancement allowed the men to do so much as they pleased that military discipline was practically absent from their commands.[38] One of the results of lax discipline was straggling and absence without leave. The Secretary of War wrote in September, 1862, " The vast amount of stragglers which now paralyze our army and defeat all attempts to reinforce it is mainly due to the inefficiency of regimental and company officers." [39] An officer of the British army who was on a visit to Mississippi in 1863 was struck by the fact that straggling took place on " a grand scale " and by the fact that officers paid little attention to it.[40] General Lee, General Bragg and General Johnston also acknowledged that straggling and absence without leave took place on a grand scale, but they were unable to get officers and men to stop it.[41] As a whole,

racks and Field (Dallas, 1906), p. 297; Freemantle, *Three Months,* p. 123; Tansill, *Free and Impartial Exposition,* pp. 10, 20; Channing, *History of the United States,* vol. vi, p. 419; *O. R.,* ser. iv, vol. ii, p. 948.

[36] *O. R.,* ser. iv, vol. ii, p. 97.

[37] March 3, 1865.

[38] Tansill, *Free and Impartial Exposition,* pp. 10-12; Beauregard to his wife, April 8, (1862) ; Jones, *Diary,* vol. i, p. 157.

[39] *O. R.,* ser. iv, vol. ii, p. 98.

[40] Freemantle, *Three Months,* p. 78.

[41] Freemantle, *Three Months,* p. 122; *O. R.,* ser. i, vol. xlii, pt. iii, p. 1213; vol. xi, pt. iii, p. 503; vol. xx, pt. ii, pp. 407, 386; vol. xix, pt. ii, pp. 622-623; vol. xvii, pt. ii, p. 622. General Lee said, " How long they

officers, doubtless because the men demanded it, were very patient with straggling and absence without leave. Three privates on the way home to north Alabama for a visit justified themselves by what they called a common reflection that no fighting was apt to take place while they were away and that they were not serving under officers who were martinets.[42]   A private from southeast Alabama wrote to his wife that he was going home for a visit because all the men who got a chance did so, and that he had consulted his company officers and been advised by them to go.[43] Many officers encouraged absence without leave not only by leniency but also by example; many officers were found among the stragglers and the absent without leave.[44]

Officers, regardless of the method by which they had been selected, who unskillfully enforced strict discipline were considered tyrannical and, consequently, disliked.   Bolling Hall, later colonel of the Fifty-ninth Alabama, in a letter to his father said that the soldiers absolutely hated a certain officer because he treated them like regulars and drank heavily, and that at reorganization many would likely refuse to serve under him.   By way of contrast, he mentioned a colonel who was surprisingly popular because he was considerate of his men, even providing them with rations of whiskey on Christmas day.[45]   From other sources, reports were made of overbearing officers who, acting as if they had a life tenure in the army, treated the men with harshness.   Whether all such reports were true or not, the result

(stragglers) will remain with us or when they will again disappear it is impossible for me to say."—*O. R.*, ser. i, vol. xix, pt. ii, pp. 622-623.

[42] J. M. Hubbard, *Notes of a Private* (St. Louis, 1913), p. 62.

[43] E. K. Flournoy to his wife, July 15, 1863.

[44] *O. R.*, ser. iv, vol. ii, p. 857, p. 1012; ser. i, vol. xix, pt. ii, p. 629: ser. i, vol. xlvi, pt. ii, p. 1239; Richmond *Examiner*, January 21, 1864.

[45] December 26, 1861.

was the same. Under tyrannical officers, privates felt that they had no method of redress of grievances and some, to save themselves from what they considered unbearable abuse, deserted.[46]

In some cases, the development of factions around candidates for office had the same disastrous effect. Two regiments which suffered from the development of factions around colonels were the Fifteenth infantry from southeast Alabama and the Ninth infantry from north Alabama. Some members of the Fifteenth Alabama declared that they would desert before they would serve under the opposing candidate, and after his appointment they made good the threat.[47] A majority of the Ninth Alabama petitioned against the removal of their colonel partly because they believed with him that the proceedings against him originated in political intrigue, and after his removal, some of them deserted.[48]

If all the officers had been appointed and if all of them had had military training, it is quite unlikely that they would have been successful in enforcing strict discipline among a high-spirited citizen soldiery like the Alabama troops. The volunteers had a strong feeling of individualism and independence which made them impatient of restraint. They had a conviction that the essential quality of a good soldier, besides which other qualities were comparatively unimportant, was bravery in battle. They never

[46] Rowland, *Jefferson Davis*, vol. v. pp. 141-142; Joseph Silver to Governor Watts, August 19, 1864; *The Independent*, January 23, 1864; *Letter Book of the Commandant of Conscripts*, p. 188; Memphis *Appeal*, March 2, 1865.

[47] W. C. Oates, *History of the Fifteenth Alabama Infantry Regiment*, chap. xix.

[48] *Proceedings of the Board of Examiners and Report upon the Case of Colonel Sam Henry*, February 12, 1863; *O. R.*, ser. i, vol. xlii, pt. ii, p. 1175.

realized the importance of obedience as a cardinal military virtue nor fully appreciated the value of discipline although they improved in discipline greatly during the latter part of the war. They believed that enthusiasm, initiative and courage of the individual were a sufficient, even a superior, substitute for discipline.[49] Consequently, as a whole, they did not consider straggling and absence without leave really serious offences. They thought that falling behind on a march or making a little visit home when opportunity afforded did not impair a soldier's efficiency nor lessen his bravery in battle. They were bound to know that straggling and absence without leave encouraged desertion by frequently shading into it and by always offering a shield to it, but still they did not give up entirely their independence of action. The war was their war. They had volunteered to fight it and they fought it well, but they insisted on fighting it their way. Probably they never entirely lost their original character, described by General Beauregard as that of " raw volunteers, without officers and without discipline, each man with an idea that he can whip the world." [50] The same spirit of individualism which permitted absence without leave caused desertion by volunteers who were convinced that they had done their share of fighting and that they should go home. The attitude of the civilian ignorant of military law except probably the state militia code, which did not contain the word " desertion," prevented the formation among Alabama soldiers of a conviction that desertion was under all circumstances a crime.[51]

A secondary feature of the organization of Confederate

---

[49] Tansill, *Free and Impartial Exposition,* pp. 19-22; Henderson, *Stonewall Jackson,* vol. i, p. 117; vol. ii, pp. 355-360; *The Independent,* January 23, 1864; Mobile *Register,* February 13, 1864.

[50] P. G. T. Beauregard to his wife, March 11, 1861.

[51] *Military Code of the State of Alabama* (Montgomery, 1861), p. 52.

troops was compulsory service, which in fact, if not in theory, applied after the first year of the war to volunteers as well as to conscripts. By act of Congress, April 16, 1862, the twelve months' volunteers were compelled to remain in service for three years and conscripts between the ages of 18 and 45 were liable to service for the same period.[52] As conscription was considered a disgrace, volunteering was stimulated by this act.[53] The Secretary of War estimated that three-fourths of the 80,000 to 100,000 men added to the army in 1863 volunteered to avoid conscription.[54] On May 28, 1862, the adjutant-general of Alabama reported that 19 regiments and a legion of 23 companies had been recently organized in the state and that the number of conscripts would be small, most of them having volunteered. He thought that 10,000 conscripts might be secured from the state, and if the enemy were expelled from north Alabama, 3,000 more.[55] In February, 1865, the superintendent of conscription reported the total number of conscripts assigned through camps of instruction in Alabama, exclusive of the operations of General Pillow, as 14,875, and said that since many volunteers had been compelled by the conscription act to join the army, they should be accredited to the operations of his department.[56] Many so-called volunteers were not in the army from choice. On the other hand, some conscripts would have been real volunteers if they had been free from private obligations to

[52] *O. R.*, ser. iv, vol. i, pp. 1095-1097.

[53] *O. R.*, ser. iv, vol. iii, pp. 1099, 1100-1101; Moore, *Conscription and Conflict*, pp. 356-357.

[54] Moore, *Conscription and Conflict*, p. 223.

[55] *O. R.*, ser. iv, vol. ii, p. 21; vol. i, p. 1131.

[56] *O. R.*, ser. iv, vol. iii, pp. 1100-1101. Professor Fleming says that much of this enrollment was only nominal and included 18 regiments (10,000 men) formed after the passage of the conscription act and in violation of it.—Fleming, *Civil War and Reconstruction*, pp. 106-107.

enter the Confederate States' service. The Governor of Alabama in his message to the legislature in 1862 said:

The far greater number of those who are now reinforcing the army as conscripts and who will hereafter enter in under the amended act of the recent session of Congress could not conveniently and in justice to others dependent upon them have enlisted at an earlier day. A large proportion of them have families whose only means of support was their own honest toil. Yielding a cheerful obedience to the call of their country, they go to join the ranks of the gallant volunteers who have preceded them to the field and side by side with them to peril their lives and all they have and are in the defense of their bleeding country.[57]

The method of enlistment, therefore, did not always determine the spirit of the soldier.

However, compulsory service was a cause of desertion of both conscripts and volunteers. Compulsory service was generally disliked. It was contrary to the spirit of the Southern people.[58] According to the Memphis *Appeal*, it was odious to free men to be treated like machines worked by government officers at the handles.[59] The conscription law was evaded and opposed. Especially in north Alabama hundreds in various ingenious ways obtained exemption and hundreds hid out in the woods to avoid conscription officers.[60] In north Alabama, opposition to conscription was so pronounced that the authorities rather than risk an armed encounter, were lax in enforcement of the law there.[61] At times, military force was used to put conscripts

[57] Mobile *Register,* October 21, 1862.

[58] Moore, *Conscription and Conflict,* p. 354.   [59] March 2, 1865.

[60] *O. R.,* ser. iv, vol. ii, pp. 403-404; Moore, *Conscription and Conflict,* p. 158; *Letter Book of the Commandant of Conscripts,* pp. 94-95; Fleming, *Civil War and Reconstruction,* p. 106.

[61] *O. R.,* ser. iv, vol. ii, pp. 207-208. See also *O. R.,* ser. iv, vol. i, p 1149.

in the army, but military force could not keep some conscripts in the army. They deserted as often as they were put in.[62] The contempt in which conscripts were held by volunteers was certainly no deterrent to desertion. It has been assumed that conscripts furnished the majority of deserters from the army. As proof of this assumption, the fact is usually cited that desertion increased soon after the passage of the conscription act to such an extent that in June and July the War Department issued orders for the apprehension of deserters.[63] But in Alabama the machinery of conscription was hardly functioning by June and July,[64] hence the increase in desertion from that state could not have been caused by desertion of conscripts. It may have been caused by desertion of volunteers who were compelled by the conscription act to remain in service or to enter it.

The conscription act in the spring of 1862 was a source of keen disappointment and even consternation to the twelve months' volunteers. The enlistment period of two-thirds of them had almost expired and they intended to go home, for a while at least. They had endured the hardships and borne the brunt of the fighting and felt that it was now the turn of others equally interested in the outcome of the war to do their share. Many, having left home hastily, felt that their business now required their attention. On the whole, the act was received with remarkable resignation and fortitude,[65] but the feeling that Congress had been guilty

[62] Benjamin Gardner to Governor Shorter, October 23, October 27, 1863; Pollard, *Life of Jefferson Davis*, pp. 326-327; *O.R.*, ser. iv, vol. ii, pp. 636-639; vol. i, p. 114; ser. i, vol. xlix, pt. i, p. 1134.

[63] Gordon, *Reminiscences*, p. 398; Appleton, *Annual Cyclopedia*, 1862, p. 245; Moore, *Conscription and Conflict*, p. 129, p. 35.

[64] *O.R.*, ser. iv, vol. i, p. 1131; vol. ii, pp. 141-142. Bragg said Nov. 3, 1862 that he had not received any conscripts in the Army of Tennessee. —*O.R.*, ser. i, vol. xx, pt. ii, p. 386.

[65] *O. R.*, ser. iv, vol. ii, pp. 280-281.

of a breach of faith in breaking the contract with them which led a part of the Stonewall brigade to mutiny and the feeling that their families were suffering because of their absence which led an East Tennessee regiment to mutiny probably animated many Alabama volunteers.[66] The Third Alabama Regiment, which had been recruited chiefly from the black belt and which was the first to go to Virginia, received the news of the conscription act, according to one of its majors, with intense excitement and with curses loud and deep on Congress and because of their disappointment at being deprived of a visit home and their indignation at being held in the same organization while new volunteers might choose organizations in which chances of promotion were better, threatened a mutiny. But they were quieted by a speech made by the commanding officer calling on them to sacrifice themselves on the altar of patriotism.[67]

In 1864, the volunteers were asked to reenlist for three years longer on pain of conscription and assignment to other organizations.[68] The reenlistment of most Alabama regiments took place unanimously, as that of the Fifty-ninth, in which some deserters in the guard-house were allowed at their request to come out and volunteer with their regiment.[69] However, it was considered advisable to have

[66] Rhodes, *History of the United States,* vol. v, p. 15; W. G. Stevenson, *Thirteen Months in the Rebel Army,* pp. 199-204. Mr. Wigfall said in the Senate, September 4, 1862, "We retain men in the army who are anxious to go home and we call them volunteers."—*Southern Historical Society Papers,* vol. viii, p. 35, "Proceedings of Congress."

[67] Brewer, *Alabama,* pp. 591-593; Union Springs *Times,* August 15, 1866, Powell, "The Third Alabama Infantry." Two years later, this regiment reenlisted unanimously.

[68] *O. R.,* ser. iv. vol. iii, pp. 178-181. For editorials on reenlistments, "The Farce of Reenlistments" and "Good Faith," see the New York *Times,* February 10, and January 29, 1864.

[69] Bolling Hall, Jr., to Bolling Hall, Sr., March 10, 1864; J. E. Hall to his sister, Laura, March 5, 1864.

speeches, urging reenlistment, made in some regiments, and it was said that unanimous reenlistment was achieved in one regiment from the southeast and the hill counties by aid of a barrel of whiskey.[70] An address, which fell into the hands of a Union spy in Calhoun county, was said to have been circulated extensively among soldiers from north Alabama. It pointed out the injustice of holding volunteers in service after the term of their enlistment had expired and declared that even the Yankees and heathen of the dark ages did not oppress their soldiers to such an extent. It called on soldiers, as silence was no longer a virtue, to assert their rights against a tyrannical government and demand their discharges, and in case of denial to go home any way to their suffering families.[71] This address expressed a discontent with the requirement for reenlistment which no doubt existed and encouraged desertion among certain soldiers. In these ways, both voluntary and compulsory service furnished an excuse or a cause to various soldiers to abandon the military service.

Features of the maintenance of the army which tended to lower its morale and cause desertion were inadequate supply of clothing and food, arrears in pay, and infrequency of furloughs.

The inadequate supply of clothing and food, combined with exposure during prolonged and hard service, caused great physical suffering among the soldiers. The Confederate government was never able to furnish an adequate supply of blankets and shoes, and only during the last year of the war furnished something like an adequate supply

---

[70] R. E. Park, *Sketch of the Twelfth Alabama Infantry* (Richmond, 1906), p. 68; *Jones Valley Times*, 1906, E. W. Jones, "History of the Eighteenth Alabama," no. 8, Dalton.

[71] Frank Moore, *Rebellion Record*, vol. viii (Incidents), pp. 45-46.

of rough clothing to its troops.[72]   The state government, in
spite of extraordinary efforts like requisitioning leather for
shoes and cutting up the carpets from the Capitol for blankets, was not able to make good the deficiencies of the Confederate government in clothing Alabama troops.[73]   Public-
spirited men contributed money and clothing, women's
organizations made socks and shirts, and many soldiers
supplied themselves with uniforms taken on the battlefield
from dead Union soldiers.[74]   The families of soldiers, so
far as they could, sent clothing to their respective members
in the army.[75]   However, irregularity of contributions, difficulty in transportation, scarcity of materials, and, in many
families, lack of means to buy clothing made the supply
from private sources also inadequate.

In the fall of 1862, the Army of Northern Virginia was
in a destitute condition.   A statement dated September 26,
Winchester, Virginia, was circulated in Alabama and other
Southern states and was used as a basis of appeal for clothing for the soldiers during the winter.   One-fifth of the
Army of Northern Virginia were barefoot, one-half in rags,
and the whole half-famished.   It was true that on the retreat from Maryland many soldiers had straggled but most
of them had done so because of hunger, exhaustion or sickness.   A great outcry about this straggling was to be ex-

[72] Fleming, *Civil War and Reconstruction*, p. 200; Appleton, *Annual
Cyclopedia*, 1864, p. 32.

[73] *Acts*, 1863, p. 83; Miller, *Alabama*, p. 167; Fleming, *Civil War and
Reconstruction*, p. 200.   Twelve of fifteen Alabama regiments were
organized without blankets.   There was not a blanket factory in the
Confederacy in 1861.—*O. R.*, ser. iv, vol. i, p. 1082; Miller, *Alabama*,
p. 167.

[74] Appleton, *Annual Cyclopedia*, 1862, p. 16; 1863, p. 216; newspapers
of Alabama, *passim*.

[75] For example see E. K. Flournoy, letters to his wife; Hall,
correspondence.

pected from "lazy cavalry men and dainty staff officers," who could forage on horseback for something to eat, but a sufficient answer to them was the "bleeding feet, tattered garments, and gaunt frames" of those who had endured hardships such as no army in this country had ever before endured. If the Army of Northern Virginia could march through the South just as it was "ragged, almost barefoot, and hatless . . . it would produce a sensation which has no parallel in history since Peter the Hermit."[76] The best of troops, wrote the army correspondent of the Mobile *Register* from Virginia, would straggle under such circumstances.[77] During the winter of 1863-64, appeals, less vivid, but equally earnest, were made for clothing for the Army of Tennessee. Captain Harris of the Twentieth Alabama in an address to the state legislature in December stated that in a recent battle fifty men of his battalion were unable to take part because they were barefoot. He said that the destitution among Alabama soldiers was so great that it could no longer be endured and requested the members of the legislature to inform their constituents of the dire need for clothing.[78] Colonel Bolling Hall, in a letter to his sister written on January 12, stated that in his regiment, the Fifty-ninth Alabama, 180 men had no shoes, 100 wore pieces of leather which exposed half the foot and that many had no blankets or covering of any kind—with the thermometer at zero to 10° above.[79] About the same time desertions from a Mississippi regiment were ascribed to suffering caused by scarcity of clothing.[80] During the next winter, the remnant of Hood's army, which had been de-

[76] Appleton, *Annual Cyclopedia*, 1862, pp. 14-15.

[77] Mobile *Register*, October 2, 1862.

[78] *The Democratic Watchtower*, December 23, 1863.

[79] Bolling Hall, Jr., to Laura Hall, January 12, 1864.

[80] Mobile *Register*, February 16, 1864.

feated in Tennessee, endured on the retreat to Mississippi great suffering caused from cold and inadequate supply of clothing, some soldiers leaving footprints in blood on the snow.[81] It is probable that the great suffering endured on such occasions as this retreat was equaled by the unromantic, but almost constant, discomfort produced, in the absence of facilities for washing, by dirt and body lice. It is probable that dirt and body lice combined to weaken the resistance of some soldiers and to cause desertion. It is certain that suffering produced by want of clothing drove many of the least hardy soldiers out of the ranks.[82]

Even greater suffering was produced by the inadequate supply of food. "Hunger," said Dr. Basil Gildersleeve, "was the dominant note of life in the Confederacy, civil as well as military."[83] During each winter of the war, the fear of famine in parts of the Confederacy appeared like a spectre.[84] As a result of war, production of food decreased and distribution of food became so difficult that plenty and scarcity frequently existed not far apart.[85] The soldiers were the worst sufferers from these conditions.[86] The government supplied them with a small and monotonous ration, consisting chiefly of meal and bacon. In 1862, the ration was one pound of beef or one-half pound of bacon and not

[81] Kate Cumming, *Gleanings from Southland* (Birmingham, 1895), p. 204; S. C. Kelley to his wife, January 16, 1864.

[82] Joseph E. Johnston, *Narrative of Military Operations Directed during the Late War between the States by Joseph E. Johnston* (New York, 1874), p. 425; *Alabama Beacon*, January 22, 1864; Lonn, *Desertion during the Civil War*, pp. 7-8.

[83] Basil Gildersleeve, *The Creed of the Old South* (Baltimore, 1915), p. 91.

[84] Tansill, *Free and Impartial Exposition*, p. 14; E. A. Pollard, *The Lost Cause* (New York, 1867), p. 480; Jones, *Diary*, vol. ii, p. 397.

[85] Fleming, *Civil War and Reconstruction*, pp. 202-203.

[86] Eggleston, *A Rebel's Recollections*, p. 208.

more than one and one-half pound of flour or meal per day; during 1864 and 1865, it was one and one-quarter pound of meal and one-third pound of bacon per day.[87] At times the ration was larger and occasionally it was varied by the addition of sorghum molasses or other articles, but on the whole it was notoriously small and deficient in vegetables. From time to time, temporary reduction of the prescribed ration was made in parts of the army; for example in November, 1863 in the Army of Tennessee, ten crackers and one-quarter of a pound of bacon constituted the ration for three days, and in March, 1865 in the Army of Northern Virginia the amount of food issued was one-sixth of a ration.[88] An indication of the amount of such reduction in 1864 was a balance in the subsistence department at the end of the year of $70,000,000, which, according to the report of the commissary-general, existed because the department had been unable to obtain the full amount of rations prescribed.[89] Moreover, the rations were frequently inferior during the last year and a half of the war; especially in the Army of Northern Virginia, where the meal was usually coarse, the pork often rancid, and where lard was occasionally substituted for meat.[90] Whenever opportunity allowed, supplies were supplemented by food sent from home or purchased by the soldiers in the neighborhood of the army.[91]

[87] *O. R.*, ser. iv, vol. ii, p. 414; Appleton, *Annual Cyclopedia; O.R.*, ser. iv, vol. iii, p. 777; Louise Wright, *A Southern Girl in 1861* (New York, 1905), p. 174.

[88] E. K. Flournoy to his wife, November 2, November 9, 1863; J. C. Wise, *The Long Arm of Lee* (Lynchburg, 1915), pp. 923-924; Gordon, *Reminiscences*, p. 385. See also the *Independent*, February 13, 1864.

[89] *O. R.*, ser. iv, vol. iii, p. 776.

[90] Tansill, *Free and Impartial Exposition*, pp. 13-14.

[91] *Ibid.;* E. K. Flournoy to his wife, November 9, 1863; February 10, February 12, 1864; Pollard, *The Lost Cause*, p. 480.

General Lee protested to various officials against the small amount of food provided for his army. To Commissary-General Northrop, he stated in August, 1863 that he feared the effect that reduction of a ration already very small would have on the army, and in December that unless the army was supplied with food it would be impossible to hold it together. To President Davis, in the following April, he expressed his anxiety about the small supply of provisions and declared that he could not operate with his present supplies, and added simply that he had "rations for to-day and to-morrow." To the Secretary of War, on January 27, 1865, he wrote that he had no doubt that there was suffering among his troops for want of food and stated that the ration was too small for men who had to undergo the exposure and labor required of his army. He protested that it would not do to reduce the ration to make up for deficiencies in the subsistence department, and stated his opinion that the efficiency of the army demanded an increase of ration.[92]

The results of insufficient food for the army were disastrous. During 1862, they were manifested chiefly in straggling, later in disease and desertion.[93] In 1863, during the siege of Vicksburg, a letter signed "Many Soldiers" was presented to General Pemberton, stating the effect of hunger on his army.

---

[92] O. R., ser. i, vol. xxix, pt. ii, p. 625, p. 862; Rowland, *Jefferson Davis, Constitutionalist*, vol. vi, p. 224; O. R., ser. i, vol. xlvi, pt. ii, p. 1143.

[93] Appleton, *Annual Cyclopedia*, 1862, pp. 13-15; Pollard, *The Lost Cause*, p. 480; W. C. Jordan, *Some Events and Incidents during the Civil War* (Montgomery, 1909), p. 102; A. P. Ford, *Life in the Confederate Army* (New York, 1905); Lonn, *Desertion during the Civil War*, pp. 9-10; New York *Times*, February 2, 1864; *Alabama Beacon*, January 22, 1864. Professor Lonn says that the most potent causes of desertion were "possibly lack of devotion to the Confederacy and personal suffering."—Lonn, *Desertion during the Civil War*, p. 19.

We have been cut down to one biscuit and a small bit of bacon per day, not enough scarcely to keep body and soul together.... If you can't feed us you had better surrender us, horrible as the idea is, than suffer this noble army to disgrace themselves by desertion. . . . Men are not going to lie here and perish even if they do love their country dearly. . . . Hunger will compel a man to do almost anything.[94]

During 1864, hunger caused disease and compelled many soldiers who were not in a state of·siege to desert. In a conversation with Postmaster-General Reagan, General Lee stated that exhaustion and want of a vegetable diet had caused the loss of more men than the bullets of the enemy. He had, he said, advised the men to eat buds of sassafras and grapevine but some of them already had scurvy.[95] A surgeon from an army hospital at Columbus, Georgia stated that a large proportion of the diseases among soldiers was caused from exposure and camp fare.[96] A nurse from an army hospital at Richmond described the patients during the summer of 1862 as " squalid pictures of famine," and to illustrate the scarcity of food in the hospital, said that nurses were compelled to count carefully the squares of corn bread and to watch the patients to prevent rats from eating poultices from wounds.[97] In February, 1865, the number of sick in Lee's army was twice the number in Grant's army although Lee's army was much smaller.[98] The physical resistance of soldiers was so lessened that slight wounds

[94] *O. R.*, ser. i, vol. xxiv, pt. iii, p. 982.

[95] J. H. Reagan, *Memoirs with Special Reference to Secession and the Civil War* (New York, 1906), p. 193 (June 3, 1864).

[96] *O. R.*, ser. iv, vol. iii, p. 719.

[97] Phoebe Y. Pember, *A Southern Woman's Story* (London, 1899), p. 120, p. 98, p. 102.

[98] *Southern Historical Society Papers*, vol. xxi (o. s.), p. 65, Thos. G. Jones, "Last Days of the Army of Northern Virginia."

frequently caused blood poisoning and death.[99]   As weakness increased, demands of service also increased.   Suffering incurred in the trenches during the eight months' siege of Petersburg caused discontent and desertion.[100]   An inspector of the trenches reported fatigue because of prolonged service requiring one man to hold four and a half feet of line, exposure in water waist-deep in trenches after rain and to rigorous cold at other times, impairment of digestive organs of the men from inferior diet, and constant presence of filth, vermin and stench as hardships which induced some of the "meaner class" to resort to desertion and even self-mutilation for escape.[101]   It was said that in March, 1865 some of General Lee's officers reported to him that many men were temporarily crazed by hunger and, in consequence, refused to obey orders and were deserting.[102] Many of these starving men, seeing other soldiers die by the roadside and reasoning, it seems, quite sanely that human endurance has its limits, determined to save themselves by going home.[103]   In 1865, the Army of Northern Virginia was melting away, and General Lee gave it as his opinion, in which all of his commanding officers concurred, that the chief cause of desertion was insufficiency of rations and arrears in pay.[104]

To many soldiers, arrears in pay represented both bad faith on the part of the government and imposition of hard-

[99] Gordon, *Remiscences*, p. 381.

[100] *O. R.*, ser. i, vol. xlii, pt. ii, pp. 1175-1176.   See also L. A. Shaver, *History of the Sixtieth Alabama Regiment* (Montgomery, 1867), pp. 81, 83.

[101] Hagood, *Memoirs*, pp. 286-287.

[102] Gordon, *Reminiscences*, p. 385; S. A. Pryor, *Reminiscences of Peace and War* (New York, 1904), p. 333.

[103] G. C. Eggleston, *History of the Confederate War* (New York, 1919), vol. ii, pp. 354-355.

[104] *O. R.*, ser. i, vol, xlvi, pt. ii, pp. 1143-1150.

ships upon themselves — and, what was far worse, upon their families. The Confederate government made no adequate arrangements to pay the bounties which it promised for enlistment and reenlistment or to pay the regular monthly wages of soldiers. The Confederate government rarely paid its soldiers. It was said that some soldiers were paid only twice in two years' service and that a large part of the soldiers were not paid at all during the last two years of the war.[105] Just before the close of the war, Congress made an appropriation of eighty million dollars to pay " all arrears " due the army and the navy.[106] This sum represented roughly pay for a year for all the soldiers, but, judged from the fact that in September, 1864, the pay due the Trans-Mississippi troops alone was sixty million dollars,[107] it was not half enough to pay all arrears due the army and the navy. But the appropriation bill did not result in the payment of even a part of the arrears; it was vetoed by the President on the ground that the large issue of paper money would inflate the currency to such an extent that the soldiers' pay would be practically worthless to them.[108]

There was some pressure upon the Confederate government to pay the soldiers because sympathy with the soldiers who did not get their pay was general. On January 29, 1862, a special committee of Congress reported that discontent had arisen among troops from a failure to pay them regularly and advised payment.[109] On April 2, 1862, Gov-

---

[105] Appleton, *Annual Cyclopedia,* 1863, p. 18; Fleming, *Civil War and Reconstruction,* p. 200; Campbell, *Reminiscences,* p. 37.

[106] *O. R.,* ser. iv, vol. iii, pp. 1154-1155 (March 17, 1865).

[107] Campbell, *Reminiscences,* p. 37. This requisition was met by the reply that the department had no funds.

[108] *O. R.,* ser. iv, vol. iii, pp. 1154-1155.

[109] *O. R.,* ser. iv, vol. i, p. 886.

ernor Shorter in a letter to the Secretary of War insisted upon payment of the bounties which had been promised for reenlistment, saying that many poor soldiers from Alabama were crying most piteously for bounties and that he feared the consequence of failure to make prompt payment.[110] In December, 1864, the General Assembly of Alabama sent in a petition urging Congress to pay the Alabama troops, many of whom were suffering want.[111] During the latter part of 1864 and the first part of 1865, certain newspapers undertook a crusade in their columns for the payment of troops. The Richmond *Examiner* published numerous letters from soldiers, some of which were written from the trenches. These letters stated that many soldiers had not received a cent for six or twelve months and asked what soldiers were to do if they were nearly naked or if they had dependent families.[112] The editor of the *Examiner* warned Congressmen not to go by the army and make speeches, assuring them that paying arrears and improving rations and clothing were more appreciated than " noble declamation," and stated that arrears in pay and oppression by officers were the chief causes of desertion.[113] A correspondent of the Montgomery *Mail* asked how, in view of such grievous wrongs as failure to pay the soldiers and provide them with sufficient food and clothing, the government expected to stop desertion and turn the complaints and indignation of oppressed men into cheerful sacrifice.[114]

[110] *O. R.*, ser. iv, vol. i, p. 1042.

[111] *Journal of the Congress of the Confederate States of America, 1861-1865* (Washington, 1904-1905), vol. iv, p. 377.

[112] Richmond *Examiner*, November 12, November 16, November 20, November 25, December 16, December 30, 1864; January 21, 1865.

[113] March 10, 1865. Since Davis affected Pollard as Mortimer did King Charles, the statement about appointment of officers should be taken with caution.

[114] February 18, 1865.

Later, the *Mail* expressed the opinion that arrangements to pay the troops in specie would add at least 100,000 men to the army.[115]

The chief justification advanced for not paying the soldiers was that the Confederate army was not a hireling army, that its soldiers were not fighting for money, but for their rights.[116] But, doubtless, many soldiers failed to understand why paper money could be printed in order to pay for other services, far less arduous than soldiers', or to appreciate the view that sufficient pay for soldiers who were in need of the necessaries of life for themselves and their families was the honor of fighting at the risk of their lives for rights which would benefit equally with themselves those who stayed at home and made money.

Infrequent furloughs were a negative hardship in denying rest from military service and a positive hardship in enforcing separation of soldiers from their families. The hardship was none the less real because it was necessary; the policy of granting few furloughs was forced upon Confederate authorities because their troops were outnumbered by those of the enemy. During the first year of the war, Congress attempted to liberalize the granting of furloughs by two acts providing that furloughs should be granted to those soldiers whose business and family affairs required their presence at home, but the operation of the first act so threatened the army with disintegration that all furloughs were revoked under the discretionary authority of the Secretary of War, and the second act was killed by a presidential veto on the ground that an army in the field

[115] March 15, 1865. See also the Montgomery *Weekly Advertiser,* September 20, 1864.

[116] Montgomery *Daily Advertiser,* November 18, 1863, Report of the Committee on Military Affairs to Congress.

could not be administered by statute.[117]   During the remainder of the war military authorities regulated the granting of furloughs on the principle that private interests must be sacrificed to military necessity and, as a rule, rigidly adhered to a stringent policy of granting few furloughs or none at all. However, at times a rather liberal system of furloughing was indulged in but military necessity invariably put a stop to it before it had been applied to all soldiers.[118]   The discretionary authority of military officers seemed at times arbitrarily used and gave rise to complaints of favoritism in granting furloughs.[119]   To the average soldier, the only certainty about the system was the uncertainty of his getting a furlough. As a result, many soldiers when opportunity allowed made visits to their homes without permission. Certain abuses in relation to furloughs added their strength to that of military necessity in compelling infrequency of furloughs and, in addition, directly encouraged absence without leave, desertion and skulking. They were laxity on the part of some hospital authorities in furloughing convalescent soldiers and on the part of some enrolling officers in furloughing conscripts, the practice of forging and selling furloughs, the habit on the part of many soldiers of overstaying their furloughs, and finally, use by some soldiers after the fall of Vicksburg of their paroles as a kind of in-

[117] *Statutes at Large of the C. S. A.,* vol. i, p. 223; Appleton, *Annual Cyclopedia,* 1862, p. 242; *O. R.,* ser. iv, vol. i, p. 1020; Rowland, *Jefferson Davis, Constitutionalist,* vol. v, p. 210; *O. R.,* ser. iv, vol. i, pp. 898-901 (veto, Feb. 1, 1862).

[118] Gordon, *Reminiscences,* p. 284; Reagan, *Memoirs,* p. 164; *Southern Historical Society Papers,* vol. vii, p. 117, " Proceedings of Congress "; *O. R.,* ser. i, vol. li, pt. ii, pp. 754-755; N. W. Davis to his wife, August 3, 1863; Maynard Haskell to his sister, April 22, 1864.

[119] Mobile *Register,* April 12, 1864; Richmond *Examiner,* February 23, 1863; Col. N. W. Davis to his wife, January 5, 1864; February 12, 1863; Lt. J. B. Mitchell to his father, August 8, 1863.

definite furlough to protect them from arrest and return to their commands.[120]

Infrequency of furloughs was not only a military and political cause of desertion, but also a social and economic cause; homesickness of soldiers and necessities of their families led many to take furloughs which could not be secured otherwise. Doubtless, it was this fact which General Lee had in mind when he wrote to President Davis on August 17, 1863 that the object of his new system of furloughs was to offer a reward for merit and to remove " all palliation from the offence of desertion." [121]

Insufficient clothing and food, arrears in pay and infrequent furloughs were primarily military, not political, causes of desertion. Although toward the end of the war, the idea that the government which could maintain its soldiers with no more efficiency was too weak to last had its effect upon the soldiers, on the whole, little blame was attached to the government for these shortcomings. However, there were certain features of the organization and maintenance of the army which caused dissatisfaction with the government and led to desertion. They were appointments to office, taxes-in-kind and impressments, and exemptions from conscription.

Retaining certain generals in command after they had lost the confidence of army and people because of defeat was assigned as a cause for desertion for which the President was responsible. After the fall of Vicksburg, General Pemberton was so discredited that many soldiers from

120 *O. R.*, ser. i, vol. xx, pt. ii, p. 502; ser. iv, vol. ii, p. 694; *Journal of Congress of C.S.A.*, vol. vi, p. 56; vol. vii, pp. 268, 290; *O.R.*, ser. iv, vol. iii, p. 749; ser. i, vol. xvii, pt. ii, p. 790; Mobile *Register*, November 27, 1863. For the story of a soldier at Chickamauga who stepped behind a tree and waved his arms at the enemy, feeling for a furlough, see J. B. Polley, *A Soldier's Letters to Charming Nellie* (New York, 1908), p. 165.

121 Freeman, *Lee's Dispatches*, p. 124, no. 65.

Mississippi and Alabama, supported by popular approval, refused to serve under him.   Some left the army without permission and others would not obey the orders for paroled men to report to camp.   One newspaper correspondent said that retaining General Pemberton in command was " an outrage."   Both the Governor and the General Assembly of Alabama requested the removal of General Pemberton, stating that the army and the people had lost confidence in him.[122]   After the defeat at Mission Ridge, where General Bragg was hissed by his fleeing soldiers, he was equally unpopular in Alabama.   In the northern part of the state, some deserters from his army swore that they would never serve under General Bragg again, but said that they would serve under another commander.   The President shared General Bragg's unpopularity especially after making him military adviser at Richmond or, according to an Alabama newspaper, " virtual commander-in-chief." [123]   After the fall of

[122] James Longstreet, *From Manassas to Appomattox* (Philadelphia, 1903), p. 470; Montgomery *Weekly Advertiser*, August 12, 1863; *O. R.*, ser. iv, vol. ii, pp. 717, 753; A. S. Abrams, *A Full and Detailed History of the Siege of Vicksburg* (Atlanta, 1863), p. 62; Richmond *Examiner*, August 5, 1863; Selma *Reporter*, March 4, 1864; *Governor's Letter Book*, August 8, 1863, p. 62; *Journal of the Called and Regular Annual Sessions of the Senate and the House of the General Assembly of Alabama*, 1861-1863 (Montgomery, 1862-1864), *Third Regular Annual Session of the Senate*, p. 6.   General Grant said that Pemberton had to march soldiers of the Vicksburg army to camps of instruction for exchange under guard to keep them from deserting.—Grant, *Memoirs*, vol. i, p. 569.

[123] H. J. Eckenrode, *Jefferson Davis, President of the South* (New York, 1923), pp. 253, 302; New York *Times*, December 18, 1863 (quoting Mr. Foote in Congress) ; Rowland, *Jefferson Davis, Constitutionalist*, vol. vi, p. 335; Alfred Battle to Governor Shorter, August 19, 1863; *The Independent*, May 7, 1864; Eckenrode, *Jefferson Davis*, p. 311.   As early as September 12, 1862 Senator Phelan defended General Bragg.   He said that General Bragg had made an army out of 80,000 men who were nothing but a mob, and that the stories of his severity originated with stragglers and deserters.—*Southern Historical Society Papers*, vol. vii, p. 115, " Proceedings of Congress."   The Mobile *Register* consistently defended Bragg.   For example, see January 16, 1863.

Atlanta, General Hood suffered a more disastrous loss of confidence. The press and the army begged for the restoration of General Johnston, who was said by an officer of an Alabama regiment to be equal to reinforcements of 10,000 men each with a twelve-pounder. The Army of Tennessee disintegrated. President Davis was censured in Alabama as the cause of the calamities of defeat and desertion.[124]

In addition, appointments to high military offices, to " bombproof " positions, and to easy " details," or special tasks, seemed to be made largely from the wealthy class.[125] The real interpretation of this fact was the superior opportunities for training in leadership in that class, but the popular interpretation of it was favoritism on the part of the government toward the rich.

The tax-in-kind fell so heavily on families whose support was derived from white labor alone that the legislature of Alabama petitioned Congress to exempt those families from payment of the tax.[126] Mr. Chilton, in presenting the resolution, expressed the opinion that the small amount of produce gained from the tax was not worth the dissatisfaction engendered by it.[127] The quartermaster-general, evidently

[124] Montgomery *Daily Mail*, July 21, 1864; Virginia Clay-Clopton, *A Belle of the Fifties* (New York, 1904), p. 237; Richmond *Examiner*, February 3, 1865; Montgomery *Weekly Advertiser*, August 3, 1864; Captain S. C. Kelly (30th Alabama) to his wife, March 2, 1865; Eckenrode, *Jefferson Davis*, p. 312; *O. R.*, ser. iv, vol. iii, p. 1065; Selma *Reporter*, July 22, 1864; Montgomery *Daily Mail*, September 27, 1864. When President Davis visited the Army of Tennessee under the command of General Hood, the soldiers shouted at him, " Give us General Johnston! "—Eckenrode, *Jefferson Davis*, p. 312.

[125] *The Independent*, April 23, 1864; Montgomery *Weekly Advertiser*, August 5, 1862; Owsley, *Defeatism in the Confederacy* (Reprinted from the *North Carolina Historical Review*, July, 1926), p. 8.

[126] Fleming, *Civil War and Reconstruction*, p. 172; *Journal of Congress of C. S. A.*, vol. iii, p. 482; vol. vi, p. 567.

[127] Richmond *Examiner*, December 29, 1863.

of the same opinion, recommended the exemption of thirteen of the counties of northern and southeastern Alabama.[128] In addition to complaints of heavy incidence on non-slaveholding families, complaints were made of discrimination against soldiers' families in collection of the tax.[129] The impressment of property tended to alienate a more influential class of citizens. Abuses of impressment raised a storm of indignation from all parts of the Confederacy.[130] Imposters, posing as state or Confederate government officials, took all kinds of property, leaving behind them in payment worthless receipts.[131] Impressing agents practically confiscated property by paying for it in currency at prices below market prices or in certificates of indebtedness at prices which after delay in honoring were also below market prices, or they confiscated property outright by neglecting in the pressure of military movements to pay anything for it.[132] They made little or no effort to distribute impressments evenly among individuals or communities, making victims sometimes of their personal enemies by impressing their property on the charge of disloyalty, and making victims more often of the helpless families of sol-

[128] *O. R.*, ser. iv, vol. ii, pp. 575-576.

[129] Johnston, *Narrative*, p. 424. See also *O. R.*, ser. iv, vol. iii, p. 572.

[130] *O. R.*, ser. iv, vol. ii, pp. 943, 988; vol. iii, p. 446 (Ga.); ser. iv, vol. ii, p. 1066 (N. C.); ser. iv, vol. ii, pp. 863-864, 901; vol. iii, pp. 405, 407 (S. C.); ser. iv, vol. ii, p. 973; vol. iii, p. 46 (Fla.); ser. iv, vol. iii, p. 37 (Ala.); ser. iv, vol. ii, pp. 875-877, 1009; Appleton, *Annual Cyclopedia*, 1863, pp. 229-230.

[131] Miller, *Alabama*, pp. 198, 199. State laws were passed making it a penal offense punishable by 1 year's to 5 years' imprisonment and by $1500 to $5000 fine to falsely represent one's self as a Confederate agent. —*Acts of the Thirty-fifth General Assembly of Alabama, 1861-1864* (1861-1865, Montgomery), *Acts*, 1864, pp. 12-13. See also *Acts*, 1863, p. 60.

[132] Fleming, *Civil War and Reconstruction*, pp. 174-176; *O. R.*, ser. iv, vol. ii, pp. 234-235, 903; E. C. Betts to Governor Watts, February 8, 1864.

diers.[133] In violation of instructions from the War Department not to impress means of support, they stripped many families of the necessaries of life.[134] The following cases of impressment of property of soldiers' families illustrate abuses of the system. In Tuscaloosa county at least 200 miles from any army, a party of impressment officers took from a family in which there was not a pound of meat their last milch cow, from another family, a horse worth $1500 for $600 and every cow, and from a third, 23 of their 28 head of cattle, leaving a note with a negro servant informing the owners of the transaction; and within a few miles of the neighborhood, traded off most of the horses and cattle impressed from these and other families of soldiers.[135] Irregular cavalry organizations were guilty of the most obnoxious abuses in impressment of property, but regular cavalry organizations committed serious depredations upon property, especially in southeast and north Alabama, sections least able to support cavalry but most exposed to invasion. From all parts of north Alabama complaints were made to the Governor that the cavalry shot down stock, stole horses, tore down fences, and appropriated corn, fodder and other supplies.[136] According to a statement of the

[133] Appleton, *Annual Cyclopedia*, 1863, p. 230; J. L. Cunningham (Post QM., 3rd Cong. Dist., Tax-in-Kind), W. T. Simpson (Capt. and E.O.) and others to Governor Watts, January 18, 1864 (They stated, " Every man with a horse is disloyal."); S. D. Cabaniss to Governor Watts, May 21, 1864; E. C. Betts to C. C. Clay, January 23, 1863; Johnston, *Narrative*, pp. 424-425.

[134] *O.R.*, ser. iv, vol. ii, pp. 875-877, 937; vol. iii, pp. 198-199, 1170; A. C. Beard, A. G. Henry, and others to Governor Watts, May 17, 1864.

[135] Richmond *Examiner*, June 1, 1864, quoting a speech made in the Senate on May 21 by Senator Robert Jemison of Tuscaloosa.

[136] H. A. Creeview to Governor Watts, February 14, 1864; J. L. Cunningham and others to Governor Watts, June 18, 1864; David Hubbard to Governor Watts, December 19, 1863; Petition of some citizens of Talladega county to Governor Watts, March 26, 1864; E. C.

adjutant-general of the state, the approach of Confederate cavalry was as much dreaded in north Alabama as invasion by the enemy.[137] It was said that some citizens felt safer in possession of their property under occupation by Federal troops than by Confederate cavalry.[138]

A disastrous result of abuses in impressments was the alienation of many citizens from the government. " They make the natural reflection," said one, " whether a good cause administered in wrong and rapacity can succeed." [139] Disaffection in the Tennessee valley was ascribed by a prominent citizen of that section not to a lack of loyalty to the Confederate cause but to a conviction that the government which allowed such depredations upon property was a despotism.[140] The system was denounced by Governor Watts as odious in principle and disastrous in practice and as liable to cause the failure of the Confederacy by breaking the spirits of the people by its acts of tyranny.[141] " The seeds of discontent," which, in the words of Senator Hill, had been sowed " broadcast over the land," produced desertions.[142] In north Alabama, many families of soldiers were reduced by impressments, which were made chiefly by

Betts to Governor Watts, February 8, 1864; A. C. Beard and others to Governor Watts, May 17, 1864; Joel Riggs (adj.-gen.) to General J. M. Withers, February 24, 1864, and enclosures of sworn statements from seven persons.

[137] Joel Riggs to Gen. J. M. Withers, February 24, 1864.

[138] E. C. Betts to C. C. Clay, January 23, 1863. The position of the cavalry was difficult. The only method by which the cavalry could secure supplies was impressment. See Miller, *History of the Eighth Confederate Calvary*, p. 50.

[139] Appleton, *Annual Cyclopedia*, 1863, p. 207.

[140] E. C. Betts to C. C. Clay, January 23, 1863; E. C. Betts to Governor Watts, February 8, 1864.

[141] *O. R.*, ser. iv, vol. iii, p. 37.

[142] Appleton, *Annual Cyclopedia*, 1863, p. 208.

cavalry, to a condition of extreme want. They wrote distressing letters to their men in the army about the maltreatment which they had received from the hands of the government and urged them to leave the army in order to save their families from starvation. Naturally, the men responded to such appeals. In a good many cases where their families had moved into the lines of the enemy in the effort to avoid starvation, soldiers deserted to the enemy; in many other cases, they returned to their homes in north Alabama.[143] The desertion of soldiers whose families had been deprived by impressing agents of support was condoned by public opinion even in the army.[144] Many of these deserters had been good soldiers [145] and they left the army only after conviction that the government whose ingratitude was so flagrant as to allow the families of its defenders to be robbed of their means of livelihood was not worthy of further sacrifices on the part of soldiers.

Abuses and inequalities of the system of exemptions from military service brought upon the Confederate government charges of corruption and favoritism. Evasions of military service by meeting technically but not actually the requirements of the laws were so widely and successfully practiced that the commandant of conscripts of Alabama said that keeping out of the army had been reduced almost to a science.[146] Among those who practised evasion, it was said there were apothecaries who knew no more of medicine than a Patagonian knows of Sunday; teachers who knew no

[143] Colonel Enoch Alldredge (48th Ala.) to Governor Watts, March 29, 1864. Governor Watts' endorsement: "Adjutant-General Riggs will have copy of letter of Col. Alldredge sent to Gen. J. E. Johnston. Write also to him stating that Col. A. is one of our best and most reliable men and his statements may be relied on implicitly. . . ."

[144] Johnston, *Narrative*, p. 425.

[145] Johnston, *Narrative*, p. 424.

[146] *Letter Book*, p. 94 (June 6, 1864).

more of books than Don Quixote of knight-errantry; militia officers who had no militia to command; bailiffs and constables who would scorn their offices but for the exemption carried with them; manufacturers who had received government contracts at big prices; laborers who were detailed to work in supply shops, on railroads, or at agricultural employment; and others who by petition for writ of *habeas corpus* or appeals to Richmond for exemption or assignment to details delayed for months or years entering the army.[147] More flagrant than such evasions were violations of the letter as well as of the spirit of the law. One of the most frequent violations took the form of collusion between enrolling officers or medical examiners and men subject to military duty and resulted in indefinite furloughs, certificates of disability, or other papers of exemption in exchange for a price.[148] Another was the forgery and sale of papers of exemption, of which it was estimated in 1863 that the fraudulent substitute papers in the Confederacy numbered 10,000.[149] The efforts of the Bureau of Conscription in 1863 to detect and punish abuses met with little success [150] and the popular belief in widespread incompetency and corruption of officials of the Bureau grew firmer during the latter part of the war.

The exemption laws presented glaring inequalities in application. In general, they exempted all the members of

[147] Moore, *Conscription and Conflict,* pp. 55, 54; N. Rowe to Governor Watts, July 22, 1864; Croom Green to Governor Watts, August 3, 1864; *O. R.,* ser. iv, vol. ii, pp. 856-858, pp. 703-704, 709; Mobile *Register,* January 13, 1864; Pollard, *Life of Jefferson Davis,* pp. 326-327; Benjamin Gardner to Governor Shorter, October 23 and 27, 1863.

[148] *O. R.,* ser. iv, vol. ii, pp. 443-444; ser. i, vol. xvii, pt. ii, p. 790; ser. iv, vol. ii, p. 582; ser. iv, vol. iii, p. 25.

[149] *O. R.,* ser. iv, vol. ii, pp. 808, 940, 947.

[150] *O. R.,* ser. iv, vol. ii, pp. 703-704, 792; Moore, *Conscription and Conflict,* p. 81.

certain occupational groups which were considered more useful in production than in military service. But all the members of these groups were not necessary to maintain the standards of production.[151] Exemptions, according to a statement in a petition of the Assembly of Alabama to Congress, were entirely too numerous and in many cases useless.[152] On the other hand, in the occupational groups which were not exempted, there were many individual cases in which need for exemption was most urgent. " Cases," wrote the Assistant Secretary of War, " founded upon misery and confusion of families when poverty, infirmity, disease, bereavement and neglect of business, and family distress in aggravated and sometimes combined forms plead for the discharge of a soldier are abundant in this Department." [153] Such cases were especially common in north and southeast Alabama among farmers who owned few or no slaves. To alleviate this condition, the Secretary of War suggested exemption of each white male who had eight or ten dependents,[154] but such exemption was never allowed. The exemption laws tended to build up a manufacturing aristocracy which profited not only by exemption from military service but also by high prices for their products.[155] The exemption laws thus shifted to the small farmers the heaviest burdens of the war, including military service by the able-bodied men, production of agricultural supplies largely by old men, women and children, and payment of exorbitant prices for the manufactured products of the exempted classes. But the most damaging evidences of favoritism on the part of the government were laws exempting

[151] *O. R.,* ser. iv, vol. ii, pp. 997, 1041.

[152] *O. R.,* ser. iv, vol. ii, p. 767.

[153] *O. R.,* ser. iv, vol. ii, pp. 220-221.

[154] *O. R.,* ser. iv, vol. ii, p. 289.

[155] Moore, *Conscription and Conflict,* p. 64.

persons who would employ substitutes and persons who owned twenty or more slaves. These laws seemed to be pure class legislation; they seemed to be framed to benefit the wealthy classes. They did benefit them in operation. The belief that the government practiced favoritism toward the wealthy classes had a pernicious effect on civilians and soldiers. It produced discontent, jealousy and demoralization, and so decreased popular support of the government and the war. It caused desertion.[156]

A political cause of desertion which had its roots in social and economic conditions was the hostility of tories to the Confederate government. This hostility was caused primarily by a desire for neutrality, not by love of the Union. The desire for neutrality was expressed by resolutions at a convention of tories held on the borders of Fayette, Winston and Marion counties in 1862.[157] It was manifested also by their reluctance to enter military service on either side. When volunteer troops were being raised for the Confederate army, "union" companies were formed by tories in Winston county with the avowed object of self-protection, and in several other counties evidently with the same object.[158] After the passage of the conscription act, organizations were maintained at home by tories and deserters to resist compulsory service and to engage in depredations upon the loyal population.[159] Service in the Union

[156] *Journal of Congress of C.S.A.*, vol. iii, p. 446; *O.R.*, ser. iv, vol. ii, p. 995; vol. iii, p. 1133; vol. ii, pp. 287, 289; Moore, *Conscription and Conflict*, p. 113; *Governor's Letter Book*, December 31, 1862, p. 294. *Cf. infra*, pp. 123-124.

[157] *O.R.*, ser. i, vol. x, pt. ii, p. 431.

[158] Dr. A. Kaeiser to Governor Moore, November 30, 1861; P. C. Winn to Governor Moore, December 7, 1861; *O.R.*, ser. i, vol. vii, p. 840; James M. Adams to Governor Moore, June 19, 1861; *O.R.*, ser. iv, vol. ii, pp. 680-681. A Senate bill to abolish the county of Winston was lost by a vote of 28 to 34.—*Journal*, 1862, p. 227.

[159] *O. R.*, ser. i, vol. xxxii, pt. iii, pp. 746-747.

army, the acid test of true unionism, was undertaken by few tories. In spite of ample opportunity afforded by Federal occupation of part of north Alabama for three years, the total number of whites from Alabama who served in the Union army, counting reenlistments, was only 2,726. As neutrality was an impossibility, most tories were disloyal to both sides.[160]

Their attitude toward the war was natural under the circumstances of their life. Most Alabama tories belonged to the least fortunate group of that class of society known as "poor whites." They lived in dire poverty and dense ignorance. Thirty tory prisoners were described by the Confederate officer who took them as "the most miserable, ignorant, poor, ragged devils I ever saw."[161] Most tories lived in isolated sections in the mountains and on sandflats of southeast Alabama.[162] In north Alabama, they were located in the northern part of the three river counties of Lauderdale, Limestone and Madison, joining Tennessee; in the southern part of the four river counties of Franklin, Lawrence, Morgan and Marshall, joining the mountain section on the south; in all of the mountain counties of Marion, Fayette, Winston, Walker, Blount, St. Clair, DeKalb and Jackson; in the western part of Cherokee and in the northern part of Calhoun, joining the mountain section on the east; in the northern part of Talladega, Jefferson and Tuscaloosa, joining the mountain section on the south; in all of the hill county of Randolph, and in a few small sections of other hill counties like southeastern Talladega and west-

---

[160] Fleming, *Civil War and Reconstruction*, p. 117.

[161] *O. R.*, ser. i, vol. iii, p. 249.

[162] Fleming, *Civil War and Reconstruction*, pp. 110, 114; *Letter Book of the Commandant of Conscripts*, pp. 86-88; A. Q. Bradley to General H. P. Watson, September 7, 1864; Miller, *Alabama*, p. 193; Mobile *Register*, September 1, 1861; Moore, *Civil War in Song and Story*, p. 215; J. P. Cannon, *Inside of Rebeldom* (Washington, 1900), p. 183.

ern Shelby and northern Bibb. They were said to be especially numerous and troublesome in Fayette, Marion, Winston, Walker, Blount, Marshall, St. Clair and De-Kalb.[163] In southeast Alabama, tories were located in the extreme southern part of five counties bordering on Florida —Conecuh, Covington, Coffee, Dale and Henry.[164]

In comparison with the whole population of these counties, the number of tories in them was small. An indication of the small number of tories was the response of these counties to the call for Confederate troops. Two recruiting agents reported that the response in north Alabama was liberal. E. H. Foster, who was recruiting a regiment in the northwest mountain counties, wrote to the Governor early in 1861 that the war spirit in the regions which had been reported disaffected was as high as elsewhere.[165] John W. Dubose, who traveled in north Alabama during the following winter, said that he did not meet a disloyal man.[166] More significant than these opinions was the part of the population which entered the Confederate army. Before the conscription act was passed, the number of volunteers reported by the probate judges as furnished by their respective

---

[163] Fleming, *Civil War and Reconstruction,* p. 110 (Map), pp. 120, 121; *Letter Book of Commandant of Conscripts,* p. 303; Merit Street to Governor Watts, September 13, 1864; J. W. Suttle to Joel Riggs, May 23, 1864.

[164] Fleming, *Civil War and Reconstruction,* pp. 110 (Map), 123; Mobile *Register,* October 27, 1863; March 19, 1864.

[165] E. H. Foster to Governor Moore, February 9, 1861.

[166] A. B. Moore, *History of Alabama and Her People* (Chicago, 1927), vol. i, p. 525. W. G. Stevenson, who after thirteen months' service in the Confederate army, part of the time in Alabama, deserted to the Union, said, "I am often asked respecting the Union feeling in the seceded states and can only answer that while I was there I did not see any . . . (They are) as sincere as ever were martyrs, going to the stake."—*Thirteen Months in the Rebel Army* (New York, 1864), pp. 132-133.

counties formed the following percentages of the total white population: Limestone, Lauderdale, Madison, Jackson, De-Kalb, 10; Franklin, 7; Marion, 6; Marshall, Calhoun, 11; Fayette, 8; Morgan, 13; Henry, 18; Coffee, 9; Covington and Conecuh, 7. The number of volunteers reported as furnished by twelve counties of the black-belt section formed percentages of the total white population from 9 to 16.[167] In view of the advantages which the black belt had in its large slave population, a productive class indirectly increasing the military class, the difference between the parts of the population furnished as volunteers by these two groups of counties seems very small and indicates that tories were neither a large nor influential element in the counties where they lived.' The relative strength of Confederate and Union sentiment in the sections which contained tories may be suggested by the fact that Jackson and Marshall counties furnished more volunteers to the Confederate army before the passage of the conscription act than the whole state furnished to the Federal army during the war.[168]

[167] *Reports of Probate Judges and Sheriffs of Counties in response to Governor Shorter's circular of March 15, 1862 of the number of companies from counties in Confederate service.* As the manuscript reports are incomplete, figures are omitted for (1) Dale, Morgan, Randolph, Walker, St. Clair and Winston and (2) Perry, Pike, Russell, Sumter, and Wilcox. In cases where reports were made in companies, calculations have been based on estimates of 100 men to a company. Population statistics were taken from the *Eighth Census, Population,* p. 8. During the war, Walker and Randolph each furnished more soldiers to the Confederate army than their voting populations.—Miller, *Alabama,* p. 193; Thomas J. Johnston to Governor Watts, April 11, 1864.

[168] *Reports of Probate Judges and Sheriffs of Counties in response to Governor Shorter's circular of March 15, 1862;* Fleming, *Civil War and Reconstruction,* p. 117. Compare also the number of soldiers furnished by Randolph to the Confederate army during the war, 3200, with the number furnished by all the counties to the Federal army during the war, 2,726. It was said after the war that Randolph furnished nearly 500 soldiers to the Federal army.—J. T. Trowbridge, *The South, A Tour of its Battle-fields and Ruined Cities* (Hartford, 1866), p. 444.

True Union sentiment among tories was not strong enough to be a major cause of desertion of Alabama troops. Those tories of military age who loved the Union enough to fight for it entered the Federal army, not the Confederate. Most tories did not wish to fight at all; they wished to remain neutral. Consequently, they resisted conscription in the Confederate army, sometimes by hiding themselves, sometimes by using force. Some " tory conscripts " who were put into the army in spite of their efforts to keep out of it deserted and probably assigned as a reason their " unionism." Naturally tories consorted with deserters, who, though they might not be hostile to the Confederacy, were equally anxious not to be put into its army. They harbored deserters and combined with them to resist capture, thus encouraging desertion. Tories with deserters committed depredations upon the defenceless loyal population, so that counties in which tories lived suffered more from lawlessness than counties in which deserters collected alone. They supported the peace movement though they were not an important part of it.[169]

The peace movement, which had as its ultimate aim the reconstruction of the Union by the restoration of the seceded states, stated usually as " reconstruction," encouraged desertion. The peace movement reflected sectionalism and manifested itself (1) in party politics and (2) in the Peace Society. The immediate background of the party politics of the war period was the secession convention with its two parties, the secession and the cooperation. The counties of south Alabama with the exception of Conecuh sent secession delegates. The counties of north Alabama above the black-belt section with the exception of Calhoun, Bibb and

[169] *O. R.*, ser. iv, vol. ii, pp. 637-638; ser. i, vol. xxxii, pp. 746-747; ser. iv, vol. ii, pp. 680-681, 726-727.

Shelby sent cooperation delegates.[170]   As the vote of the
state for Breckenridge in the presidential election had indicated, the secessionists secured a majority — 54 to 46.[171]
The secessionists favored immediate separate secession by
the state. The cooperationists were divided; some favored
cooperation by the state with the other Southern states or
with the other cotton states to secure protection of their
rights in the Union; others favored cooperation with other
states in secession and the formation of a Confederacy.[172]
Although the white counties sent 70 of the 100 delegates,
both parties were agreed on the need of some action to protect their rights against a sectional party pledged to exter-
minate slavery and at the opening of the convention passed
a resolution by a unanimous vote that the state would not
submit to the administration of Lincoln.[173]   The passage of
this resolution seemed to make secession doubly sure but the
cooperationists delayed it for a few days.   In an effort to
secure united action in the South, they made a minority
report proposing that a convention of the slaveholding
states should be called to meet February 22 to consider
remedies for certain grievances which they listed, but the
report was rejected by a strict party vote.[174]   They insisted
that any ordinance of secession which should be adopted by
the convention should be submitted by referendum to the
people, but the secessionists opposed a referendum on the
ground that it was unnecessary and would involve delay.

[170] Fleming, *Civil War and Reconstruction*, p. 359.

[171] W. R. Smith, *The History and Debates of the Convention of the
People of Alabama* (Montgomery, 1861), p. 23. Contests in Mobile,
Autauga and Shelby were close.

[172] Smith, *Debates*, p. 25; Fleming, *Civil War and Reconstruction*, p.
28; Hodgson, *Cradle of the Confederacy*, p. 488.

[173] Smith, *Debates*, pp. 24-30; Fleming, *Civil War and Reconstruction*,
pp. 29, 30-31.

[174] Smith, *Debates*, pp. 77-80.

The cooperationists talked a good deal but not very clearly about the feelings of their constituents, but much of their talk probably came out of the obstruction tactics of a minority party and from the long habit of opposition of north Alabama to south Alabama. With the exception of one incident in debate, great harmony prevailed between the parties in the convention.[175] They were united on the ground of resistance to a common enemy, the Black Republican party. The cooperation delegates made not one strong appeal for the union and expressed no love of it. They said, on the other hand, that they and their constituents preferred secession to " submission." [176] The vote on the ordinance was 69 to 31. Fifteen of the cooperationists voted for it, and 9 of the 31 who voted against it signed it. In eloquent and patriotic speeches, the cooperationist leaders pledged themselves to support the ordinance of secession and thus show to the common enemy a people united in loyalty to their sovereign state.[177]

[175] Smith, *Debates, passim;* Fleming, *Civil War and Reconstruction,* pp. 31, 37-38, 53-54. At one time Yancey warned the cooperationists that resistance to the ordinance after it should have been passed would be treason and should be punished as such. He predicted that the name " tory " would be revived to apply to those who should offer resistance. Jemison, a cooperationist leader, resented Yancey's speech as a slur on " great popular masses in certain sections " and accused him of proposing the inauguration of a reign of terror by wholesale hangings. Yancey explained that he had reference only to certain localities, not to all north Alabama. The localities to which he referred were doubtless those in which tories were later found. They had only one representative in the convention, Sheets. In 1862, Sheets was expelled from the state legislature for giving aid to the enemy.—Smith, *Debates,* pp. 68-74; *Journal of House,* 1862, p. 122.

[176] Smith, *Debates,* pp. 87, 96, 98, 99, 101, 103, 104, 105, 106, 109, 110, 117, *passim;* Fleming, *Civil War and Reconstruction,* pp. 32-34, 37, 55-56.

[177] Smith, *Debates,* p. 122; Fleming, *Civil War and Reconstruction,* p. 57; Owsley, *Defeatism,* p. 4; Montgomery *Daily Mail,* April 5, 1861; Jere Clemens to Governor Moore, February 2, 1861; *Democratic Watchtower,* January 30, 1861.

Secession was received by the people of the state with enthusiasm with some exceptions in north Alabama. Expressions of discontent there included meetings of protest in Franklin and Marion; the burning of Yancey in effigy in Limestone; talk of hostility among the mountaineers in Lauderdale; and plans, which had been discussed before the convention, for the formation, by secession of extreme north Alabama and part of Tennessee, of a new state, Nickajack, which should be neutral in the coming conflict.[178]

Then President Lincoln's call for 75,000 volunteers shocked the people of Alabama into practically unanimous realization that secession was not a domestic issue upon which they might differ, but a declaration of independence which could be made good only by fighting. Invasion by the army of the abolitionist North menaced the dissolution of their social system and threatened the spoliation of their homes. Confronted by such danger, the people forgot party and sectional lines and responded together. Within a year, they sent 60,000 volunteers out of a voting population of 90,000 to fight in self-defense. But following this outburst of patriotism, old habits of political differences began to reassert themselves. In 1862, opposition to the war emerged in north Alabama and from 1863 to the end of the war formed a minority party which was rather formidable. It existed in the same counties in which the cooperation party had been strong.[179]

The peace party, or the reconstructionists, though differ-

---

[178] Moore, *Rebellion Record*, vol. i (Diary of Events), pp. 19-20; Montgomery *Daily Mail*, April 5, 1861; Jere Clemens to Governor Moore, February 15, 1861; Mobile *Register*, January 16, 1861; Smith, *Debates*, p. 84; Betts, *Early History of Huntsville*, p. 95; Wm. Jackson to Gov. Moore, Feb. 3, 1861.

[179] Owsley, *Defeatism in the Confederacy*, p. 5; Tansill, *Free and Impartial Exposition*, pp. 12-13; *The South Atlantic Quarterly*, vol. ii, pp. 114-124, W. L. Fleming, "The Peace Movement in Alabama."

ing somewhat among themselves, believed that the Confederate States could not establish their independence and that they should lay down their arms and assume their former position in the Union. The war party, or the secessionists, believed that the Confederate States would establish their independence and that they could make an honorable peace and avoid " subjugation " only with independence. The leaders of the peace party came largely from the old cooperation party. They varied from former cooperation leaders, who saw nothing but disaster in continuing the war and hoped by immediate peace to save something out of the wreck, to unscrupulous demagogues, who, caring nothing for public interests, used any appeals, including those to sectional and class prejudice, which might advance their own immediate political fortunes. Most of the leaders of the peace party were men of small talent and of limited experience in public affairs, but they had a field which was practically free from competition because of the absence of the ablest former leaders, volunteers in the army, and which was full of discontent because of the hardships entailed by war.[180] The members of the party were malcontents, including tories. They were described by a secession newspaper as " the doubting, the despondent, the croaking, and the dissatisfied." [181] The peace party were dissatisfied with Confederate and state administrations on account of the ardent support which both governments had given to the war. Because of serious military reverses, beginning with Vicksburg, the peace party despaired of success in the war and although they had some fears of the resentment of soldiers, disfranchised by service in the army, they

---

[180] Moore, *History of Alabama*, vol. i, p. 544; Mobile *Daily News*, October 20, 1865, quoting Wm. R. Smith; Crenshaw Hall to his father, June 4, 1863.

[181] Montgomery *Weekly Advertiser*, August 5, 1863.

planned to replace secession officers with peace men. The peace party were dissatisfied also with Confederate and state administrations on account of certain military and civil policies. The chief grievances charged against the Confederate administration were those already described in connection with conscription, exemption, soldiers' pay, taxes-in-kind and impressments.[182] The chief grievances charged against the state administration were (1) discrimination between north and south Alabama in providing military protection and (2) failure to make adequate provisions for the families of poor soldiers.[183] The fact that most of these grievances were felt more severely by the poor tended to make the peace party a social movement.

Though a " minority of malcontents," the peace party was strong in voting and had considerable success in the election of August, 1863.[184] Governor Shorter, who had been an enthusiastic supporter of the Confederate cause, was overwhelmingly defeated by Thomas Hill Watts, who was said to be a reconstructionist. Governor Shorter himself attributed his defeat to his zeal in " holding up the state to its high resolves and crowding the people to a performance of their duty." [185] The report was current that Watts was

[182] *O. R.,* ser. iv, vol. ii, p. 727; Mobile *Register,* March 22, 1864; Montgomery *Weekly Advertiser,* August 5, 1863; *Democratic Watchtower,* July 8, 1863; *Alabama Beacon,* May 20, 1864; John Clisby to Governor Shorter, July 22, 1863; Moore, *Rebellion Record,* vol. viii (Incidents), pp. 45-46. In sections which were invaded or threatened with invasion, some men advocated peace in order to save their property.— Jones, *Diary,* vol. i, p. 208; vol. ii, p. 16; Mobile *Register,* June 12, 1862.

[183] *Alabama Beacon,* July 24, 1863 (circular address of Governor Shorter) ; Jacksonville *Republican,* July 11, 1863; E. C. Betts to Governor Watts, February 8, 1864.

[184] Fleming, *Civil War and Reconstruction,* p. 135.

[185] *Governor's Letter Book,* September 8, 1863, p. 69; July 24, 1863, p. 55.

in favor of reconstruction.[186]   An officer in the army deplored the bad reports of the issues upon which Watts beat
Shorter among the lower classes.[187]   Another keen observer
assigned as the chief reason for Watts' election the belief
that he would make adequate provisions for the poor families of the soldiers.[188]   The vote showed no sectionalism by
counties, as Watts carried all the counties in the state but
four in north Alabama.[189]   After his election, Governor
Watts refuted " the slander " that he had been in favor of
reconstruction, saying that after a searching canvas, he was
convinced that there were few people in the state base enough
to live with Yankees again on any terms and that he would
prefer the desolation of the Confederacy by fire and sword
to its reunion with the North.[190]

The success of the peace party was greater in the election
of members of Congress.   It was said that six of the twelve
members of Congress elected from Alabama were in favor
of reconstruction.[191]   In the third district, in extreme northeast Alabama, a tory was elected—W. R. W. Cobb, called a
perfect type of demagogue with the art of inspiring devotion among the simple-minded and ignorant classes.[192]   In
the fourth district, directly south of the third, Cruikshank,

[186] Mobile *Register,* October 10, 1863; Montgomery *Weekly Mail,*
September 23, 1863; Appleton, *Annual Cyclopedia,* 1863, p. 8.

[187] Bolling Hall, Jr., to his father, August 10, 1863.

[188] J. W. Dubose, *The Life and Times of William L. Yancey* (Birmingham, 1892), p. 674. See also the Montgomery *Weekly Advertiser,*
August 5, 1863.

[189] *Journal of House,* 1863, p. 110.

[190] Montgomery *Daily Advertiser,* November 18, 1863; Appleton,
Annual Cyclopedia, 1863, p. 8. It was said that as a secessionist he out-
Heroded Herod.

[191] Fleming, *Civil War and Reconstruction,* pp. 138-139.

[192] Brewer, *Alabama,* pp. 285, 287. In 1864, Cobb was expelled from
Congress for giving aid and comfort to the enemy.—*Journal of Congress,*
vol. vii, pp. 275-278.

a little known editor and, by reputation, a reconstructionist, defeated the incumbent, J. L. M. Curry, a national figure and a personal friend of President Davis. Peace was an important issue in this contest. Cruikshank, it was said, leaned toward peace and played upon the hopelessness and hardships of the war.[193] Curry denounced the belief that peace could be made without the sacrifice of liberty and independence as " an ignorant delusion," and the attempt to organize a peace party as " unjust to our sister states, grossly wrongful to the army, and an encouragement to our enemies to persevere in their unhallowed designs." [194] The election of Cruikshank was attributed by one secession journal to his patriotic efforts to aid the poor families of soldiers, but it was generally looked on as a victory for the peace party and as an indication among the people of a tendency to let down.[195] In south Alabama each of the sixth, seventh, and eighth congressional districts, which included two kinds of counties, the vote, though in favor of continuing the war, showed a perfect division of the rich, slave-holding counties against the poor, white counties.[196] At the same time, a number of unknown men of doubtful zeal for the Confederacy were elected to the state legislature.[197]

[193] Montgomery *Weekly Mail,* September 16, 1863; Mobile *Evening News,* July 21, 1865; J. L. Underwood, *Women of the Confederacy* (New York, 1906), p. 191.

[194] *Democratic Watchtower,* July 8, 1863 (speech of Curry).

[195] Selma *Reporter,* August 11, August 19, 1863; Montgomery *Weekly Mail,* September 23, 1863; *Democratic Watchtower,* July 22, 1863; *O.R.,* ser. iv, vol. ii, p. 726; Polk, *Leonidas Polk,* vol. ii, p. 230. Curry wrote to Governor Watts, January 23, 1865, that the peace feeling which had defeated him was "ill-concealed unionism." Calhoun county, which had sent secession delegates to the convention, gave a majority to Curry.— Montgomery *Weekly Advertiser,* September 23, 1863 (official returns).

[196] See the official returns in the Montgomery *Weekly Advertiser,* September 23, 1863.

[197] *O.R.,* ser. iv, vol. ii, p. 726. See also: Mobile *Register,* April 19, 1864 (Holley of Covington) ; Selma *Reporter,* August 19, 1863.

Encouraged by their success in the election of 1863, the peace party continued their activities during 1864 and 1865. They elected a good many men to local offices, gaining control of the government in several counties in north Alabama, and expected to elect a governor in 1865.[198] They held public meetings, at which they usually passed resolutions for peace and occasionally made plans for reconstruction.[199] During the fall of 1864, their members in the state legislature introduced resolutions proposing peace on the terms laid down by the platform of the Republican convention in Chicago and suggested the appointment of a commission from the state to the Lincoln government. The resolutions, after a heated debate in the legislature and after an earnest message from Governor Watts, were tabled.[200] Near the close of the war, certain leaders of the peace party were carrying on some kind of negotiations with the Federals, looking toward the reconstruction of at least three-fourths of Alabama, if not all of it.[201]

As an expression of demoralization at home, the peace party increased demoralization in the army. It convinced some soldiers, who probably wanted to be convinced, of the

[198] John Clisby to Governor Watts, October 17, 1864 (Randolph); A. Hester to Governor Watts, May 18, 1864 (Coosa); M. J. Turnley to Governor Watts, March 14, 1865 (Calhoun); *Clarke County Journal,* December 22, 1864.

[199] *South Atlantic Quarterly,* vol. ii, p. 257, W. L. Fleming, " The Peace Movement in Alabama"; Appleton, *Annual Cyclopedia,* 1864, pp. 10-11; Mobile *Register,* March 27, 1864 (talk of secession of Jackson county); Mobile *Register,* May 8, 1864 (talk of a new state in north Alabama).

[200] Fleming, *Civil War and Reconstruction,* p. 136; *Garfield Collection of Pamphlets,* p. 474, "Record of Governor Parsons of Alabama"; Memphis *Appeal,* October 7, 1864; New York *Times,* October 29, 1864; January 29, 1865.

[201] *South Atlantic Quarterly,* vol. ii, p. 257, Fleming, "Peace Movement in Alabama"; *O. R.,* ser. i, vol. xlix, pt. i, pp. 590-593.

uselessness of fighting longer for a cause which was doomed to defeat and for a government whose policies were shot through with injustice if not tyranny.[202] They held out to wavering soldiers the alluring prospect of an end to the almost unbearable hardships of war. As a means of protection to deserters, the peace party had more influence in encouraging desertion. The party issued a trumpet call to disaffected elements and received into its ranks the conscripts and deserters who answered it. With open or tacit approval, it accepted the aid of such reinforcements, and in some cases in the election of 1863 owed its success to the votes of paroled men from Vicksburg and deserters.[203] By its success in elections, the peace party gave the impression in the army that it represented the wishes of the majority in certain sections, if not in the entire state, and so assured deserters of a public opinion which would not only accept them as voting members of the community but protect them from any attempts from the outside to return them to the army.[204] It helped to create the immunity which allowed deserters to come and go at pleasure in twenty-five counties of the state in 1865.[205] The result of the activities of the peace party was stated in May, 1864 in a report to Congress from the committee on the judiciary which, after making an enumeration of the difficulties of the Confederacy including invasion, exhaustion, scarcity of the necessaries of life, deranged currency and doubtful public credit, and military defeats, read:

But the timid began to despond, the wavering to incline against

---

[202] *Speech of Thomas Gholson* (Va.) *on Employing Negroes in the Army*, 1865, p. 17.

[203] *O. R.*, ser. iv, vol. ii, p. 727.

[204] Bolling Hall to his father, August 17, 1863; *O. R.*, ser. iv, vol. ii, p. 727.

[205] *O. R.*, ser. iv, vol. iii, p. 1065.

us, and the unscrupulous to prepare to sell their country's independence. Designing men, while they disguised a treasonable aim, thought a season of distress was opportune for denouncing the war although we had no alternative but submission to a foreign yoke. They exaggerated our misfortunes and the power of the enemy. . . . Under the sinister influences of the times, our army was thinned by desertions and the deserters were protected at home.[206]

The Peace Society was the collective name usually given to several semi-political, secret societies which existed in the state during the latter half of the war. The Peace Society had no written constitution and kept no written records; it elected no officers and held no meetings. Although these conditions admitted considerable variety and flexibility, the Peace Society was a strong organization with the same general features everywhere in the state. Whether it had its origin with the enemy or with the politicians at home, it grew in the same dissatisfaction which produced the peace party. The object of the Peace Society, as its name indicated, was peace. To some members, who stated that they were hostile to Lincoln and the abolitionists, the object was an " honorable " peace followed by the restoration of the union as it was under Jefferson; to others, probably a majority, it was peace at any price. With a view to ending the war, the members of the Peace Society pledged themselves (1) to overthrow the Confederate government and (2) to break up the army. To overthrow the Confederate government, all of the members advocated the use of the usual party methods of electing men to offices with the unusual object of abolishing the offices, and some of the members advocated the use of the revolutionary methods of disobedience and force. To break up the army, the members

[206] *Report of the Committee on the Judiciary upon Suspension of the Writ of Habeas Corpus,* May 21, 1864, p. 8.

took an oath to resist conscription, to encourage desertion
and to protect deserters from arrest. Some members who
were in the army took an oath to desert, to encourage desertion and never to fight the enemy. Near the Federal lines,
the Peace Society encouraged fraternization with the enemy.
Whether the objects were treasonable or not depended upon
the point of view. The Peace Society embraced at least
three organizations of the state. One was found in southeast Alabama in the counties of Conecuh, Covington, Coffee, Dale, Henry, Barbour and Pike, and two others were
found in north Alabama in the counties lying between the
black-belt section and Tennessee. Of the last two, one,
which was said to include among its policies the encouragement of desertion to the Federal army, was found in the
extreme northern part of the state, including four counties
north of the Tennessee river in which few deserters collected, and the other, the largest in the state, was found in
the northern counties below this area and was especially
strong in the hill counties of Talladega, Shelby, Coosa,
Tallapoosa, Randolph and Calhoun, and in the mountain
counties of Blount, Winston and Walker. Thus the Peace
Society was located in the same sections in which deserters
collected.[207]

The members of the Peace Society embraced about one-
half of the active men left in the state [208] and formed a
majority of the population in some counties — Randolph,
Coosa, Tallapoosa, and probably others.[209] Its members

[207] *O. R.*, ser. iv, vol. ii, pp. 726-727; ser. iv, vol. iii, pp. 393-398; ser.
i, vol. xxiv, pt. ii, pp 548-557; ser. i, vol. xxxii, pt. iii, pp. 681-683, pp.
855-856; Fleming, *Civil War and Reconstruction,* pp. 141-142; *South
Atlantic Quarterly,* vol. ii, pp. 247-256, Fleming, "Peace Movement in
Alabama"; Bolling Hall to his father, July 18, 1863; Lt.-Col. John W.
Estes to Maj. J. C. Lewis, April 28, 1864.

[208] Fleming, *Civil War and Reconstruction,* p. 138.

[209] *O. R.*, ser. iv, vol. iii, p. 393. Two members of the Peace Society

came from the poorer classes of the population, which had little share in public affairs.[210] But the Peace Society was said to contain some men of ability and influence. The report was current that L. E. Parsons, later provisional governor of the state, was head of the order and that other politicians, prominent in the state, were members of it.[211] Investigations by agents of the Confederate army revealed the fact that the Peace Society included some lawyers, preachers, justices of the peace, members of the legislature, enrolling and conscripting officers, members of boards of surgeons, men and officers in the county reserves, and officers in camps of instruction.[212] The Peace Society also entered the army. In June, 1863, because of the large number of desertions, the Peace Society was discovered in Hilliard's Legion, Gracie's Brigade, which was then stationed near Knoxville, Tennessee. After a quiet investigation, officers of the Legion reached the conclusion that the soldiers who had joined the Peace Society had been the ignorant dupes of politicians and harbored no treasonable designs. As a punishment for having the Peace Society in it, Colonel Bolling Hall's regiment, which had been recruited largely in southeast and north Alabama, was ordered to the front. At Chickamauga, the regiment fought with such gallantry that its colors were pierced with eighty-two holes.[213] In December, 1863, the Peace Society was discovered in General Clanton's brigade, which had been recruited largely

said that nearly all of the deserters and conscripts evading service were members.—Lt.-Col. John W. Estes to Maj. J. C. Lewis, April 28, 1864.

[210] O. R., ser. iv, vol. xxvi, pt. ii, p. 550; Fleming, *Civil War and Reconstruction*, p. 142.

[211] O. R., ser. iv, vol. iii, pp. 384, 396, 398.

[212] O. R., ser. i, vol. xxxii, pt. iii, p. 682; ser. iv, vol. iii, pp. 397-398.

[213] Bolling Hall, Jr., to his father, July 18, 1863; Crenshaw Hall to his father, June 4, 1863; O. R., ser. i, vol. xxvi, pt. ii, p. 556; Brewer, *Alabama*, p. 671.

from the counties of southeast Alabama and was then stationed in one of them. It was discovered through the mutiny of about a hundred men, which proved to be a premature attempt at the execution of a plan for a general mutiny to take place on Christmas day. Seventy of the men were sent in irons by General Clanton to Mobile for trial but investigations by the court-martial showed that few had joined the army for treasonable purposes. To improve its loyalty, the brigade was scattered. Two regiments were ordered to the front and obeyed without a single desertion.[214] Few members of the Peace Society were in the army. Although the Peace Society had no regular officers, certain active workers, called "eminents," secured new members and initiated them. Members took an oath upon penalty of death for its violation to observe strict secrecy, assumed obligations to aid members of the order and to work for its objects, and were taught passwords for different occasions and grip and signs for recognition of members.[215]

The Peace Society carried on an active propaganda at home and in the army. It had workers at home, who, adapting their arguments to every shade of disaffection, secured new members and fanned the flames of discontent. It had agents in the Army of Northern Virginia and in the Army of Tennessee and probably in the Federal army.[216] They participated in politics in order to elect men friendly to their aim. They formed the most aggressive part of the peace party. They wrote letters to soldiers in the army, urging them to come home in time to vote in August, 1863, with

[214] *O. R.*, ser. i, vol. xxvi, pt. ii, pp. 548-557. They were poor men and were distressed by the suffering of their families.

[215] *O. R.*, ser. i, vol. xxxii, pt. iii, p. 682; ser. iv, vol. iii, pp. 393, 395, 397.

[216] *O. R.*, ser. iv, vol. iii, pp. 393-396.

the result that many soldiers came home—with their canteens filled with powder—and voted. The success of the peace party in that election was due largely to the Peace Society. An indication of their activity in the election of 1863 may be given by a comparison of the number of votes for governor cast in each county in 1861 with the number cast in each county in 1863. As soldiers in the army could not vote, the number of votes cast in 1863 was smaller with the exception of two counties than the number cast in 1861, ranging from 19% to 101%. In spite of the fact that many factors operate in bringing out the vote, it is striking that with three exceptions the twelve counties in which the percentages were highest, from 71 to 101, were in the sections of the peace societies—(1) Lauderdale, (2) St. Clair, Talladega, Randolph, Tallapoosa and Coosa, and (3) Coffee, Covington and Baldwin. In 1864 and 1865, they succeeded in electing some conscripts and deserters to local offices.[217]

The methods used to break up the army were encouragement of disaffection and desertion and protection of deserters from arrest. The exact relation between the Peace Society and the enemy was not known. It was reported that the Peace Society was in communication with the enemy and offered protection to their prisoners and spies, helping them to maintain a line of spies in 1864 from Tennessee to Tallapoosa county.[218] It was reported that the Peace Society was in cooperation with a similar society in the Union army.[219]

---

[217] *O. R.*, ser. iv, vol. ii, pp. 726-727; John Clisby to Governor Shorter, July 22, 1863; A. Hester to Governor Watts, May 18, 1864; M. J. Turnley to Governor Watts, March 14, 1865. For the number of votes cast for governor in 1861 and in 1863, upon which the percentages were computed, see: *Journal of Senate and House*, 1861, pp. 91-92; *Journal of the House*, 1863, p. 110.

[218] *O. R.*, ser. i, vol. xxxii, pt. iii, p. 682; ser. iv, vol. ii, p. 726; Montgomery *Weekly Advertiser*, July 6, 1864.

[219] *O. R.*, ser. i, vol. xxxii, pt. iii, p. 681; Lt. Col. John W. Estes to

One of the signs of the Peace Society, holding the gun at an angle of forty-five degrees with the right hip and then placing it on the left shoulder, was given to members to be used in battle to keep them from being fired at.[220] One of the passwords was given to be used in prison to effect their release.[221] Some members took an oath never to fight the enemy. The Peace Society claimed that Vicksburg was surrendered and Mission Ridge lost through their instrumentality.[222] To encourage desertion, members wrote to soldiers in the army and talked to soldiers at home on furlough or parole, urging them to desert. To keep conscripts out of the army and to protect deserters from arrest, they relied mainly upon their control of the agencies of conscription. Enrolling officers declined to arrest conscripts; boards of surgeons discharged them as physically unfit for military service. Enrolling officers gave passes good for a year to deserters; officers of prisons and conscription camps released them; members and officers of the reserves made only a pretense at looking for deserters and admitted them as members of the organization.[223] One illustration will

Major J. C. Lewis (Provost-Marshal General, Lt.-Gen. Polk's Dept.), April 28, 1864. This letter, which was written from the Chief Provost Marshal's Office, First District, North Alabama, contains an account of the confession of two prisoners who had been initiated into the society in Franklin county, Alabama. They made the statement, which they probably believed, that all of the Northern army and one-third of the Southern army belonged to the society, the name of which was the Knights of the Golden Circle. For an account from Union sources of the Knights of the Golden Circle, see *O. R.*, ser. ii, vol. v, pp. 363-367.

[220] *O. R.*, ser. iv, vol. iii, p. 397; ser. i, vol. xxxii, pt. iii, p. 681; ser. ii, vol. v, p. 364; Lt.-Col. John W. Estes to Maj. J. C. Lewis, April 28, 1864.

[221] *O. R.*, ser. i, vol. xxxii, pt. iii, p. 681.

[222] *O. R.*, ser. iv, vol. iii, p. 398.

[223] *O. R.*, ser. iv, vol. iii, pp. 394-398; ser. iv, vol. ii, pp. 258, 727; ser. i, vol. xxxii, pt. iii, p. 681; Jno. W. Estes to J. C. Lewis, April 8, 1864.

show how the system worked. In 1864 in Randolph county, a loyal officer of the reserves arrested a deserter who had a forged furlough and took him to the conscript camp at Talladega, but the deserter, after giving the sign of the Peace Society to a lieutenant at the camp, was released and got back home by the time the officer who arrested him did.[224] Because of its general character and objects, its organization and methods, the Peace Society was a potent cause of desertion.

[224] *O. R.*, ser. iv, vol. iii, p. 398.

CHAPTER IV

SOCIAL AND ECONOMIC CAUSES OF DESERTION

THE belief that the war was "a rich man's war and a poor man's fight" was a cause of desertion. This belief grew in the soil of class distinctions, which was well prepared in Alabama before the war. On top, the slaveholders formed an aristocratic class, which, though courteous in its treatment of the non-slaveholding class, felt a decided superiority to them. At the bottom, the non-slaveholders who lived in the mountains and sandhills formed the class known as the "poor white trash," who were as ignorant and superstitious as they were poor and who hated "niggers" and "nigger lords." The non-slaveholders in moderate circumstances and the "poor whites" formed the middle class, which changed gradually in economic and social interests from the aristocracy to the "poor white trash."[1] The hardships of the war, falling with greater severity upon the poor, increased the differences between rich and poor, slaveholder and non-slaveholder. From the beginning of the war, the belief that the war was "a rich man's war and a poor man's fight" was held by most of the lowest class, the tory faction in Alabama, which was willing to see the slaves freed to humiliate the owners, and from 1862 to the

[1] Moore, *History of Alabama*, vol. i, p. 540; H. R. Helper, *The Impending Crisis of the South* (New York, 1860), pp. 381-382. The attitude of the aristocracy is suggested in the following references: M. B. Chestnut, *A Diary from Dixie* (New York, 1905), pp. 14, 401; Pryor, *Reminiscences*, p. 237.

end of the war, it was accepted by many other members of the non-slaveholding class.[2]   Most of them supported the peace movement.   The belief was assiduously cultivated by demagogues who made effective use of it in the election of 1863 and afterwards.[3]   From the extreme view, the war was the rich man's war because he brought it on to protect his peculiar property; he plunged the country into civil war to preserve " the divine institution of slavery even to the territories "; but it was the poor man's fight because he had to fight for those who brought on the fight; he had to stop the bullets; " they think all you are fit for is to stop bullets for them, your betters, who call you poor white trash." [4] From the moderate view, the war was the rich man's war because he had more to gain from it; though the war was fought for the liberty of the poor, it was fought for the liberty and the property of the rich; the man of moderate means and the poor working man prized liberty as highly as any " swell-headed aristocrat " but for its intrinsic value; they had no plantations nor slaves to lose; but the war was

[2] Mrs. Chestnut, *Diary*, p. 58; *O. R.*, ser. iv, vol. iii, pp. 1040-1042; Resolutions of a meeting of citizens of Choctaw county (sent to the Governor), January 5, 1862; Cannon, *Inside Rebeldom*, p. 183; Selma *Reporter*, September 18, 1863.

[3] Tansill, *Free and Impartial Exposition*, p. 16; *Our Women in the War* (Charleston, 1885), p. 276; Montgomery *Weekly Advertiser*, January 21, November 18, 1863; *O. R.*, ser. iv, vol. i, pp. 318-319. A candidate for a local office in one of the counties of north Alabama asked his constituents to support him because he was a poor man. " As a poor man, I only ask to be tried in this position."—Jacksonville *Republican*, July 8, 1863.

[4] Mobile *Register*, April 30, 1862; J. A. Hill to Governor Shorter, February 21, 1862; Montgomery *Weekly Mail*, September 16, 1863; Montgomery *Daily Mail*, January 4, 1865; R. S. Tharin, *Arbitrary Arrests* (New York, 1863), p. 157. Tharin had been run out of Lowndes county for " negro-phobia " and was living in Coosa county when the war came on. He went North.—Montgomery *Daily Advertiser*, March 10, 1863.

the poor man's fight because he had to bear the heaviest burdens, which the rich man shifted to him.[5]

These beliefs were strengthened by exemptions which seemed to prove that the rich, in spite of their greater stake in the war, were unwilling to fight it. It was said in Richmond that it was easier for a camel to go through the eye of a needle than for a rich man to enter Camp Lee. It was believed that some rich men secured exemption by giving huge bribes to enrolling officers, surgeons and other officials, and that others secured exemption by paying large fees to lawyers who knew the intricacies of exemption laws. It was reported that a certain lawyer in Richmond, who as a member of Congress advocated continuing the war until the last man fell in the last ditch, made $2,000 a day as fees for his services in securing exemptions. It was believed that other rich men who would not use these methods secured safe positions in the military service, " bomb-proofs," for themselves and their sons. One soldier said that a black list should be published of the sons of rich men, pets of the government, who had never shouldered a gun; another said that it made him feel like " cussing " to see the miserable favoritism displayed everywhere in the army to the rich.[6] But such exemptions did not cause as deep resentment as exemptions under the twenty-negro law and the law allowing substitutes. The twenty-negro law was obnoxious on its face because it made the peculiar property of the rich, which the poor had to fight for, the basis of exemption. Its defense by Confederate leaders as a necessary

---

[5] *Southwestern Baptist*, November 27, 1862; Jones, *Diary*, vol. ii, p. 367; Montgomery *Weekly Advertiser*, August 5, 1863.

[6] Pollard, *The Lost Cause*, p. 646; Jones, *Diary*, vol. ii, pp. 271, 108, 243; W. G. Prather to Governor Shorter, August 24, 1862; Pollard, *Life of Jefferson Davis*, p. 327; Mobile *Daily News*, July 21, 1865; Selma *Reporter*, February 13, September 5, 1864.

police measure and its modification by Congress did not stop its use in the propaganda of a rich man's war and a poor man's fight.[7]   The substitute law found no defenders but its beneficiaries; it was the most unpopular act of the Confederate government.   Although in theory it allowed exemption to all who would furnish a substitute, in practice it allowed exemption only to the rich because only they could afford to pay several thousand dollars for a substitute. Its repeal did not, as Senator Wigfall hoped it would, stop the mouths of demagogues.[8]   To many the twenty-negro law and the substitute law appeared to be pure class legislation, convicting the government of favoritism toward the rich.   They caused, it was said, the wholesale withdrawal of the rich men from the army, leaving the poor men to carry on the fight.   The fact that the government allowed exemption and that men accepted it on the basis of property for the protection of which the war was being fought created serious discontent in the army and at home, and deepened class animosity.   Many poor soldiers, feeling bitterly that they had as much right to be at home as the rich men, decided that they would not fight any longer " the rich man's war " and went home.[9]

Another cause for the division of rich against poor was profiteering, or extortion.   Extortion was condemned by

[7] Richmond *Examiner*, February 17, February 20, 1863; President Davis in an address in Jackson, Miss., December 27, 1862, said that he would never have given his consent to any law intended to bear unfairly upon the poor, " even to a feather's weight.   The poor *have* fought our battles and so have the rich."—Selma *Reporter*, January 1, 1863.

[8] Appleton, *Annual Cyclopedia*, 1864, p. 206; Richmond *Examiner*, December 31, 1863.

[9] Jones, *Diary*, vol. ii, pp. 271, 277, 281, 347, 123; *The Independent*, August 1, 1863; *O. R.*, ser. iv, vol. ii, pp. 287-289; Moore, *Conscription and Conflict*, pp. 33, 49-51; Channing, *History of the United States*, vol. vi, p. 418; *O. R.*, ser. iv, vol. ii, p. 996.

government officers, preachers and others in Alabama as a sin and a crime but it flourished from 1861 to 1865.[10] Extortion was closely related to exemption because among the extortioners were many men who had evaded military service by furnishing a substitute or by owning slaves or by meeting some other requirement of the exemption law. To the offense of skulking, these men added the crime of extortion. They not only refused to fight and stayed at home in comfort, but they made money out of the opportunities offered by the war. Among the worst extortioners, it was said, were the farmers who, exempted from the army, raised provisions and sold them at fabulous prices. Hundreds of them in Alabama, it was said, piled up so much money that they did not know what to do with it.[11] The fact was generally recognized — and deplored — that the worst sufferers from extortion were the army and the poor families of soldiers.[12] The government, though acknowledging that it was hindered in securing supplies, stood between the army and extortioners, but the poor families of soldiers were helpless. Their only alternative to paying exorbitant prices was starv-

[10] O. R., ser. iv, vol. i, p. 701; vol. ii, pp. 211-212, 902; Jacksonville Republican, October 17, 1861 (a sermon on Achan); October 31, 1861; The Independent, October 3, 1863; Clarke County Journal, April 9, 1863; Appleton, Annual Cyclopedia, 1862, p. 15. "As vile extortion is an abominable sin against humanity, all good men are earnestly urged to denounce its practice and to crush out its spirit."—Governor Shorter, Proclamation Book A, pp. 35-36.

[11] The Independent, September 19, 1863; C. G. Millican to Governor Watts, June 18, 1864; Appleton, Annual Cyclopedia, 1863, pp. 230-232; 1864, p. 206; Montgomery Weekly Advertiser, September 30, 1863'; Democratic Watchtower, May 11, 1864; Southwestern Baptist, April 30, 1863; Jones, Diary, vol. ii, pp. 367, 43; Selma Dispatch, December 20, 1863; Mobile Register, January 3, 1864.

[12] O. R., ser. iv, vol. ii, pp. 900-901, 212; Jones, Diary, vol. i, p. 298; Minutes of the Fortieth Annual Session of the Alabama Baptist Convention, 1862 (Tuskegee, 1862), pp. 17-18.

ing. Thus, it was said, they were ground beneath the heels
of extortioners. Rich men were making money out of the
necessities of soldiers and their families. They were traitors, treating the families of soldiers as if they were enemies
to be starved out, and like leeches, sucking the life blood
out of the defenders of themselves and their money. They
were Shylocks exacting the pound of flesh from the families
of those who were fighting for their country. They had
bowed the knee to Baal and were sacrificing their rights and
the rights of soldiers' families to the almighty dollar. The
rich were getting richer and the poor were getting poorer.
The poor man gave; the rich man sold.[13] The effects upon
the army were disastrous. Indignation and bitterness, dissatisfaction and demoralization seized many poor soldiers.
They might endure skulking, which was injustice to themselves, but not extortion, which was oppression of their
families. They made threats of dealing out terrible punishment to extortioners after the war was over, or if necessary,
before. Thousands of poor soldiers—good and loyal soldiers—went home to see about their suffering families.[14]
This result is stated in the following extracts from letters
to the Governor of Alabama:

. . . he (a rich man who was asked by the writer, aged 73, to
relieve the distress of certain poor families) berry indifferently

[13] Montgomery *Weekly Advertiser*, October 1, 1862; Montgomery *Daily
Advertiser,* March 8, August 5, 1863; *Magazine of History,* vol. ix, p. 37,
"In the 'Back Country' of South Carolina, 1862-1864"; Montgomery
Weekly Mail, September 2, 1863; *Southwestern Baptist,* November 27,
1862; Appleton, *Annual Cyclopedia,* 1863, p. 231; Selma *Reporter,* March
3, 1863; *The Independent*, August 29, 1863.

[14] Montgomery *Weekly Advertiser*, April 22, August 5, September 30,
1863; October 1, 1862; Jones, *Diary,* vol. ii, pp. 288, 441, 94, 464; *Diary
of Lt.-Col. John G. Pressley,* p. 50; *The Independent,* December 19, 1863;
Selma *Reporter,* February 16, 1863; March 9, 1864; *Southwestern Baptist,*
April 9, September 3, 1863.

replied that he new meny familys haas children war picking Berreys to keap from Starving. . . . She (the wife of a man who boasted that he had made $100,000 out of the Confederacy) heard a good menney famileys was Boilling Potatoes Vines To Subsist on . . . the cruelty of the (rich) to the Soldiers famileys is the caus of thear deserting.[15]

Is it any wonder that our armies are decimated by desertion and dissatisfaction prevails throughout the poorer classes when such nefarious practices (i.e. buying up corn in middle Alabama and selling it at eight dollars a bushel) are allowed to be carried on at home by wealthy men and officers . . . how many families who have not means to purchase . . . and are suffering while Messrs. ———— and ———— wealthy citizens and one of them a Government official of conscript age, hiding in a bomb-proof behind a miserable little tax collector's office, are speculating upon the bread that ought to go into the mouths of poor women and children, many of whom have husbands and sons now for four years defending the lives, liberty and property of these miserable, avaricious and cold blooded speculators.[16]

Probably the result justified the fear that the breach between rich and poor would do more injury to the Confederate cause than the Union army.[17]

The chief cause for the desertion of Alabama soldiers from the Confederate army was poverty in the families of soldiers. The number of indigent families of soldiers was

15 J. A. Sullivan to Governor Watts, February 28, 1864.

16 Lt. A. H. Burch to Governor Watts, February 20, 1865.

17 *Southwestern Baptist*, November 27, 1862. See also Rowland, *Jefferson Davis, Constitutionalist*, vol. v, pp. 59-60. Efforts of Confederate leaders to suppress the belief show their uneasiness over its effects. See: Mobile *Register*, October 8, 1863 (speech of Governor Brown to the Army of Tennessee); Montgomery *Daily Advertiser*, November 18, 1863 (speech of General Magruder to his army); Richmond *Examiner*, February 17, 1865 (speech of Senator Wigfall to his old command); J. L. M. Curry, *Civil History of the Government of the Confederate States* (Richmond, 1901), pp. 145-251.

large. Early in 1861, many families began to be in want
soon after their breadwinners went into the army so that in
the fall the state adopted the policy of giving aid to them.[18]
There are no records of the number of indigent families in
1861; the following table shows the number who received
state aid in 1862, 1863 and 1864: [19]

INDIGENT FAMILIES OF SOLDIERS WHO RECEIVED STATE AID

Year	Number of families	Percentage of the total number of families
1862	10,263	10.6%
1863	31,915	33.3%
1864	37,521	37.0%

The reports of indigent families for 1862 with the exception of a few supplements were made before the conscription act was passed on April 16 and so include with not
more than a thousand exceptions the families of the first
group of volunteers.[20] The reports for 1863 show a large
increase, reflecting the effects of the conscription act in

[18] O. R., ser. iv, vol. i, pp. 51, 197.

[19] Reports of Commissioners' Courts to the State-Comptroller under
the act approved November 11, 1861, 1862. (A report from each of the
52 counties was sent in but there were no returns from one district in
Walker and from two districts in DeKalb) ; Annual Report of the Comptroller of Public Accounts to the General Assembly, November, 1863,
p. 38, statement no. 7; Report of the Quartermaster-General, 1864, for
the fiscal year ending September 30, Table H, Report by judges of
probate of the number of indigent families of soldiers in their counties,
etc.; Report of Abstracts of Disbursements made by Duff Green,
Q. M.-G., in 1864 under the act approved December 8, 1863. Percentages
were computed from statistics from these sources and from the Eighth
Census, Mortality and Miscellaneous Statistics, p. 340.

[20] Most of the reports were made in January and February. Exceptions
to those made before April 16 were the entire report of Choctaw, July
2 (264 families) and supplementary reports of Autauga, August 18 (72
families) ; Butler, May 27 and August 11 (113 families) ; Calhoun, May
20 (259 families) ; Fayette, April 21 (68 families) ; Henry, June 12
(169 families) ; Jackson, May 23 (4 families) ; Tallapoosa, July 18,
(141 families).

forcing men whose families depended upon them for support to volunteer. The reports for 1864 show an increase from 1862 of 255%.

The indigent families of soldiers were distributed unevenly among the counties of the state. They formed proportions of the total number of families which varied in 1862, from 1% in Sumter county to 32% in Mobile county; in 1863, from 10% in Dallas to 59% in Walker; in 1864, from 10% in Dallas to 66% in Shelby; and which represented median averages of 7% in 1862, 34% in 1863, and 39% in 1864. They were concentrated in the white counties in the northern and southeastern sections of the state. The distribution of indigent families of soldiers in 1863 is shown on Map D.[21] Of the fifty-two counties in the state, there were in 1863 twenty-nine counties in which more than one-third of the families received state aid as indigent families of soldiers. There were in 1864 thirty-five counties in which more than one-third of the families received state aid as indigent families of soldiers.[22] These thirty-five counties embraced all of the counties in which deserters collected with two exceptions, Marion (30%) and DeKalb (32%). A probable explanation of these two exceptions lies in the inefficient administration of state aid by the officer in charge, the probate judge. In 1864, the probate judge of DeKalb county, who had been accused of disloyalty to the Confederacy, was captured and carried off by the Federals. In the same year, the Governor of the state advised impeachment of the probate judge of Marion county for maladministration of funds appropriated to indigent families of soldiers.[23]

[21] Computed from statistics from sources cited on p. 128, *supra*.

[22] Seven counties were added and one county, DeKalb, was subtracted.

[23] Col. M. C. Reid to Gov. Watts, May 2, 1864; *Acts*, 1864, p. 141; *Governor's Letter Book*, May 17, 1864, pp. 144-145. For an account of destitution in DeKalb, see Governor Watts to Captain Davenport, April 2, 1864.

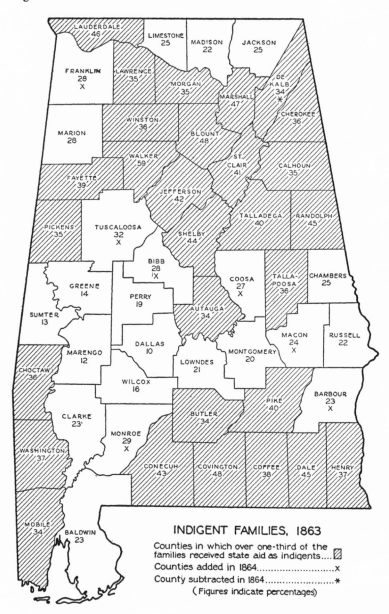

INDIGENT FAMILIES, 1863

Counties in which over one-third of the families received state aid as indigents.... ▨

Counties added in 1864............................x

County subtracted in 1864........................*

(Figures indicate percentages)

But if the reports for Marion and DeKalb were accurate, it is still true that in all the counties in which deserters collected nearly one-third to nearly two-thirds of the families in 1864 received state aid as indigent families of soldiers.

The degree of indigence among the families of soldiers was high and in many cases reached destitution. Those war conditions which compelled the wealthy in the state to do without customary luxuries [24] deprived the poor of many necessaries of life. As farming was the chief occupation, the decrease in agricultural stock and machinery is a good indication of the lowered economic status of the people. Five years after the war, there were in Alabama only two-thirds as many horses and mules, three-fourths as many cattle, two-fifths as many hogs, and four-ninths as much agricultural machinery as in 1860.[25] In 1865 and 1866, farmers cultivated thousands of acres of land with no implements but hoes; they had no horses, mules or oxen to draw plows.[26] During the war, the scarcity of farm machinery and animals in north and in southeast Alabama occasioned serious complaint — fences were down and women could not split rails; mills were out of repair and mill-wrights were in the army; plows and wagons were worn out and there was no iron to mend them; horses, mules and hogs were driven off to supply the armies and the wives of soldiers had to do as they could without them.[27] There

[24] Virginia Clay-Clopton, *A Belle of the Fifties*; Victoria Clayton, *Black and White under the Old Regime* (London, 1899) ; Frances Howard, *In and Out of the Lines* (New York, 1905); A. H. Gay, *Life in Dixie during the War* (Atlanta, 1887) ; Parthenia Hague, *A Blockaded Family* (Boston, 1888) ; *Our Women in the War*.

[25] Computed from statistics from: *Eighth Census, Agriculture*, pp. 2-3; *Census of 1870*, vol. iii, pp. 94-95.

[26] Miller, *Alabama*, p. 228.

[27] J. A. Sullivan to Governor Watts, February 28, 1864; Robert M. Tosey to Governor Watts, April 23, 1864; W. Garrett to Governor

was much suffering among the families of soldiers for clothing and for food—even for bread.[28]   Some of the families
who received state aid were partially indigent; others were
wholly indigent; for example, in 1864 the returns from
Barbour stated that 280 families were "half-supplied,"
649 destitute; from Coosa, over half were destitute; from
Washington, three-fourths were destitute; from Jefferson,
"all actually indigent"; from Fayette, "these cannot live
without help."

From 1862 to 1865 unofficial reports of destitution came
from north and southeast Alabama to the Governor.   The
reports came from Shelby county in March, 1862 that 300
women were at the handles of the plow; from Marshall
county in July, 1862 that corn was $1.25 a bushel and that
women and children were crying for bread; and from
Coffee county a week later that some families of soldiers
were living on bread alone without salt.[29]   Early in 1863,
the city of Mobile was said to be in a starving condition
chiefly on account of an embargo on the shipment of grain
from Mississippi, placed by General Pemberton to preserve
supplies for his army.   Bread riots were said to have
occurred in Mobile in April and September when women
whose husbands were in the army raided provisions shops
on Dauphin and Whitehall streets and paraded on Spring
Hill avenue with a banner inscribed with the legend " Bread

Watts, June 4, 1864; Leona E. Moore to Governor Watts, April 16, 1864;
"Rev. Dr." Willoughby (18th Ala.) to Governor Watts, October 29, 1864.

[28] Senator Jemison said in 1863 that thousands of families of soldiers
in north Alabama had no meat.—Richmond *Examiner*, June 1, 1864.

[29] Lawrence M. Jones to Governor Shorter, March 17, 1862; S. K.
Rayburn to Governor Shorter, July 10, 1862; Lucreesy Simmons to
Governor Shorter, July 17, 1862.   See also: J. L. Holt to Governor
Shorter, July 29, 1862 (Barbour, Henry and Dale); Charles Gibson to
Governor Shorter, September 2, 1862 (Winston); *Governor's Letter
Book*, December 4, 1862, p. 274 (Randolph).

or Blood." [30] In July, 1863, D. P. Lewis wrote to the Governor from Lawrence county that women, many of whom had been in ease and affluence before the war, were plowing, grubbing, rolling logs and milling.[31] In 1864, the reports were most distressing. The women of Bibb and Shelby, barefoot, were begging for corn in the canebrake country to the south; the women and children of Randolph were " in a suffering condition "; many families of soldiers in Fayette and other upper counties were destitute of corn, which was selling at $5 a bushel and had to be hauled from the Tombigbee valley, and all were destitute of salt; the families in the interior of Coosa whose former support was in the army were in absolute want—begging corn, which was selling at $8 or $9 a bushel.[32] On April 15, 1864, Colonel J. L. Sheffield of the Forty-eighth Alabama wrote to Governor Watts:

I take the liberty of writing you that you may know the condition of things in this section of the state (Marshall, St. Clair, Blount, DeKalb). I have, sir, made it my business to go through the country to ascertain the condition of families of *poor men* who are in the service. I find *hundreds* of them entirely destitute of everything upon which to live, not even *Bread*. Nor is it to be had in the Country. . . . Something should be done else they are bound to suffer. All they ask for is *Bread*.

Of these and similar letters, Governor Watts said on December 9, " The cries of the starving people are coming up to me almost every day from counties in that section of

[30] *Governor's Letter Book*, February 28, 1863, pp. 329-330; Richmond *Examiner*, April 4, 1863; Appleton, *Annual Cyclopedia*, 1863, pp. 811-818, 6-8; Moore, *Rebellion Record*, vol. vii (Diary of Events), p. 48.

[31] February 9, 1863.

[32] Selma *Reporter*, April 25, May 7, 1864; D. M. Robison (E. O.) to Governor Watts, June 5, 1864; Leona E. Moore to Governor Watts, April 16, 1864; W. Garrett to Governor Watts, June 4, 1864.

Alabama (north)." [33]   From Coffee county, John G. Moore, member of the state legislature, wrote to Governor Watts on March 5 that the enormous sacrifices of southeast Alabama for the war had produced such destitution in that section that he feared that unless the counties where abundance prevailed came to their assistance the " cry will be here, give us bread or give us blood." [34]   The official reports and the unofficial reports, even with allowance for exaggeration, represent a condition of soldiers' families which was a tragedy.

The unusual amount of poverty in the northern and the southeastern sections of the state during the war may be accounted for largely by decrease in production, which was caused by unfavorable seasons, invasions of the enemy, impressments and taxes-in-kind, and withdrawal of a large part of the laboring population for the army.   In 1862, a severe drouth produced a shortage in the grain crop of the state.   According to statistics collected by the Governor, in that year twenty counties failed to make enough corn to supply their own needs—six of the southwest, three of the southeast, nine hill and two mountain counties of north Alabama.   To conserve the food supply, the Governor issued a proclamation in December, forbidding the distillation of grain, either domestic or imported, in any of these counties. Other counties of north Alabama raised less grain than usual in 1862.[35]   In 1863, all the counties of southeast Ala-

[33] *Governor's Letter Book*, December 9, 1864, p. 187.

[34] John G. Moore to Governor Watts, March 5, 1864; Brewer, *Alabama*, p. 186.

[35] *Proclamation Book A*, pp. 56-58; Charles Gibson to Governor Shorter, September 3, 1862; S. K. Rayburn to Governor Shorter, July 10, 1862; James F. Redus to Governor Shorter, October 12, 1862. It was reported that southeast Alabama produced an unusually large quantity of grain and hogs; probably the three counties which escaped the drouth did so.—Appleton, *Annual Cyclopedia*, 1863, p. 211.

bama suffered from drouth and subsequent shortage in the grain supply. It was estimated that Coffee county lacked 50,000 bushels to supply its own needs.[36] In 1864, some of the counties of north Alabama again made only a small crop of corn on account of drouth.[37] In each of the three years, the drouth-stricken areas imported corn from the black-belt section.

The black-belt section was also fortunate in escaping the invasions of the enemy until 1865. Southeast Alabama suffered from invasions in 1863 and 1865, and north Alabama every year from 1861 to 1865, inclusive. The counties which suffered most severely were Lauderdale, Limestone, Madison, Jackson, Franklin, Morgan, Lawrence, Marshall, Marion and Cherokee.[38] The theory upon which Federal officers in Alabama, with few exceptions, seemed to have acted was that stated by General Sherman in a letter of instructions written January 1, 1863 to an officer at Huntsville, Alabama: This war was a war between peoples, not between rulers with hired armies. Since the people were combatants, they had no property rights. " The government of the United States has in north Alabama any and all rights which they choose to enforce in war, to take their lives, their horses, their lands, their everything." [39] In accord with this theory, the destruction of property, whether required by military necessity or not, was thorough. The report of a Federal officer of a raid near Town Creek in

[36] John G. Moore to Governor Watts, March 5, 1864; L. J. Cole to Governor Moore, October 30, 1863.

[37] Joseph D. McCain to Governor Watts, October 22, 1864.

[38] Fleming, *Civil War and Reconstruction*, pp. 256, 77, 75. Conecuh in the southeast was invaded in 1864.

[39] Miller, *Alabama*, pp. 182-183. Exception, General Buell. Sherman set the example by ordering confiscation of provisions and forage in Jackson county.

May, 1863 suggests the devastation which north Alabama suffered from three years of such warfare:

We destroyed or carried off 1½ million bushels of corn, 500,000 pounds of bacon, quantities of wheat, oats, rye, and fodder, captured and brought out horses and mules and an equal number of cattle, sheep, and hogs, besides thousands that the army consumed in three weeks. We also brought out 1,500 negroes, destroyed tan yards, flouring mills and we left the country in such a devastated condition that no crop can be raised during the year.[40]

By such methods the Tennessee valley, which was said to have been capable of maintaining an army of 100,000 men, was made a naked country.[41] The effect of invasions in decreasing production should be measured not only by actual devastation but also by discouragement of efforts at production.

Confederate cavalry, stationed in those sections where invasion was expected, became a heavy burden upon the communities which they were designed to protect. They required large amounts of provision and forage, consuming, it was said, not only the surplus products, but also those necessary for the support of the indigent families of soldiers. They used many horses and oxen, thereby decreasing the means of transporting food from the black-belt section. They secured their supplies by impressment. Protests that the cavalry were impoverishing the upper country were made from all parts of north Alabama, but were especially earnest from St. Clair, DeKalb, Marshall, Blount, Chero-

[40] Miller, *Alabama*, p. 178. Refugees from north Alabama to the central and southern counties increased the number of indigent families in those counties.—Fleming, *Civil War and Reconstruction*, p. 197.

[41] Miller, *Alabama*, p. 213; Fleming, *Civil War and Reconstruction*, pp. 74-76, 255-257.

kee and Talladega.[42] For example, Governor Watts in 1864 wrote to General Taylor that the four or five companies of cavalry in Walker county were doing no good, but were depriving the poor of bread.[43] The support of cavalry was an additional war tax upon north Alabama. Regular war taxes were heavy there as elsewhere. Impressments of supplies were made for the army as well as for the cavalry at government prices, which were always lower than market prices and which were frequently ruinous to producers. Impressments not only removed supplies from home consumption, but they also caused the withdrawal of supplies from the market and discouraged further production. They were a direct cause of destitution in those cases—and they were not uncommon—in which they took away all the means of support provided by soldiers for their families.[44] Taxes-in-kind, which were tithes on agricultural products, fell so heavily on the white counties that the state legislature petitioned Congress to exempt from payment of these taxes the families of soldiers whose support was derived from white labor alone.[45]

More disastrous to production than drouth, invasions or war taxes was the withdrawal of a large part of the laboring population for the army. Statistics, though partial and, in some cases, probably exaggerated, show that the quotas furnished by the various counties to the army were large. Before the passage of the compulsory military service act,

[42] W. J. Haralson to Governor Watts, March 23, 1864; M. C. Reid to Governor Watts, May 2, 1864; J. W. Jones to Governor Shorter, February 4, 1863; Dr. Willoughby to Governor Watts, October 29, 1864; Leona E. Moore to Governor Watts, April 16, 1864.

[43] *Governor's Letter Book*, December 9, 1864, p. 187.

[44] Appleton, *Annual Cyclopedia*, 1863, p. 208; Johnston, *Narrative*, p. 425; *Governor's Letter Book*, March 8, 1864, pp. 120-121.

[45] *Acts*, 1863, p. 217. Approved November 28.

April, 1862, twelve of the counties of north Alabama and three of the counties of southeast Alabama had sent one volunteer out of every ten white men, women and children.[46] Two other counties of north Alabama, Tallapoosa and Shelby, were said to have sent at the same time 14% and 15% of their white population.[47] Before the end of 1864 the quotas had greatly increased; for example, Marshall sent by April, 1862, 11% of its white population; by April, 1864, 17%; Tallapoosa sent by April, 1862, 12% of its white population; by April, 1864, 19%.[48] Three counties for which statistics for 1862 are not available, Talladega, Randolph and Walker, sent before the end of 1864, 17%, 17% and 25%, respectively, of their white population.[49] By January 25, 1864, the state as a whole had furnished to the Confederate army 17% of its white population, as many soldiers as its voting population.[50] By the end of 1864, the counties of southeast Alabama and many of the counties of north Alabama had furnished more soldiers to the Confederate army than their voting population.[51]

[46] Computed from statistics from: *Reports of the Probate Judges and Sheriffs of the Counties in response to Governor Shorter's Circular of March 15, 1862 of the number of companies from counties in Confederate service* (Reports from 11 counties of these sections are missing) ; *Eighth Census, Population*, p. 8.

[47] James M. Pearson to Governor Shorter, April 12, 1862 (Tallapoosa) ; Lawrence M. Jones to Governor Shorter, March 17, 1862; John W. Pitts to Governor Shorter, April 4, 1862. Henry county in southeast Alabama reported to the Governor 18%.

[48] *Reports of Probate Judges and Sheriffs*, 1862; Governor Watts, April 25, 1864, introducing A. H. Hayes; John Rowe and others to Governor Watts, April 7, 1864 (also A. J. Sturdivant to Governor Watts, June 9, 1864).

[49] Miller, *Alabama*, p. 198; Thomas J. Johnston (chairman of mass meeting) to Governor Watts, April 11, 1864; Miller, *Alabama*, p. 193.

[50] *O. R.*, ser. iv, vol. iii, p. 103.

[51] John G. Moore to Governor Watts, March 5, 1864; Selma *Reporter,*

The withdrawal of so many men from the army caused a serious scarcity of labor. In these counties where the slave population was small, the men who entered the army had been the chief productive laborers. As two-thirds of the families owned no slaves, they were supported by white labor alone. In these counties where the land was less fertile, the majority of the people were poor and were dependent for support upon their daily labors. Many families gave up to the army their only means of support. Frequently, one man who was left at home had to look after a half-dozen or more families of women and children. In the absence of the men of military age, old men, women and children did the farming. Although women did plowing and other heavy work, they were not able to get as big returns or to cultivate as much land as men.[52] For example, in 1862 it was estimated that in spite of the fact that many women of Coosa were daily following the plow, 15,000 acres of land would be thrown out of cultivation by the withdrawal of 800 volunteers, thereby decreasing the corn crop by at least 150,000 bushels.[53] The result of such conditions, which the Secretary of War feared when in January, 1863 he proposed the exemption of

May 7, 1864, letter by J. W. Lapsley; D. P. Lewis to Governor Shorter, February 9, 1863; John W. Pitts to Governor Shorter, April 2, 1862; J. H. Davis (secretary of a mass meeting) to Governor Shorter, November 28, 1862; Thomas J. Johnston to Governor Watts, April 11, 1864. See also *O. R.*, ser. iv. vol. ii, p. 681.

[52] James M. Pearson to Governor Shorter, April 12, 1862 (Tallapoosa); *Governor's Letter Book*, April 11, 1864, p. 125 (Talladega); Thomas H. Watts, introducing A. H. Hayes, April 25, 1864 (Marshall); Gainesville *Independent*, August 16, 1862 (Butler); Edward Davis to Governor Shorter, April 7, 1862 (Shelby); James Montgomery to Governor Shorter, April 12, 1862; B. M. Long to Governor Moore, ——, 1861 (Walker); Owsley, *Defeatism in the Confederacy*, p. 5; Montgomery *Weekly Mail*, September 12, 1862.

[53] Petition of the Coosa Confederates, Robert J. Wise Guards, Joe Calloway Guards and Coosa Rangers (437 men) to Governor Shorter, 1862.

men who had each eight or ten helpless females dependent upon them, was scarcity, even destitution, among the families of soldiers.[54]

In spite of decrease in production in certain sections, enough food was raised in the state to supply all the people. But it was not distributed; frequently plenty existed in one place and scarcity in another only fifty or seventy-five miles away. The difficulty was transportation. As the railroad from Selma into Bibb and Shelby was the only one connecting the poorer counties with the black-belt counties, wagons and mules or horses or oxen had to be used. They were very scarce in north and southeast Alabama in 1863 and 1864. They had been sold voluntarily or involuntarily— or seized—to supply the armies. Means of transportation were so scarce that families of soldiers who had enough money sometimes could not get teams to haul corn and the Governor threatened to impress teams to haul corn for the indigent families of soldiers.[55]

Decrease in production and difficulty in transportation were accompanied by increase in prices. Scarcity and specu-

[54] *O. R.*, ser. iv, vol. ii, pp. 287-288; Thomas J. Johnston (chairman of a mass meeting) to Governor Watts, April 11, 1864; A. Bowen (chairman of a mass meeting) to Governor Shorter, November 28, 1862; John Rowe to Governor Watts, April 7, 1864; John G. Moore to Governor Watts, March 5, 1864; Selma *Reporter*, February 16, 1863. The Senate Committee on Military Affairs estimated in the spring of 1863 that not more than one-fourth of the soldiers had neither means nor friends to support their families.—Richmond *Examiner*, April 20, 1863.

[55] *Governor's Letter Book*, December 31, 1862, p. 295; April 21, 1864, p. 131; *Southwestern Baptist*, August 6, 1863; Appleton, *Annual Cyclopedia*, 1864, p. 209; Fleming, *Civil War and Reconstruction*, pp. 202-203; Miller, *Alabama*, p. 230; Tuomey, *Geology of Alabama*, frontispiece, map; W. Garrett to Governor Shorter, June 4, 1864; John G. Moore to Governor Watts, March 5, 1864; Leona E. Moore to Governor Watts, April 16, 1864; A. H. Burch to Governor Watts, February 20, 1865; *Governor's Letter Book*, April 21, 1864, p. 131. See also *Acts*, 1864, p. 167.

lation contributed to the increase in prices but the chief cause was inflation of the currency by both state and Confederate governments. The values of Confederate currency in gold, which were published by a Mobile banking house, show the depreciation of currency in south Alabama: January, 1862, 120; 1863, 310; 1864, 1,800; 1865, 3,400.[56] In north Alabama, currency was worth less. A corresponding appreciation in prices took place, which began to be seriously felt in 1862. Some quotations of prices of clothing, food and transportation suggest the effects on living conditions. In Mobile, the price of a pair of shoes in 1862 was $25; in 1864, $150 to $175; in east Alabama, in 1863-1864, a calico dress, $108; a plain straw hat, $100;[57] in the black belt, in October, 1862, jeans, $20 a yard; in north Alabama, in 1863, cotton cards, $100 a pair; wool, $5 a pound; cotton, $1 a pound.[58] In Mobile, in 1862, the price of flour was $40 to $60 a barrel; in 1864, $250 to $300.[59] The staple articles of food, bacon and corn, which sold before the war at 10 cents a pound and 50 cents a bushel, were advertised in Mobile papers at the following prices:

	1862	*1863*	*1864*	*1865*
Corn per bushel	$1	$3	$:—	$7
Bacon per pound	.21	1.30	3.25	3.75 [60]

In northern counties the prices were generally higher; for example, prices of corn per bushel in Jefferson, February, 1863, $5; Coosa, June, 1864, $8 or $9; St. Clair, October, 1864, $10.[61] In southwest Alabama in 1864, a mule, worth

[56] Kate Cumming, *Gleanings from Southland*, p. 276.

[57] Fleming, *Civil War and Reconstruction*, pp. 180-181.

[58] Gainesville *Independent*, October 13, 1862; December 19, 1863; D. P. Lewis to Governor Shorter, February 9, 1863.

[59] Fleming, *Civil War and Reconstruction*, pp. 180-181.

[60] Cumming, *Gleanings from Southland*, p. 276.

[61] Fleming, *Civil War and Reconstruction*, p. 204; Selma *Reporter*,

$75 to $120 before the war, sold for $800 to $1200; a horse, worth $120 to $250 before the war, sold for $1,200 to $2,500; a wagon and team, $2,940.[62] In Tallapoosa county in 1862, the price of corn was $1 a bushel and the price of sacking and hauling it from an adjoining county, $1 a bushel; in Lawrence county in 1863, the price for hauling 3 barrels of corn 45 miles was $100.[63]

The effects of such prices were most disastrous on the families of soldiers who owned no slaves. Their income was small and precarious. They raised few or no surplus products to sell to share in the advantages of the increase in prices and the wages of soldiers, which only in some cases were supplemented by earnings of women for work like sewing and weaving,[64] were fixed and payable in a depreciating currency. At the beginning of the war, the soldier's pay of $11 a month represented a living wage; in 1860 the average monthly wages of a farm laborer in Alabama were $12.41 with board.[65] But in 1862, $11 would not buy one-fourth of the articles which it would buy at the beginning of the war [66] and its purchasing power declined more sharply in 1863 and 1864. The soldier's pay, though it was increased in June, 1864 to $18 a month, was a trifle in

February 16, 1863; W. Garrett to Governor Watts, June 4, 1864; Dr. Willoughby to Governor Watts, October 29, 1864.

[62] Fleming, *Civil War and Reconstruction*, p. 181.

[63] A. J. Sturdevant to Governor Shorter, November 5, 1862; D. P. Lewis to Governor Watts, February 9, 1863. Sometimes certain goods were not to be had at any price. See quotation of prices in the Montgomery *Daily Mail*, March 21, 1863 for a statement that no pork, Irish potatoes, fodder or wheat were on the market.

[64] *Minutes of the Fortieth Annual Session of the Alabama Baptist State Convention*, 1862, pp. 19-20; Moore, *Rebellion Record*, vol. iii (Documents), p. 349.

[65] *Eighth Census, Mortality and Miscellaneous Statistics*, p. 512.

[66] *Speeches of William L. Yancey* (Montgomery, 1862), pp. 52-54. On the Senate bill to increase the pay of soldiers, October 6, 1862.

comparison with other wages and with prices.[67] For example, in east Alabama in 1863-1864, the wages of a working man were $30 a day. With one day's wages, he could buy two bushels of corn which was then selling in that section at $13 a bushel,[68] but the soldier could not buy two bushels of corn with one month's pay. With his pay, the soldier could not buy even bread for his family. Moreover, the soldier's pay was usually in arrears, often two years, and when it was given to him it was in treasury notes which were heavily discounted by money-changers.[69] To the soldier with an indigent family, the result was the same whether the government paid him $11 or $18 or nothing at all; in the army, he could not keep his family from want.

The fact that the causes of poverty among the families of soldiers were beyond the control of soldiers, did not lessen the keen distress which they felt about their families. Before entering the army, men with dependent families were solicitous about making provisions to care for them during their absence.[70] The first volunteers, believing that the war would last only two or three months, made provisions for their families for only a short time. When they were held in the army for three years and other men who had been entrusted with the care of their families were also put into

---

[67] *Statutes at Large*, vol. iv, p. 262. Compare the soldier's pay with the assistant commissary's pay of $140 a month (1865) and with the iron moulder's pay of $5 a day (1862).—*O. R.*, ser. iv, vol. iii, p. 775; Colin J. McRae, *Letter Book*, p. 71.

[68] Fleming, *Civil War and Reconstruction*, p. 181.

[69] Moore, *Conscription and Conflict*, p. 151.

[70] W. J. Whisenhunt to Governor Moore, ——, 1861; B. M. Long and others to Governor Moore, June 16, 1861; Petition of certain citizens of Sumter county to Governor Shorter, April 3, 1862; Edward Davis to Governor Shorter, April 7, 1862; Frank Moore, *The Civil War in Song and Story* (New York, 1889), pp. 431-432; Stevenson, *Thirteen Months in the Rebel Army*, pp. 199-200.

the army, the men with dependent families felt great anxiety. A group of several hundred soldiers wrote earnestly to the Governor that if they should be silent about the helpless condition of their families, they deserved to " lose our characters for humanity." [71]   Many men with dependent families delayed entering the army until they were forced to volunteer to avoid the disgrace of conscription.[72]   Volunteers were assured by private individuals and by the state government that their families would be provided for during their absence.[73]   Thus, men with dependent families, fortified by private arrangements and by assurances of friends and government, met the utmost demand of patriotism.   But the families of many of them came to want.   By the fall of 1863, soldiers were showering Congress with letters, telling of their distress over the want and suffering among their families.[74]

It was universally recognized that the distress which soldiers felt about want and suffering among their families had dangerous effects upon the army.   It caused loss of fighting spirit among the soldiers.[75]   According to resolutions of a mass meeting held in Montgomery in 1865, it was the only thing which would completely unnerve the arm of a freeman in a struggle for liberty.[76]   It caused desertion.   Upon

[71] Petition of the Coosa Confederates, Robert J. Wise Guards, Joe Calloway Guards and Coosa Rangers to Governor Shorter, 1862.

[72] *Journal of the Senate*, 1862, p. 15.

[73] *Cf. infra*, p. 161.

[74] Appleton, *Annual Cyclopedia*, 1863, p. 16.

[75] *Southwestern Baptist*, June 11, 1863; *Alabama Beacon*, December 26, 1862; April 17, 1863; January 30, 1864; Montgomery *Daily Advertiser*, October 2, October 14, 1863; March 3, 1865; Mobile *Register*, January 11, 1863 (address of President Davis); Varina Davis, *Jefferson Davis, Ex-President of the Confederate States* (New York, 1890), p. 495.

[76] Memphis *Appeal*, February 28, 1865.   General Clanton was chairman of the committee on resolutions.

this fact, leaders of the press, church, government and army were agreed. No government regulations, one newspaper insisted, could hold soldiers in the army when they knew that their families were suffering for the necessaries of life.[77] "Let our soldiers realize," read the report of a committee appointed by a religious organization to investigate poverty in soldiers' families, "that the danger from the rear is greater than the danger in front and can we expect any other result but that our armies will melt away like the morning dew?"[78] Thousands of soldiers, said Colonel Harry Maury of the Thirty-second Alabama, went home because their wives wrote to them that they had nothing to eat or wear.[79] In north Alabama, many good soldiers who had come home on furlough declared that they could not go back into the army as long as their families were uncared for.[80] Hundreds of good soldiers, who had been ardent secessionists, returned to their homes in southeast Alabama to provide for their families, who were in want of the necessaries of life.[81] The Governor and the state legislature, sympathizing with such soldiers, in October, 1864, issued proclamations of amnesty to deserters. The Governor addressed his proclamation especially to those who had left the army "under the mistaken notion that the highest duty required you to provide sustenance and protection to your families."[82] In 1865, the Assistant Secretary of

[77] *Southwestern Baptist*, April 9, September 3, 1863.

[78] *Southwestern Baptist*, October 11, 1863. Tuskegee Baptist Association. Report of the committee on indigent families of soldiers to the Tuskegee Baptist Association.

[79] Montgomery *Weekly Mail*, September 30, 1863.

[80] Colonel J. L. Sheffield to Governor Watts, April 15, 1864.

[81] *O. R.*, ser. iv, vol. iii, p. 1043; John G. Moore to Governor Watts, March 5, 1864.

[82] *Acts*, 1864, p. 44; *Clarke County Journal*, October 13, 1864.

War, Judge Campbell of Alabama, enumerated several causes for desertion, naming last the sufferings of soldiers' families.[83] A similar condition was assigned as a cause for desertion in the neighboring states of Mississippi, Georgia, Florida, Tennessee, and in the more distant states of South Carolina, North Carolina and Texas.[84]

In the opinion of contemporaries, poverty in the families of soldiers was the chief cause of desertion.   September 16, 1863, the *Democratic Watchtower* of north Alabama asked, " What brings home half the deserters?   It is the cries of mothers, sisters, wives, daughters." January 16, 1864, the Mobile *Register* quoted the Richmond *Whig*, " The want of food with their families at home is the cause of over half the desertions." A. S. Abrams, an ex-soldier and a writer, in reply to one of Pollard's attacks on Jefferson Davis' administration, called it " one great cause of absenteeism and desertion from the Confederate army," and said, " The other causes which lead to desertion and absenteeism are but small when brought in comparison. . . "[85] General Pillow, Chief of the Volunteer and Conscript Bureau, the organization which was charged with the duty of collecting deserters in Alabama, Mississippi and Tennessee, was quoted as follows: ". . . desertion, which in most cases springs from solicitude about family support."[86] A committee appointed by a religious organization in Alabama to investi-

[83] Campbell, *Reminiscences*, p. 30.

[84] *O. R.*, ser. i, vol. xxxix, pt. iii, p. 806; pt. ii, p. 856; Frances Howard, *In and Out of the Lines*, p. 152; *O. R.*, ser. iv, vol. ii, p. 973; vol. iii, pp. 46-47; Mobile *Register*, March 29, 1864; *Magazine of American History*, vol. ix, p. 37, "In the 'Back Country' of South Carolina, 1862-1864"; *O. R.*, ser. iv, vol. ii, p. 247; H. Washington to S. D. Yancey, February 3, 1864.

[85] A. S. Abrams, *President Davis and His Administration* (Atlanta, 1864), pp. 15-16. See Pollard, *Rival Administrations*, p. 11.

[86] Montgomery *Weekly Mail*, November 25, 1863.

gate poverty in soldiers' families reported, " The most pro-
lific cause of desertion from our army is found in this
very state of things at home." [87]   President Davis wrote
to General Holmes of the Trans-Mississippi Department on
January 28, 1863:

I regret . . . that desertions have become so frequent. I had
hoped that the liberal provisions understood to have been made
by the state legislature would to a great extent have relieved the
suffering of the poor and have quieted the anxiety of the
soldiers in regard to the condition of their families.[88]

The appeals to soldiers from their families to come to
their relief were so strong that they were almost irresistible.
They were made in letters, many of which were read by
" letter men " to soldiers who could not read or by officers
whose advice the recipients sought, and hundreds of which
were intercepted and sent to the headquarters of General
Lee and of other commanders. In these letters, mothers,
wives and sisters told of destitution and despair. They
told of the cries of children for bread and implored the
soldiers by all they held dear to come home and save them
from starvation. Almost crazed by suffering, they begged
the soldiers to observe the sacred obligations which they
owed to their families and to rescue them from death.[89]
The following extracts from letters which were received by

[87] *Southwestern Baptist*, October 11, 1863 (Tuskegee Baptist Association).

[88] Rowland, *Jefferson Davis, Constitutionalist*, vol. v, p. 425.

[89] Stiles, *Four Years under Marse Robert*, pp. 349-350; Cumming,
Hospital Life, p. 191; Hagood, *Memoirs*, p. 332; Gordon, *Reminiscences*,
p. 348; Oates, *War between the Union and the Confederacy*, p. 493;
Clarke County Journal, February 19, 1863; Montgomery *Daily Adver-
tiser*, December 9, 1863; *The Independent*, October 10, 1863; J. E.
Saunders, *Early Settlers of North Alabama* (New Orleans, 1899), p. 174;
Unwritten reminiscences of the President of the Confederate Veterans,
1929; Underwood, *Women of the Confederacy*, pp. 167-168, 132-133.

two soldiers serve as illustrations of thousands of such appeals:

December 17, 1864.

. . . Everything me and the children's got is patched. Both of them is in bed now covered up with old comferters and old pieces of karpet to keep them warm . . . for their feets on the ground and they have got no clothes neither . . . me and the children have broke up all the rails roun the yard and picked up all the chips there is. We haven't got nothing in the house to eat but a little bit o meal. . . . I don't want you to stop fighting them Yankees . . . but try and get off and come home and fix us all up some and then you can go back . . . my dear, if you put off a-coming, 'twont be no use to come, for we'll all hands of us be out there in the garden in the old grave yard with your ma and mine. . . .[90]

. . . I would not have you do anything wrong for the world, but before God, Edward, unless you come home, we must die. Last night I was aroused by little Eddie's crying. I called and said, " What is the matter, Eddie? " and he said, " O, mama, I am so hungry! " And Lucy, Edward, your darling Lucy, is growing thinner every day. And before God, Edward, unless you come home we must die.[91]

A woman who served as nurse in soldiers' hospitals in Virginia, Georgia and Alabama said that when she saw the agony that such a letter caused she understood why soldiers deserted.[92] An officer in the Army of Northern Virginia said

[90] L. C. Pickett, *Pickett and His Men* (Atlanta, 1900), p. 368 (read by Mrs. Pickett).

[91] Underwood, *Women of the Confederacy*, p. 169 (read by General C. A. Battle). Each of the soldiers who received these letters deserted, was arrested on his return, and was condemned to death, but was pardoned. Later, " Edward " died at his gun, which was the last in the battery to be silenced.

[92] Fannie A. Beers, *Memories* (Philadelphia, 1891), p. 199.

that the strain was enough to unsettle the reason and break the heart-strings of a strong man.[93] A soldier who received such a letter was confronted by conflicting duties—to his country and to his family. He was a soldier fighting in defense of his country; he had taken an oath not to desert; he knew that the penalty for desertion was death. But he was a husband and a father; he had binding obligations to his family; he feared that if he did not go to their aid, they might die. He could not get a furlough. He had to decide whether a man's first duty was to his country or to his family.[94] Doubtless, he asked himself the question which a soldier in a similar crisis asked, " If I lose all that life holds dear to me, what is my country or any country to me?" [95] Usually, his duty to his family seemed paramount to his duty to the military service. He went home. General Joseph E. Johnston stated in the following words the dilemma of the soldiers of the laboring class, who " formed the body of the army ":

. . . in all the last period of ten or twelve months, — those soldiers of the laboring class who had families were compelled to choose between their military service and the strongest obligations men know—their duties to their wives and children. They

93 Stiles, *Four Years under Marse Robert*, p. 341.

94 Taylor, *Four Years with General Lee,* p. 144; DeLeon, *Four Years in Rebel Capitals,* p. 186; Stiles, *Four Years under Marse Robert*, pp. 323, pp. 349-351. See also; Moore, *Rebellion Record*, vol. viii (Incidents), pp. 45-46; *Confederate Veteran*, vol. xviii, pp. 517-518, Cheney, " War Reminiscences "; Oates, *War between the Union and the Confederacy,* pp. 492-493; Gordon, *Reminiscences,* p. 384.

95 *Confederate Veteran*, vol. xviii, p. 519, Cheney, " War Reminiscences." He left his dying child and returned to the army within his leave. A man wrote to the Governor, " What is independence to a man when those that are most near and dear to him are famished and died for want of his assistance at home? "—James F. Redus to Governor Shorter, October 24, 1862.

obeyed the strongest of those obligations, left the army, and returned to their homes to support their families.[96]

It was said that the conflict between duties was so well understood by fellow soldiers that they would not prevent the going of a man who had received a letter begging him to come home and that they did not think he should be punished by death. It was said that some officers felt more of pity than condemnation for such deserters and shuddered as if accessories to murder when they passed the death penalty upon those arrested.[97]   No doubt, sympathy with deserters who went home to take care of their suffering families and who, as a rule, had been good soldiers, was a cause of the leniency of public and government toward desertion.   Colonel Oates of the Twenty-sixth Alabama Regiment, in speaking of the conflicting duties of poor soldiers, expressed in the following words his opinion, which was probably held by many: " Was he criminally a deserter? No, a hero, until heroism in his estimation ceased to be a virtue." [98]   On February 3, 1864, Major Washington, one of Major-General Magruder's staff officers, a part of whose duties was securing the return of deserters to the army, made the following report, which would apply to part of Alabama as well as to part of Texas:

. . . I am satisfied that desertion in this part of Texas arises not from disloyalty but poverty and destitution.   The deserters

[96] Johnston, *Narrative*, pp. 423-424.

[97] Stiles, *Four Years under Marse Robert*, pp. 350-351; J. R. Maxwell, *Autobiography of James R. Maxwell of Tuscaloosa* (New York, 1926), p. 156; *Confederate Veteran*, vol. x, p. 68, Ridley, " Camp Scenes around Dalton." Jefferson Davis wrote to his wife that there was one sacrifice that he could not make for the Confederacy—his wife and children.— Rowland, *Jefferson Davis, Constitutionalist*, vol. vi, p. 562.

[98] Oates, *War between the Union and the Confederacy*, p. 493.

belong almost entirely to the poorest class of non slaveholders whose labor is indispensable to the daily support of their families, and who are too poor and friendless to hope for help from others in their absence.   When the father, husband or son is forced into the service, the suffering at home with them is inevitable.   It is not in the nature of these men to remain quiet in the ranks under such circumstances.   They have not the enlarged views of patriotism and self-sacrifice which belong to the higher classes.   They will go to their suffering families, and remain near them whether they can aid them or not.   This war is peculiar in its intensity and the new features it presents. Laws made for desertion under different circumstances cannot be rigidly enforced, when whole classes are forced out, who have counter duties calling them back, so strong that they will risk death rather than resist them. . . .[99]

Mental suffering of soldiers from the want of necessaries of life among their families was often increased by dread of the lack of protection to their families against Federal troops, tory outlaws and, sometimes, Confederate cavalry. As no men but the aged and infirm were left at home in the white counties, most women were unprotected and afraid.[100]

[99] H. Washington to S. D. Yancey, Adjutant General of Major General John B. Magruder, commanding the District of Texas, New Mexico and Arizona.

[100] Fleming, *Civil War and Reconstruction*, p. 66; Owsley, *Defeatism in the Confederacy*, p. 6.   Three examples will illustrate the scarcity of men.   In a certain place in Coosa county, only one adult male was left in five families of kinspeople, numbering twenty-one persons.   In a large and populous beat in the southeast corner of Talladega there were only four boys under 17 years and 36 men over 50 years.   There one man had put up houses on his farm for his kinspeople.   In 1864, an officer of Blount county wrote the Governor that at the spring term of circuit court he had been unable to get enough men for a grand jury.— Owsley, *Defeatism in the Confederacy*, p. 6; John Lucius, statement made on oath to the probate judge, 1864 (Governor's Papers); L. E. Parsons to Governor Watts, March 27, 1864; A. M. Gibson to Governor Watts, August 29, 1864.

" You say you are not afeared, no never," wrote a soldier
to his wife, who was living alone, " but I am all the time
uneasy about you." [101]   The irregular mail service of the
Confederacy, said a petition from some soldiers, was the
most successful system of torture ever devised; the inability
to hear from home was the cause of half the agony of the
war as well as half the desertions.[102]   When soldiers did
get letters from home, they sometimes heard the worst they
had feared.   Outrages attending Federal invasions were
notorious.   North Alabama suffered especially because, as it
was not of strategic importance, only the worst disciplined
Federal troops were stationed there and because officers in
command there made little or no effort to restrain troops.[103]
For example, one officer in turning a city over for sack said
to his soldiers, " I shut mine eyes for an hour "; and another on a similar occasion said, " The country is yours,
enjoy it." [104]   It was believed in Alabama that General
Buell was removed because he attempted to restrain soldiers
and that General Sherman, his successor, made no effort
whatever to restrain them.[105]   The liberty allowed in the
destruction of property easily merged into license in violation of personal rights.   General Mitchell, a Federal officer,
wrote from north Alabama in May, 1862, ". . . the most
terrible outrages—robberies, rapes, arson and plundering—
are being committed by lawless brigands and vagabonds

[101] E. K. Flournoy to his wife, April 15, 1864.

[102] Richmond *Examiner*, August 14, 1863. See also *Examiner*, August
18, 1863; *Confederate Veteran*, vol. xviii, p. 517, Cheney, " War Reminiscences."

[103] Fleming, *Civil War and Reconstruction*, pp. 62-67.

[104] Selma *Reporter*, July 26, 1863 (This officer was cashiered but later
promoted) ; Montgomery *Daily Mail*, November 26, 1862.

[105] Montgomery *Daily Mail*, December 14, 1862; Saunders, *Early
Settlers of North Alabama*, p. 287.

connected with the army." [106] Alabama newspapers from 1861 to 1865 gave accounts of the same kinds of outrages and others, including scourging and murder, committed by Federal troops, white and colored, in Alabama and in other states.[107] A select committee of Congress made a report of the same kinds of outrages in Alabama and other states.[108] General Clanton from north Alabama wrote to the Governor in April, 1864, " The Yankees spare neither age, sex, nor condition." [109] Such violations, like a spectre, day and night haunted soldiers whose homes were in invaded districts. Imagination brought to them, one said, the shriek of wife, turned out of doors with her children, destitute of food and clothing and insulted by the light of her own burning dwelling. Overpowered by suspense or by a desire for revenge, many soldiers went home to their families in invaded districts, sometimes bushwhacking the enemy, sometimes quietly hiding, but refusing to return to the army.[110]

Depredations committed by tory outlaws, often banded with deserters, followed by reprisals by irregular Confed-

---

[106] *O. R.*, ser. i, vol. x, pt. ii, p. 204. (General O. M. Mitchell).

[107] *Southwestern Baptist*, April 30, 1863; Selma *Reporter*, August 29, 1863; February 11, 1864; Richmond *Examiner*, January 3, 1863 (by a correspondent from Alabama); Montgomery *Weekly Advertiser*, September 16, 1863; January 6, March 23, June 23, June 29, 1864; Montgomery *Daily Advertiser*, January 27, 1865; Montgomery *Daily Mail*, November 20, 1862; March 8, 1863; June 23, 1864; Memphis *Appeal*, October 16, 1864 (published in Alabama). See also Freemantle, *Three Months in the Southern States*, p. 141.

[108] Montgomery *Daily Mail*, May 7, 1863.

[109] Fleming, *Civil War and Reconstruction*, p. 75.

[110] Owsley, *Defeatism in the Confederacy*, p. 6; Goodloe, *Confederate Echoes*, p. 300; DeLeon, *Four Years in Rebel Capitals*, p. 186; Wise, *The Long Arm of Lee*, p. 923; Bruce, *Lee*, p. 282; Rowland, *Jefferson Davis, Constitutionalist*, vol. v, p. 564; vol. vi, pp. 172-175; *O. R.*, ser. iv, vol. ii, p. 671; E. Kilpatrick, *The Political History of Alabama during the War of Secession* (Paris, 1924), p. 99.

erate cavalry, kept north Alabama in a condition of anarchy.
" Sheriffs and constables," wrote Edward Betts to the Governor, " are as extinct as geological specimens." [111] The
Governor acknowledged as much when he said that since
constables and militia officers were subject to conscription,
the state was powerless to enforce laws in certain sections
by civil or military process.[112] Sometimes Confederate cavalry, irregularly organized and indifferently disciplined, only
made matters worse and were themselves charged with serious abuses.[113] Bands of tories, combined with deserters,
defied both state and Confederate governments. They
robbed, plundered and committed all the outrages which a
lawless band could commit. They so terrorized parts of
north and southeast Alabama that many families of soldiers
became refugees and Confederate soldiers on furlough were
compelled to hide to save their lives. When soldiers in the
army received news from their wives and sisters of the
outrages and abuses to which they had been subjected by
outlaws, they were indignant and painfully uneasy. Many
deserted in order to punish the perpetrators of such outrages or to protect their families from similar treatment in
the future. But by desertion, they became outlaws themselves, and sometimes they became allies of the very bands
which had caused them to come home, thereby aggravating
the danger to the community and offering immunity to other

[111] February 8, 1864.

[112] *Governor's Letter Book*, July 24, 1863, p. 55; July 28, 1863, p. 56.

[113] *Governor's Letter Book*, 1864, p. 133, pp. 148-149; Montgomery
Weekly Advertiser, August 17, 1864 (for a contradictory statement, see
September 14) ; H. A. Creeview to Governor Watts, February 14, 1864;
Thomas P. Cottle to Governor Watts, April 21, 1864. On April 3, 1862,
a resolution was offered in Congress proposing legislation for the punishment of "crimes of murder and of rape committed by our soldiers upon
citizens in certain localities."—*Southern Historical Society Papers*, vol.
vii, p. 66, " Proceedings of Congress."

deserters. The condition was the more deplorable because most of the deserters who went home to protect their families had been good soldiers.[114]

Another cause of desertion was depression. Hunger and fatigue among soldiers, though gallantly borne, lessened their physical resistance and made them more susceptible to depression. Homesickness also caused depression and, in extreme cases, the death of its victims. Officers of the army agreed that discipline and efficiency among troops, even veteran troops, were improved by distance from their homes. Nearness to their homes presented a temptation so strong that many soldiers yielded to it. They went home for a visit and frequently they stayed. In 1863, General Pillow said, after he had put some deserters of north Alabama into the Army of Tennessee three or four times, that it was impossible to keep them in an army near their homes. During the latter part of the war, long absence, often a year or two, increased the natural longing of soldiers to go home.[115]

Hopelessness of winning the war was a more potent cause of depression. Despondency of the people at home affected the soldiers seriously although the morale of the army was always higher than that of the people.[116] The chief factor

[114] E. J. Kirksey to Governor Shorter, July —, 1863; Bush Jones (Lt.-Col. of the Ninth Alabama Battalion) to Governor Shorter, July 16, 1863; Catharine Powell to Governor Watts, June 13, 1864; *O. R.*, ser. i, vol. xv, p. 939; Cannon, *Inside of Rebeldom*, p. 194; Fleming, *Civil War and Reconstruction*, p. 129; Montgomery *Weekly Advertiser*, September 14, 1864; *Governor's Letter Book*, March 28, 1863, p. 354; May 18, 1863, p. 7; July 24, 1863, p. 55; July 28, 1863, pp. 56-57.

[115] *Review of Reviews*, vol. xliii, p. 435, Randolph Harrison McKim, "Glimpses of the Confederate Army"; Montgomery *Weekly Advertiser*, February 4, 1863; Rowland, *Jefferson Davis, Constitutionalist*, vol. v, pp. 462-463; vol. vi, pp. 161-162; Mobile *Register*, May 12, 1864; *O. R.*, ser. iv, vol. ii, pp. 680, 853; vol. iii, p. 796.

[116] *Clarke County Journal*, September 3, 1863; *Southwestern Baptist*,

in producing despondency was military defeat. The three periods of deepest popular depression in Alabama followed the fall of Fort Donelson in February, 1862; the fall of Vicksburg in July, 1863; and the fall of Atlanta in November, 1864, after each of which the state was subjected to invasion.[117] The first two periods were followed by recovery of the hope that the Confederacy would win the war; the third was not. The people were stunned by the unexpected fall of Fort Donelson, followed soon by Shiloh, but after the army was doubled by the conscription law, they supported the war with a hopeful determination though not with their early buoyancy. They were covered with intense gloom by the fall of Vicksburg, followed soon by the defeat at Mission Ridge, but after the reenlistment of soldiers early in 1864 and the improvement of the morale of the Army of Tennessee by General Johnston, they supported the war with desperation. They were fighting for peace rather than for victory. In 1864, the people of Alabama were as ardent in their desire for independence and more furious in their resentment of Federal invasion, but they began to realize that by a process of attrition they would finally be defeated. They were filled with despair by the fall of Atlanta. Though the war continued six months, they never recovered the hope of winning it.[118] During this period despondency was in-

August 13, 1863; December 18, 1862; *Alabama Beacon*, October 9, 1863; Montgomery *Weekly Advertiser*, September 30, 1863; January 13, 1864.

[117] Grant, *Memoirs*, vol. i, p. 374; Mobile *Register*, January 3, 1863; Stephenson, *Day of the Confederacy*, p. 114; Polk, *Leonidas Polk*, pp. 230-231; Fleming, *Civil War and Reconstruction*, p. 137; Mobile *Register*, January 27 and 31, 1864; *Alabama Beacon*, July 31, 1863; Eckenrode, *Jefferson Davis*, p. 227; Sallie Putnam, *Richmond during the War* (New York, 1867), p. 339. For references on periods of desertion, cf. *supra*, pp. 26-28.

[118] The rise and fall of depression in Alabama was traced in newspapers. See also: Gildersleeve, *The Creed of the Old South*, p. 31;

creased by exhaustion. " Pressed as we are for means of all description," reported the inspector-general of the Division of the West, December 31, 1864, " it is not in the power of men to continue such a struggle much longer." [119] In 1865, officers high in command acknowledged to themselves that the people were tired.[120] January 23, 1865, J. L. M. Curry wrote to the Governor from north Alabama, " The public mind is depressed beyond what I have known at any antecedent period of this war. The demoralization in the Army, fearful beyond description, is exceeded by demoralization at home." The next month, General Lee reported that despondency among the people was causing a great increase in desertion, and urged that leaders try to revive something of the spirit which animated the people during the first two years of the war.[121]

To the people and the soldiers who during the latter part of 1864 were convinced that the war was over, further fighting seemed both useless and cruel. The great mortality among Confederate troops in 1864 had a very depressing effect. "Another series of victories," wrote the Richmond

Eckenrode, *Jefferson Davis*, p. 315; Stiles, *Four Years under Marse Robert*, p. 242; E. K. Flournoy to his wife, June 14 and July 5, 1864; P. A. Bruce, *Robert E. Lee* (Philadelphia, 1907), pp. 299, 283.

[119] *Letter Book of Major Henry Bryan* (to General Beauregard). The New York *Times* of May 9, 1864 said that the rebels were using their life blood.

[120] Taylor, *Four Years with General Lee*, p. 144 (March 5). Early in March, 1865, General Lee suggested to Confederate authorities that they make peace.—Pryor, *Reminiscences*, pp. 334.

[121] *O. R.*, ser. i, vol. xlvi, pt. ii, p. 1254; vol. xlvii, pt. ii, pp. 1270-1271. See also: *O. R.*, ser. i, vol. xlvii, pt. ii, pp. 1312, 1296; Hagood, *Memoirs*, pp. 332, 64; Rowland, *Jefferson Davis, Constitutionalist*, vol. vi, p. 574; *Alabama Beacon*, January 22, 1864. The New York *Times*, January 22, 1864, stated that popular depression in the South was a cause of desertion and expressed the opinion that it was not human nature to make a protracted sacrifice for a hopeless cause.

Examiner in May, 1864, "another outburst of grief throughout the Confederacy." [122]   Some people at home began to say that the few men who were left ought to be saved.   Soldiers saw nothing before them but certain death. Since there was no hope of winning the war, the sacrifice of their lives seemed useless to their country and unjust to their families.   To fight longer was to become a martyr to no purpose.[123]   Soldiers went home by the thousands.   Under the contagion of desertion,[124] General Hood's army disintegrated rapidly and General Lee's army disintegrated less rapidly but as surely.[125]

The periods of deepest popular depression coincided with the periods of greatest desertion.   So the barometer of popular depression was desertion.

The various causes for desertion, military and political, social and economic, which have been named in succession, usually operated in groups of two or more.[126]   For example, short rations, reconstruction sentiment at home and the belief that the government showed favoritism toward the rich would lead one soldier to desert; suffering in his family for the necessaries of life and conviction that the war was over would lead another to desert.   Any combination of causes might be reinforced by popular depression and by a gener-

[122] Channing, *History of the United States*, vol. vi, p. 623, quoting the Richmond *Examiner*.

[123] Channing, *History of the United States,* vol. vi, pp. 615, 621-623; Oates, *The War between the Union and the Confederacy*, pp. 429-430; Grant, *Memoirs*, vol. ii, p. 477; Pryor, *Reminiscences*, pp. 293, 326.

[124] "The evil fed upon itself."—Lonn, *Desertion during the Civil War*, p. 17.

[125] Goodloe, *Confederate Echoes*, p. 129; Rhodes, *History of the United States*, vol. v, pp. 43-44; Hood, *Advance and Retreat*, p. 71; Grant, *Memoirs*, vol. ii, p. 480; Pollard, *Southern History of the War*, vol. ii, p. 507.

[126] A close parallel may be seen between these causes and the causes for desertion during the Revolution.

ally lenient attitude toward infractions of discipline in an army of volunteers. The combination was made to suit the individual and reflected much of the background of his life. Thus causes for desertion were usually complex, varying not only with external circumstances but also with the characters of the men responding to them. If an analysis of these complex causes were possible, it would doubtless show that poverty in the families of soldiers was the element which was dominating and which best accounts for the sectional distribution of deserters in the state.

CHAPTER V

Efforts to Check Desertion: Prevention

ONLY a few efforts of military authorities were directed immediately toward preventing desertion. Some changes in military organization were made to improve discipline. To secure more efficient officers, in 1862 the method of selecting higher company and regimental officers was changed from election to appointment, and provision was made for removal upon grounds of inefficiency by recommendation of a board of examiners, and in 1864 by recommendation of the general commanding. To provide for better administration of army regulations, standing military courts, supplementary to courts-martial, were organized in each corps in 1862 and in various divisions in 1863, and were given more extended jurisdiction in 1864. These changes, according to the report of the Secretary of War, were effective in improving the morale of the army.[1] Severity of punishment of deserters as an example to deter others from committing the crime was insisted upon by Generals Bragg, Johnston and Lee. It was also practiced by them as consistently as possible. General Lee's opinion was that inexorable execution of the death penalty upon soldiers convicted of desertion was one of the most effective methods of preventing

[1] *O. R.*, ser. iv, vol. ii, pp. 205-206; vol. i, p. 1096; vol. ii, pp. 80-81, 288, 202-203, 691; vol. iii, pp. 497, 498, 327, 333. Withholding pay of absentees had little effect. Most of the efforts of military authorities were directed toward securing the return of deserters, probably with the ultimate objective of preventing desertion by insuring certainty of punishment. For these efforts, see Chap. VI.

desertion and truly merciful in the end.[2] Upon the insistent request of General Pillow, transfers of some deserters from north Alabama from the Army of Tennessee to the Army of Northern Virginia in order to increase the distance between them and their homes were allowed by the War Department in the fall of 1863.[3] A system of furloughs based on merit and designed to lessen homesickness was put into effect in both of the great armies during the latter part of 1863 and the first part of 1864. In both of the armies, precedence in claims to furloughs was given to soldiers whose family necessities were most pressing. This system of furloughs was considered very successful in preventing absenteeism and desertion.[4]

More effective than these features of military organization in preventing desertion were measures of social relief. There was in Alabama a general recognition of the fact that justice to the poor soldiers demanded measures of social relief. When soldiers with dependent families entered the army, they were assured that while they were fighting for the country their families would be taken care of. These promises were one of the chief methods of raising volunteers in 1861 and 1862. They were pledges that the soldiers had taken in good faith, it was said, and they deserved to be kept.[5] Supporting the families of poor soldiers was not

[2] Freeman, *Lee's Dispatches*, pp. 124, 154-158; Mobile *Register*, Jan. 27, 1863; T. B. Hall to his sister, July 12, 1862; *General Orders* no. 33, 1864, Hdqrs. Army of Tenn.

[3] *O. R.*, ser. iv, vol. ii, pp. 638, 680, 742, 830-831.

[4] *O. R.*, ser. i, vol. xxix, pt. ii, p. 650; Park, *The Twelfth Alabama*, p. 68; Col. N. W. Davis to his wife, Apr. 6, 1864; *G. O.* no. 21, 1864, Dept. and Army of No. Va.; Johnston, *Narrative*, p. 280; Capt. S. C. Kelly to his wife, Jan. 17, 1864; J. E. Hall to his father, Feb. 8, 1865.

[5] *The Democratic Watchtower*, Oct. 28, 1863; *The Alabama Beacon*, Dec. 26, 1862; Apr. 17, 1863; Selma *Reporter*, March 31, July 31, 1863; *Southwestern Baptist*, Sept. 10, 1863. See also Dillon Jordan to Gov. Shorter, March 25, 1863.

only redeeming a pledge but also paying a debt. At home these men could have supported their families in comfort, but they had given up their homes and were defending with their lives the liberty of all the people. Their sacrifices made them the real patriots and placed those for whom they fought under so great a debt that aid to their families could pay it only in part.[6]

There was also a general recognition of the fact that expediency for property owners demanded measures of social relief. Planters and merchants were urged to aid the indigent families of soldiers in order to avert defeat in the field and to protect their property at home. Soldiers whose families were dependent upon them for support formed a large part—if not the larger part—of the army and they could not fight when their families were in want. The serious military reverses of 1864, said Governor Watts, were due partially to the sins of the people at home in neglecting soldiers' families.[7] The army alone protected the fields of planters from devastation, and the integrity of the army depended upon the liberality of planters to the families of soldiers. Planters must give to save.[8] Furthermore, fail-

[6] *Democratic Watchtower*, Oct. 28, 1863; Montgomery *Advertiser*, Nov. 18, 1863; *Southwestern Baptist*, Nov. 6, 1862; Apr. 30, 1863; Selma *Reporter*, March 31, 1863; May 7, 1864; Mobile *Register*, Sept. 30, 1863; *Journal of Senate*, 1862, p. 15; *Journal of House*, 1862, p. 22; *Acts of the Called and the First Regular Annual Session of the General Assembly of Alabama*, 1863, pp. 22-23.

[7] Montgomery *Advertiser*, March 3, 1865 (speech, Feb. 25).

[8] *Democratic Watchtower*, Jan. 20, 1864; Mobile *Register*, Apr. 19, 1864; *Alabama Beacon*, Dec. 26, 1862; Apr. 17, 1863; Jan. 30, 1864; *The Independent*, Oct. 24, 1863; *Southwestern Baptist*, June 11, 1863. " Many of them have absolutely nothing with which to buy. In this aspect of the case, is it at all astonishing that so many of our soldiers are deserting and coming home to look after the wants of their families? We tell you, fellow countrymen, that unless you contribute your substance to this purpose promptly and liberally, the time is not distant when it

ure to care for the poor families of soldiers might precipi-
tate a social revolution at home in which property would
vanish. Scenes in Richmond and nearer home in 1863,
though a cloud no larger than a man's hand, wrote a wealthy
planter of Greene county, might result in a storm which
would burst in ruin over all.[9] In the fall of 1863, Governor-
elect Watts, in a tour of the state, urged upon the people
the " sacred duty we owe," and in December in his in-
augural address, called upon central and middle Alabama,
" the seat of wealth and plenty," to discharge their duty
to the destitute families of soldiers from other parts of the
state, saying that men with property had a double obligation
to feed and clothe the families of soldiers who were forming with their bodies breastworks against Yankee invasion
and outrage.[10]

From 1861 to 1865, measures of social relief were undertaken by private organizations and individuals. In Mobile,
the largest city in the state, several private organizations
distributed aid to the indigent families of soldiers. The
Military Aid Society, organized in May, 1861, offered employment to soldiers' wives making uniforms under contract with the government and gave money to the more
needy wives.[11] The Samaritan Society, organized in June,
1861, rendered medical aid to the indigent families of sol-

will be destroyed by our enemies. Our only defense is in the armies of
the Confederate States and if from our indifference to these home necessities, these armies are so weakened by desertions as to subject our whole
country to the mercy of our enemies, we shall have nobody to blame but
ourselves."—*Southwestern Baptist,* Aug. 6, 1863.

[9] Appleton, *Annual Cyclopedia,* 1863, p. 18; *Southwestern Baptist,* Sept.
17, 1863; *Alabama Beacon,* Apr. 17, 1863 (H. T.).

[10] *The Independent,* Oct. 24, 1863 (" sacred duty ") ; *Democratic Watchtower,* Nov. 4, 1863; Selma *Reporter,* Oct. 24, 1863; *Journal of Senate,
Ala.,* 1863, pp. 204-205.

[11] Mobile *Register,* Nov. 2, 1862.

diers, paying the annual salary of a physician and the cost of the prescribed medicines.[12]   In September, 1863, a Confederate Aid Society was organized in Mobile which advocated as the best means of raising money to support the families of soldiers an assessment upon all owners of property exceeding $10,000 in value.[13]

The most important of these and similar organizations was the Citizens' Relief Association.   It was organized in October, 1861, and carried on its constantly enlarging work till 1865.   The president of the Citizens' Relief Association was the mayor of the city.   The executive, or general, committee was composed of seven ward committees, each member of which was responsible for a district of the city. These committees were assisted when the need arose by special temporary committees.   Other officers of the organization were inspectors who ascertained the needs of families and agents who collected and distributed supplies.[14]

The Citizens' Relief Association was financed by private subscriptions.   At first, the Association called only upon the citizens of Mobile for contributions of money and preferably of supplies.   Their response was generous, but the needs of indigent families increased so greatly that the Association in December, 1861, made an appeal to the people of Alabama and adjoining states for aid in performing " the sacred duty " which " the war has devolved upon society."   People outside gave help then and later, but the burden of financing the Association fell upon the citizens of Mobile.   They made liberal contributions, which were acknowledged frequently in the newspapers.   These were

[12] *Ibid.*, June 9, 1863.

[13] Montgomery *Weekly Mail*, Sept. 30, 1863; Montgomery *Advertiser*, Oct. 14, 1863.

[14] Mobile *Register,* Oct. 8, 12, 22, 1861; June 12, 1862; Jan. 4, 1863; Oct. 3, 1863.

sometimes supplemented by contributions from odd sources, like proceeds from a benefit performance of the Mobile Theatre and from an amateur minstrel show and fees sent to the Mobile *Register* for matrimonial advertisements. The Relief Association occasionally faced crises when raising funds seemed hopeless but it never appealed to the citizens of Mobile without success.[15]

The Citizens' Relief Association maintained a Free Market, at which bread, vegetables, meat, provisions, candles, wood and other necessaries were sold at low prices or given away to the holders of tickets issued by the ward committees or the secretary of the Association. The Free Market on the day of its opening, October 14, 1861, supplied 400 persons and in three weeks three times as many. By December 19, it was supplying daily 1800 persons, including indigent families of soldiers and some unemployed persons. According to its official report, the Relief Association dispensed during the year 1862, $120,000 worth of supplies to the indigent families of soldiers, many of whom it was believed could not live without such aid. According to an unofficial report, it dispensed during 1863 $200,000 for food and clothing. In that year, the Relief Association made two " drives " for clothing and appointed a special agent to purchase clothing in factories at wholesale prices. It employed a meat contractor with about a dozen assistants. It sent agents into other counties to solicit contributions of money and food and to buy supplies. Its agents went to Mississippi, Tennessee, and as far north as Charleston, South Carolina, buying supplies for the Free Market.[16]

---

[15] Mobile *Register*, Dec. 4, Oct. 29, Dec. 19, 1861; Oct. 22, March 1, June 3, Nov. 13, 1863; May 18, March 24, 1864; Dec. 18, 1863; Apr. 2, 1864; Feb. 7, March 28, Apr. 5, Dec. 4, 1862.

[16] Mobile *Register*, Oct. 15, 17, 25, 29, Dec. 19, 1861; March 28, 1862; Jan. 18, 1863 (report); Fleming, *Civil War and Reconstruction*, p. 198,

The city government cooperated with the Citizens' Relief Association and to some extent supplemented its efforts.[17]

In Montgomery, second in size among the cities of Alabama, but much smaller than Mobile, the chief organization for giving aid to the indigent families of soldiers was the Soldiers' Fund Committee or the Montgomery Indigent Relief Committee. The Soldiers' Fund Committee was organized April 26, 1861 at a meeting of citizens called to take measures to raise funds for the families of volunteers whose resources were slender. In the fall of 1863, apparently, it was reorganized as the Montgomery Indigent Relief Committee, each ward of the city having one member. The methods and work of these committees were similar to those of the Mobile Citizens' Relief Association. Subscription lists were opened and contributions of supplies were called for to aid " the needy families of our gallant volunteers." Appeals in articles in the newspapers and in speeches in the churches were made by the chairman, who said that the number of the poor was increased by refugees from abandoned farms and that, in many cases, destitution was extreme. In November, 1863, a contribution of $10,000 was made by the commissioners' court. In 1861, the Committee had a stall at the municipal market where citizens were requested to send vegetables, and later it opened a store where provisions and clothing were received and distributed. It contracted with wood haulers to deliver wood at reduced prices to the holders of tickets and later established a woodyard of its own.[18] The Supply Association, which was

quoting the N. Y. *Herald*, Dec. 26, 1863; Mobile *Register*, Nov. 14, Oct. 6, 22, 1863; Louis P. Waganer to T. P. Owen, June 1, 1909; P. J. Hamilton, *Mobile of the Five Flags* (Mobile, 1913), p. 308.

[17] Mobile *Register*, Oct. 12, 1861; Hamilton, *Mobile of the Five Flags*, p. 302.

[18] Montgomery *Weekly Advertiser*, May 1, 1861; Montgomery *Daily Mail*, Oct. 25, 1862; Jan. 28, Apr. 30, July 24, 1863; Montgomery *Adver-*

organized in April, 1863, was a joint stock company which sold supplies at cost to the indigent families of soldiers. The capital, $50,000, which was raised by selling shares of $500, was to be returned to stockholders without interest at the close of the enterprise.[19]

In Selma, at a meeting of citizens held April 24, 1861, a solemn promise was given to soldiers in the following words: " Resolved that the city council and the citizens of Selma pledge themselves to support, protect and defend the families of those who have (taken) or may take up arms for the defense of the cause of our country." [20]   On the same day, another meeting of citizens was held to consider a systematic way of raising money to keep the pledge.   The result was the Soldiers' Relief Association, the executive part of which consisted of a committee of seven with sub-committees for each precinct in Dallas county.   The Association received gifts from individuals and in October, 1863, requested the city council to make an appropriation and to levy a property tax.[21]   In December of the same year, the Selma Supply Association, similar to the Montgomery Supply Association, was organized by the citizens of Selma and the mechanics in the Confederate States' iron works there.   It was a joint stock company, the capital of which was raised by subscription to be finally returned without interest and the object of which was to secure by purchase or gift, food, clothing and fuel, and to sell them at cost to persons designated by a committee of the Supply Association.[22]

tiser, Nov. 18, 1863; Sept. 10, 18, 1864; Montgomery *Daily Mail*, Oct. 10, 1864.

[19] Montgomery *Daily Mail*, Apr. 17, 1863.

[20] Selma *Reporter*, Apr. 25, 1861.

[21] Selma *Reporter*, Apr. 25, 1861; Jan. 6, 1862; Oct. 26, 28, 1863.

[22] Selma *Reporter*, Sept. 24, 1863.   It was said that mechanics agreed to give one day's wages each month.—Mobile *Register*, Dec. 19, 1863.

Unique among the organizations for the relief of soldiers' families was the Citizens' Supply Association, organized in Selma in March, 1863. The system of committees was exactly like that of the Soldiers' Relief Fund, but the object of the Association was to raise food in Dallas county for the suffering families in the upper counties, Bibb, Shelby, Blount and others, which had experienced a drouth in 1862 and which had sent large numbers of volunteers, nearly all of whom were poor men. In two weeks the Association raised $40,000 and large amounts of corn, salt, meat and other provisions. Unfortunately, the Citizens' Relief Association was inactive in 1864.[23]

Private aid to the indigent families of soldiers was better organized in the cities than in the counties of the state; but a good many counties had organizations similar to those of cities. The best known of the county organizations was the Central Aid Society of Talladega. It was organized in 1861 to carry out the pledge made by the citizens to volunteers that $20,000, if necessary, would be raised annually for the support of their families. By this pledge, at least 27 companies of volunteers were raised by April 1, 1864, but the county was strained to care for their families, many of whom became destitute in the absence of the bread-winners. In May, 1861 only 30 persons received aid, but in April, 1864, 3,979 needed aid and received it. The county raised part of the necessary funds by taxation, part by contributions. The central executive committee was assisted by beat committees and occasionally by mass meetings of citizens. In 1863, the citizens raised $7,276 in cash, 2570 bushels of corn, 16 sacks of salt, and 102 bushels of wheat, besides selling to the government for the poor families of soldiers 21,755 bushels of corn at 50 cents a bushel when

[23] Selma *Reporter*, March 31, 1863; *Alabama Beacon*, Apr. 17, 1863; Selma *Reporter*, May 7, 1864.

corn was worth $3 a bushel and 233 sacks of salt at $20 a sack when salt was worth $80 a sack. They were obliged to haul some of the corn forty miles. As a result, it was said many soldiers from Vicksburg returned to the army and many women who received supplies stated to the officer distributing them that they intended to write to their husbands in the Army of Tennessee or the Army of Northern Virginia not to come home.[24] In Calhoun county, a relief association was organized in 1861 with an executive committee and beat committees.[25] The following southern counties organized relief associations from 1861 to 1863: Lowndes, Perry, Sumter, Greene, Macon and Marengo. The organization of these associations was similar to that of associations in cities, and the methods were the same.[26] Frequently, the leaders of the county organizations were men who were prominent in public life or who became prominent in public life because of their activities on behalf of the poor families of soldiers. In 1861 optimistic newspaper reports were made of the formation of organizations for aid to the indigent families of soldiers in cities and counties all over the state.[27] These lists of organizations in three cities and in several counties are doubtless incomplete, but they are indicative of the important fact that better pro-

[24] *Democratic Watchtower*, May 8, 15, Oct. 9, 1861; Nov. 11, 18, 1862; Selma *Reporter*, Aug. 11, 1863; Jacksonville *Republican*, May 9, 1863; J. W. DuBose, *Eighth Confederate Cavalry*, pp. 1-2; Miller, *Alabama,* pp. 198-199; Mobile *Register,* Oct. 4, 1863. Parsons was president; Cruikshank, secretary.

[25] Jacksonville *Republican*, Oct. 17, 1861.

[26] Montgomery *Weekly Advertiser*, May 15, 1861; Gainesville *Indebendent,* June 1, 1861; Oct. 13, Nov. 8, 1862; *Alabama Beacon*, March 14, 21, Nov. 7, 1862; Montgomery *Advertiser*, Nov. 18, 1863; *Southvestern Baptist*, Oct. 29, 1863; Selma *Reporter*, Sept. 24, 1863.

[27] Montgomery *Weekly Advertiser*, May 1, May 29, 1861; Mobile *Register,* June 11, 1861.

visions for indigent families of soldiers were made in the southern part of the state.

Church organizations contributed to the aid of indigent families of soldiers, directly and indirectly. They cared for many indigent families through church funds administered by church committees. And during the latter part of the war they assumed practically the entire burden of caring for the orphan children of soldiers. But indirectly, the churches probably gave greater aid. From the pulpit and from convention committees, their leaders continually urged upon individuals the spirit and the practice of charity toward the poor and tried to secure from them pledges to sell the necessaries of life to soldiers' families at prices approaching pre-war prices.[28] The aid of churches, like that of relief organizations, was more effective in the richer counties of the state.

A large part of the aid to the indigent families of soldiers was unorganized. According to the very scanty records, it was given by men of means in various ways. Planters sold supplies for indigent families of soldiers below market prices. For example, in 1863 the state government secured in Talladega county a limited amount of corn at 50 cents a bushel when the market price was $3, and of salt at $10 when the market price was $80, and it secured in the black-belt counties through ex-Governor Moore as special agent, a partial supply of corn at $1.25 a bushel.[29] In 1863, a movement, which probably had some success, was started

[28] Fleming, *Civil War and Reconst.*, p. 224; *Minutes of the 40th Annual Session of the Alabama Baptist State Convention*, 1862, pp. 17-18, 19-20; *Minutes of 44th Session of Alabama Baptist Association* (Montgomery, 1863), pp. 6, 11; *Southwestern Baptist*, Oct. 11, 22, 1863. For mention of sermons, see newspapers, *passim*.

[29] Miller, *Ala.*, p. 198; Geo. W. Jones to Gov. Watts, enclosing a printed broadside to probate judges, Oct. 29, 1863. See also Jacksonville *Republican*, May 9, 1863.

to secure through the cooperative effort of churches, the adoption of a schedule of prices to indigent families of soldiers: corn $1 a bushel, wheat $2.50 a bushel, and bacon 25 cents a pound.[30] Planters contributed to agents who were soliciting funds for the poorer counties and for the city of Mobile. For example, in 1863 the agent of Clarke, who was a member of Congress, collected 2600 bushels of corn, $595, and 100 pounds of bacon from Wilcox and Marengo. To relieve the destitution of southeastern counties, in 1863 the Governor suggested the appointment by the counties of agents to Lowndes, Dallas and Montgomery.[31] Planters gave to " corn women " from the up-country. In 1863 and 1864 " corn women " with their sacks were familiar figures in Perry, Dallas and other black-belt counties near the hill counties. They came on trains and steamboats, representing themselves as wives of soldiers and begging corn to save their children from starvation. They always received corn. Their sacks were not only filled but sent to the station for them. Many of them, finding begging corn easier than raising it, took advantage of the generosity of planters and imposed upon it. In 1864, they came in droves from ten to twenty with several sacks apiece and scoured the country for corn. When sacks gave out, they brought bed-ticks which held ten bushels or more. Some of the " corn women " were wives of deserters, and others were wives of men who had never been in the army at all. It was said that they used some of the corn they got by begging to pay taxes-in-kind and some to distill into whiskey. Overseers hated " the corn women " as nuisances and even

---

[30] *Southwestern Baptist*, Oct. 11, 22, 1863; *Minutes of 44th Session of Alabama Baptist Association*, 1863, pp. 6, 11.

[31] Montgomery *Mail*, March 21, 1863 (Dickinson) ; Jno. G. Moore to Gov. Watts, March 5, 1864, endorsement; see also *Alabama Beacon*, Apr. 22, 1864 and Mobile *Register*, Oct. 22, 1863.

planters began to lose patience with them in 1864. But since they could not tell imposters from genuine " corn women," they gave to all. In 1864, planters of Perry county gave hundreds of bushels of corn to these women.[32] Planters took care of poor families in their neighborhoods. In some cases, they had their land plowed and did similar services which women could not do well for themselves. In other cases, they furnished practically the entire support year after year.[33]

Other wealthy men in the state also gave liberally. Railroad and steamboat companies transported supplies for various relief organizations and for the government at reduced rates or free of charge. They also carried the " corn women " with their sacks free of charge.[34] Merchants and manufacturers sometimes distributed goods. For example, in December, 1862, a company of Eastboga gave shoes to all the women in the beat whose husbands were in the army and who had no slaves, and several times a company of Oakfuskee distributed cotton and woolen thread to the poor of Randolph county.[35]

It is impossible to determine exactly the total amount of private aid given to indigent families of soldiers through organized and unorganized sources, but it was undoubtedly

[32] Selma *Reporter*, Apr. 25, May 7, 1864; Jno. H. Chapman to Gov. Watts, May 14, 1864; *Our Women in the War* (Mrs. Rhodes of Ala.), p. 276.

[33] *Southwestern Baptist*, June 11, Sept. 10, 17, 1863; Selma *Reporter*, Feb. 16, March 31, 1863; *Independent*, Oct. 13, 1862; Montgomery *Weekly Mail*, Sept. 30, 1863; Fleming, *Civil War and Reconst.*, p. 202. See also Selma *Reporter*, Mar. 30, 1864; Mobile *Register*, March 28, 1862; *Governor's Letter Book*, March, 1863, pp. 352-353.

[34] Selma *Reporter*, Nov. 14, 1862; May 7, 1864; *Our Women in the War*, p. 276; Hamilton, *Mobile of Five Flags*, p. 302.

[35] *Democratic Watchtower*, Dec. 9, 1862; Jacksonville *Republican*, Feb. 13, 1864.

very large. One contemporary observer estimated the amount as "many more millions" than the state appropriations.[36] Another spoke enthusiastically of "the God-like munificence" of planters, which intensified patriotism at home and in the field.[37] The liberality of men of means is indeed striking when it is remembered that they not only gave large sums but also paid heavy taxes for the support of indigent families of soldiers. In spite of the talk of a "rich man's war," it seems that rich men who did not give to this cause were rare. Practically all of the owners of property valued at $20,000 and more who applied for amnesty in 1865 and 1866 acknowledged that they had aided the rebellion by contributing to the support of the indigent families of soldiers.[38] However, the more generous doubtless carried the heaviest burden. It is also impossible to determine exactly the results of this aid. It is certain that it prevented much suffering. It is equally certain that it helped to hold many men in the army. However, the measures of social relief undertaken by private organizations and individuals, since they depended upon emotional appeals, were lacking in regularity. And, since they depended upon the wealth of citizens, they were not evenly distributed among the counties of the state. For example, the thirteen counties which contained the largest number of the owners of property worth $20,000 and up who acknowledged in their applications for amnesty to contributing to indigent families were located, with the exception of Tuscaloosa and Talladega, in the southern part of the state. The four counties of Perry, Greene, Mobile and Dallas contained over half of these men; thirteen of the counties of north

---

[36] Jacksonville *Republican*, Feb. 13, 1864.

[37] Selma *Reporter*, June 9, 1864.

[38] *Register of Applications for Amnesty and Pardon*, Aug. 5, 1865– July 12, 1866, vols. i-ii, *passim*.

Alabama contained not one. Concentration of wealth in the southern counties meant more effective measures of relief for the poor of that section.

From 1861 to 1865, measures of social relief were undertaken also by state and county governments. The first act of the General Assembly making an appropriation for the indigent families of soldiers was approved November 11, 1861. A special tax of 25% upon the amount already imposed on taxable property should be collected in the same way as the annual state and county taxes and paid into the state treasury as " a fund for the aid of the indigent families of volunteers." To apportion the fund among the counties, reports showing the number of members, the means of support, and the needs of each indigent family should be made within a specified time to the probate judges by agents appointed for each precinct by the county commissioners. From these reports, estimates of the number of families and their needs should be returned by the commissioners to the state comptroller of public accounts. From these estimates, the apportionment among the counties of the 25% tax should be made by the comptroller. The funds paid by him to each county, according to the apportionment, should be administered by the probate judge under the supervision of the commissioners' court.[39] The reports by precincts giving the name of the volunteer, the number of persons in his family, and the amount of money estimated to meet their needs for the fiscal year ending September 30 were sent in during January and February, 1862, supplemented by a few scattering lists submitted later.[40]

[39] *Acts of the Second Called Session, 1861 and of the First Regular Annual Session of the General Assembly of Alabama*, 1861, pp. 4-8.

[40] *Reports of Commissioners' Courts to the Comptroller under the act approved Nov. 11, 1861*. The following extracts from the *Record Book of Blount County*, Jan. 6, 1862-April, 1880, pp. 25 and 69, illustrate the

The reports of the counties showed great variation in estimates of the amounts required to meet the needs of indigent families and great uniformity in placing the estimates high above the income from the special 25% tax. The comptroller, making no effort to equalize the estimates of the counties, apportioned to each county one-third of the estimates sent in under the act, thus making the apportionment roughly equal to the 25% tax of each county. It happened that about a dozen of the richer counties received considerably less and about a dozen and a half of the poorer counties and the rich county of Mobile received more than their 25% tax.[41] On the basis of contribution to the fund, the apportionment appeared fair, but on the basis of the needs of families, it was grossly uneven. The annual amounts apportioned varied from $4 per family in Blount and Winston to $66 per family in Dallas. All the counties of north Alabama but six and the counties of extreme southeast Alabama fell below the median average of $19 per family. Thus the distribution favored the southern counties and gave to them that had. Naturally, the unequal distribution created dissatisfaction among the poorer counties. Again, the tax yielded a total sum smaller than was expected, only $197,044.68, and the sums apportioned to the counties were only one-third of the amounts estimated to meet the needs. Thus the aid under the act was inequitably distributed among the counties and entirely inadequate to the needs of the indigent families.[42]

difficulty of making these reports: (1) "Wife, children 6, from 17 yrs. to 4 yrs. has corn to do 3 mos. and meat to do 5 mos. cotton and cotton cards needed and salt needed. leather needed $5 worth. has 1 cow Giving milk 12 A. of land under cultivation." (2) "Mother aged 40, Sisters 17 and 7, Bro. 9 and 4, has no means whatever . . .$75."

[41] *Annual Report of the Comptroller of Public Accounts to the Assembly*, 1862, pp. 5, 7, 17.

[42] Commissioners' Court of Pike to the Gov. Aug. 25, 1862; H. J.

A minor act of the General Assembly which was designed to aid the poorer soldiers exempted volunteers from payment of poll tax and of tax on property to the amount of $500.[43] In addition, joint resolutions were passed, asking Congress to increase the pay of soldiers.[44]

Before the legislation of the General Assembly in the fall of 1861, many counties had adopted measures of aid to the indigent families of soldiers. The acts passed by commissioners' courts of the counties to aid indigent families were legalized by acts of the General Assembly November 9 and November 30, and future appropriations by commissioners' courts for the same object were authorized by act of the Assembly November 29.[49] Under acts of the counties more speedy relief could be given than under state legislation. In addition, legislation for certain counties for aid of indigent families was passed by the Assembly. Butler (southern) was allowed to place an additional tax of 25% upon the amount of the state tax, if needed; Choctaw (southern) was authorized to use the sum in its treasury with a reservation of $2000; Cherokee (northern) was allowed to impose a special tax to equalize the amounts spent by individuals in equipping volunteers and aiding their families; and Talladega (northern), to lay a special tax to meet the liabilities incurred by the central committee above the amounts raised by voluntary contributions.[46]

Marley to Gov., July 20, 1862; *Journal of Senate,* Ala., 1862, p. 15; *Gov.'s Letter Book,* Dec. 31, 1862, p. 295; *Annual Report of Comptroller,* 1862, p. 5.

[43] *Acts of Second Called and First Regular Sess. of Gen. Ass. of Ala.,* 1861, p. 81.

[44] *Ibid.,* p. 270, Dec. 10.

[45] *Ibid.,* pp. 170-171, 74.

[46] *Ibid.,* p. 199 (Dec. 7) ; *Acts of Called and Second Regular Annual Session of Gen. Ass.,* 1862, pp. 198-199, Dec. 4 (omitted by mistake in 1861) ; *Acts,* 1861, p. 201 (Nov. 27) ; p. 229 (Nov. 29).

In October, 1862, the Governor called a special session of the General Assembly for the purpose of making provisions for the indigent families of soldiers.[47]   An act was passed by a unanimous vote in each house and approved by the Governor November 12, 1862, making an appropriation of two million dollars to the indigent families, including dependent mothers, fathers, brothers, and sisters of volunteers and conscripts in the Confederate army and of volunteers in the state militia, with the exception of the families of substitutes and the families of deserters while it was known that deserters were not in the army.   The act provided that a registration of the indigent families should be made in each county according to some efficient plan of the county commissioners, that the apportionment of the two million dollars be made by the state comptroller according to the number of indigent families in each county and that the funds, paid by him in quarterly installments, beginning immediately, be distributed by the probate judge for a fee of ½ of 1% under the supervision of the county commissioners, who should be bound by an oath for faithful administration of the funds and who should keep written records of their transactions.   The act provided that, whenever practicable, aid should be given in the form of supplies.[48]   In the course of debate in the Assembly, several proposals were made for raising the necessary funds—a suspension of the public schools of the state and transfer of their appropriation; a tax on incomes; a tax on cotton raised by slave labor; a graded tax on persons exempted from military service.[49]   However, no taxes were laid to meet the appropriation, but in a night session just before

[47] *Journal of Senate*, 1862, pp. 14-15.

[48] *Acts*, 1862, pp. 26-29; *Journal of House*, 1862, p. 78; *Journal of Senate*, 1862, p. 68.   The act of Nov. 11, 1861 was repealed.

[49] *Journal of Senate*, 1862, p. 27; *Journal of House*, pp. 23, 25, 52, 181.

adjournment, an act was passed providing for the issue of 20-year bonds, bearing interest at 6%.[50] The registration of indigent families made under this act of November 12 was so thorough that it was changed during the rest of the war only by additions. The comptroller, ignoring the estimates of necessary amounts which had been submitted, determined the apportionment among the counties on the basis of the number of indigent families, obtaining a quotient of $62.66 $^{13}/_{20}$ as the annual amount for each family, an amount larger than any appropriation under the 25% tax except that to Dallas county.[51] The bonds sold quickly at a premium of 50% to 100%.[52] Yet the appropriation, as liberal as it seemed, fell short of the needs of the indigent families.[53] The act of November 12, 1862, however, formed the basis of subsequent acts having the same object.

Several acts, one of which carried an appropriation of $100,000, provided for the distribution of salt at cost among the counties in proportion to population, giving preference to the families of soldiers. Another act, approved November 8, carrying an appropriation of $60,000, provided for the purchase in foreign markets of cotton and wool cards and for the distribution of them among the counties in proportion to white population.[54] In addition,

[50] *Journal of House*, 1862, pp. 233, 264; *Acts*, 1862, pp. 30-33. Any profits accruing to the state from distillation of grain should be applied to relief of indigent families.—*Acts*, 1862, pp. 43-44.

[51] *Report of Comptroller*, 1863, pp. 25, 38.

[52] Fleming, *Civil War and Reconst.*, pp. 164-165.

[53] *Acts*, 1863, pp. 50-51.

[54] *Acts*, 1862, pp. 56-58, 58-61, 49; Miller, *Alabama*, pp. 167-168. The reports of probate judges in regard to the needs of indigent families for salt were so incomplete by Nov. 12 that they were not printed.—*Journal of House*, 1862, p. 101. Reports of the quartermaster-general showed the quantity of salt received by him, Jan. 1—Aug. 27, 1863, from state works for general distribution to be 6759 bu. and from lessees, 7115 bu.—*Jour. of House*, 1863, p. 50.

the House passed resolutions urging the Confederate Congress to increase the pay of soldiers.[55]

Again, it had been necessary for the counties to take measures to aid the indigent families. The appropriations and the borrowing of money on issues of bonds and county scrip by the county commissioners were legalized by acts of the Assembly November 7 and November 8, and future taxes by the same officers not exceeding 100% on the state tax were authorized by act of the Assembly November 8.[56] In addition to this general legislation for the counties, the following special legislation for aid to indigent families of soldiers was authorized or legalized: Autauga (southern), a special tax on all taxable property; Morgan (northern) and Fayette (northern), a tax on dogs above the number of two in one family; Macon (southern), a tax of 65% of the county taxes; Monroe (southern), a tax not exceeding 100% on state taxes; Marshall (northern), Fayette (northern) and Barbour (southern), a special tax on all taxable property (legalized); Morgan (northern), a special tax for refunding to individuals money advanced to equip volunteers and buy provisions for their families (legalized); Walker (northern), hiring and rehiring slaves through an agent, receiving pay in provisions; Sumter (northern) and Walker (northern), borrowing $10,000 each; and Sumter, a tax of 50% of the state tax to retire its bonds.[57]

In 1863, a change of policy was stated in the following extract from the joint resolutions, approved August 27:

Whereas, the appropriation made at the session of the legis-

---

[55] *Journal of House*, 1862, p. 233.

[56] *Acts*, 1862, pp. 17-18, 25-26.

[57] *Acts*, 1862, p. 150 (Nov. 7); pp. 155-156 (Dec. 6); p. 158 (Nov. 7); p. 163 (Dec. 6); pp. 158-159 (Nov. 5); p. 165 (Dec. 2); p. 168 (Nov. 26); p. 179 (Nov. 28). The tax on dogs was repealed Aug. 27, 1863.—*Acts*, 1863, p. 30.

lature of 1862, and approved November 12, 1862, for the support of the indigent families of soldiers has been found insufficient for said object; and whereas in consequence of said inefficiency the commissioners' courts of the various counties of the State have been compelled to levy an additional tax to supply the deficit of said appropriation for the support of said families; and whereas the counties furnishing the largest number of soldiers are in the main the least able to supply said deficit, in consequence thereof the said families in some of the counties are very inadequately supported and whereas, all the soldiers of the State are alike battling for the rights and liberties of the State and Confederacy, therefore be it

1. Resolved by the Senate and House of Representatives of the State of Alabama in General Assembly convened, That the indigent families of soldiers of this state be treated with the same consideration and that taxation for the support of the same be equally borne by the people of the State and an amount necessary for such support be appropriated from the treasury of the State.[58]

Two days later an act was approved making an appropriation of $1,000,000 to the indigent families of soldiers including families of deceased and disabled soldiers but excluding families of substitutes, to be paid in equal amounts in October, November and December, under the regulations of the act of 1862, reinforced by the addition of penalties for misapplication of funds. The Governor was authorized to use any unappropriated funds in the treasury or, if necessary, to issue treasury notes.[59] As the funds were insufficient, he issued treasury notes.[60] The rate of apportionment under this appropriation was about $31 per family.[61] On

[58] *Acts,* 1863, pp. 50-51. (During the second period of desertion.)

[59] *Ibid.,* pp. 16-17.

[60] Montgomery *Advertiser,* Nov. 11, 1863, message of Governor; Fleming, *Civil War and Reconst.,* p. 165.

[61] *Report of Comptroller,* 1864, p. 19.

the day upon which this appropriation was made, an act was approved authorizing probate judges to impress provisions under certain conditions.[62] At the regular session of the legislature, an act was passed making an appropriation of $3,000,000 to be paid in equal amounts in January, May and October, 1864 under the regulations of the act of 1862 to the beneficiaries of the act of the special session of 1863 with the addition of the families of substitutes who received less than $1,500. To make administration more effective, stricter regulations of the local agents were adopted, and the central management was transferred from the comptroller to the quartermaster-general.[63] To raise funds, the committee on ways and means was instructed to consider the expediency of levying a tax-in-kind, but the policy of making paper money was continued and treasury notes were issued again. This issue of notes was delayed because the treasurer and the comptroller were not able to sign them fast enough. Pressing calls were made for the installments due the counties.[64] Under this appropriation, the apportionment was about $81 per family.[65]

The policy of acquiring supplies of necessities which were very scarce was continued with a view to rendering aid especially to the indigent families of soldiers. The salt which was manufactured by the state or secured from

[62] *Acts*, 1863, p. 26.

[63] *Acts*, 1863, pp. 81-82, 84, 87-89, 26.

[64] *Journal of House*, 1863, pp. 102, 120; Montgomery *Weekly Advertiser*, Aug. 3, 1864; Selma *Reporter*, July 27, 1864; *Governor's Letter Book*, May 5, 1864, pp. 139, 141, 145; to Col. Shilleha, 1864, p. 167. Another cause of delay was a derangement in currency produced by legislation of Congress. There was no delay in printing as the state had three public printers who could print money.—Fleming, *Civil War and Reconst.*, p. 277.

[65] *Report of the Quartermaster-general*, 1864, ending Sept. 30, Table G, Disbursements.

lessees of state works or from other sources was to be distributed at cost to the indigent families of soldiers except substitutes and deserters to the amount of 25 pounds a person.   Counties were authorized to engage in the manufacture and sale of salt and cotton yarn, raising the necessary capital by taxation.[66]   By an act, approved December 8, but repealed a year later, counties were ordered to pay for medicines prescribed by physicians as necessary for the indigent families of soldiers.[67]   In addition, resolutions were passed by both houses of the legislature, urging Congress to increase the pay of soldiers to enable them to take care of their families.[68]

Under the resolutions of August 27, the probate judges were called upon to make, in addition to reports of the number of indigent families and estimates of their needs for the coming year, reports of the amounts raised by the counties during the fiscal year 1864 for the support of indigent families.   By September 30, 1864, nineteen counties of the state made reports which showed a total amount raised by them for the support of indigent families of soldiers of $380,070.20.[69]   Most of these counties were located in the black-belt section; five black-belt counties raised over one-half of the total amount.   To the counties of the state which had been overrun by the enemy, special aid was extended in 1863.   The Governor was authorized to suspend the collec-

[66] *Acts*, 1863, pp. 17-18 (Aug. 29) ; pp. 83-84 (Dec. 3).

[67] *Acts*, 1863, pp. 84-85 ; *Acts*, 1864, p. 82.

[68] *Journal of Senate*, 1863, pp. 20, 24, 245.

[69] *Report of the Quartermaster-general* for 1864 ending Sept. 30, Table H, Reports of Probate Judges.   Eleven counties made no reports by Sept. 30.   A few made reports after this date and a few made reports before this date in such terms that they could not be tabulated.   The report of Cherokee (northern), dated Nov. 27, 1863, of $154,000 was not included in the Quartermaster's Report for 1864.

tion of state taxes in all counties in which occupation by the enemy prevented the making of the ordinary crops. The Confederate Congress was petitioned to exempt the counties overrun by the enemy from payment of the tax-in-kind. Congress did so. An appropriation of one-half million dollars was made December 8 to soldiers' families made destitute by invasion with the exception of recent refugees, tories, harborers of deserters, and families of deserters.[70] In addition, Washington (southern) was authorized to borrow $10,000 and to levy a tax of not over 50% for indigent families of soldiers; Baldwin (southern), to use $4,000 of the money accruing to its treasury in fines; Mobile (southern), to levy a tax of not over 50% of the state tax; Macon (southern), to levy a tax-in-kind on corn, meat and potatoes; Pike (southeastern), to levy a tax-in-kind and a tax on incomes; and Dale (southeastern), to levy a tax of 10% of the state tax to pay for medical services rendered during an epidemic of smallpox.[71]

The acts of the legislature of 1864, making provisions for the indigent families of soldiers, appropriated larger sums of money, formulated stricter regulations for distributing them, and prescribed the administration of aid in the form of supplies whenever possible. October 7, an appropriation of $2,000,000 was made to be paid in November through an issue of bonds or treasury notes, and December 13 an appropriation of $3,000,000 was made to be paid in equal amounts in March and September, 1865. Penalties were fixed for embezzlement of funds, for false returns of

[70] *Acts*, 1863, pp. 75-76 (Dec. 5) ; p. 216 (Nov. 28) ; pp. 86-87 (Dec. 8) ; *Statutes at Large of Con. States*, 1st Cong. 4th Sess., p. 186. Joint resolutions petitioning Congress to exempt from payment of tax-in-kind families whose support was derived from white labor alone were approved Nov. 28.—*Acts*, 1863, p. 217.

[71] *Acts*, 1863, pp. 46-47 (Aug. 27) ; p. 117 (Nov. 19) ; p. 141 (Nov. 30) ; p. 117 (Dec. 7 and Dec. 4) ; p. 167 (Nov. 27).

the enumeration of families, and for partial distribution of aid among indigent families. A system of auditing the books of probate judges was devised and semi-annual reports were required to be made under oath by the probate judge and certified to by the commissioners' court. The quartermaster-general was to be replaced by the comptroller of state accounts. To equalize the distribution of salt and cotton and wool cards, salt was to be sold at a fixed uniform price in all of the counties and cards were to be distributed in each beat according to the number of indigent families. Probate judges were ordered to make special inquiry to ascertain what efforts were being made by the indigent families of soldiers to support themselves. Probate judges and commissioners' courts were directed to purchase supplies of food and distribute them instead of money. Special agents might be employed to purchase supplies in other counties and sheriffs might be ordered to employ wagons, teams and drivers to transport supplies. Negotiations with the Confederate government were authorized for an arrangement by which tithe corn collected by the Confederate government in counties remote from navigable rivers and railroads might be exchanged for corn delivered by the state at depots on rivers and railroads.[72] Such an arrangement had been made in 1863.[73] In addition, joint resolutions, approved November 30, urged upon the Confederate government the importance and necessity of immediate payment of the amounts due to soldiers, stating that " a large proportion of the officers and privates in the military service of the Confederate States are men of limited means, many having families at home who are in straightened circumstances and in want of the necessaries of life." [74]

[72] *Acts*, 1864, pp. 5-7, 58-61, 61-62, 12, 17-18, 167-168, 47-48.

[73] Printed broadside to Probate Judges by Controlling Quartermaster of Ala., Marion, Oct. 29, 1863.

[74] *Acts*, 1864, p. 189. (During the third period of desertion.)

As usual, acts—though fewer—were passed relating only to certain counties. An appropriation of $180,000 was made to Cherokee, DeKalb, Morgan, St. Clair, Marshall and Blount, because they had been overrun by the enemy and were faced with starvation. Autauga (southern) was authorized to expend any surplus funds secured from fines and forfeiture, and Pike (southeastern), to levy a tax-in-kind on corn, meat, potatoes and sorghum for the indigent families of soldiers. An appropriation of $6087.50 was made to reimburse Lawrence for funds for indigent families of soldiers which had been twice taken by the enemy.[75]

It is impossible to determine the total amount of the appropriations made by the counties to the indigent families of soldiers, but the legislation summarized above indicates that the sums were large. The total amount of the appropriations made by the state, excluding appropriations for salt and cards, was $11.8 million. But in the face of enormous appropriations and of cooperative services in securing supplies below market prices, want and destitution persisted among the families of soldiers. The legislature was compelled each year at a special session to make an extra appropriation to give immediate relief to them. There were complaints from various sources of inefficiency, unfairness, and graft on the part of some officers who administered state aid.[76] For example, it was said that probate judges

[75] *Acts*, 1864, pp. 133, 141, 159-161, 151. Proposals were made from time to time in the Confederate Congress for legislation to aid indigent families of soldiers, but they did not amount to anything because social legislation was not within the sphere of the Confederate government. See *Journal of Cong. of C. S.*, vol. ii, pp. 428-429; vol. v, pp. 231, 307; vol. vi, p. 57. Senator Yancey declared that he was opposed to such legislation because it would be " of an agrarian tendency."—*Speeches of William L. Yancey*, pp. 52-54, speech delivered in the Senate on October 6, 1862.

[76] *Gov.'s Letter Book*, June 20, 1864, p. 160; Jno. Gurganey to Gov.,

were not active in buying corn in the cheapest markets at the earliest time, that state agents speculated in salt, and that tory judges gave aid to families of deserters and of soldiers in the Union army. It was said that by their insistence upon technical interpretation of the laws, officers deprived some meritorious families of aid, as in cases of change of residence by a family to a county in which they were not registered.[77] It is probable that some of these complaints arose out of a kind of bewilderment at the ineffectiveness of such large appropriations; it is probable that some of them arose out of a solid foundation of facts. There was also some abuse of state aid by the recipients— by women whose husbands were deserters or tories, by women who had the corn received made into whiskey, and by women who refused to work.[78] But it is probable that the inefficiency and the abuse attending the administration of state aid to the indigent families of soldiers were no more than were to be expected in a great experiment of social legislation tried under the pressure of war. The real cause for the inadequacy of state aid was the increase in

June 10, 1862; Jno. Ware to Gov. Shorter, Sept. 11, 1862; W. E. Clarke to Gov., March 25, 1864; Selma *Reporter*, May 7, 1864. J. W. Lapsley proposed an investigation of officers and the conscription of offenders.

[77] Jno. H. Chapman to Gov., May 14, 1864; *Gov.'s Letter Book*, Apr. 25, 1864, p. 132; Josiah Patterson to Gov. Watts, Feb. 1, 1864, giving an account of the execution by cavalry of the probate judge of Winston county who had given state supplies for indigent families to families of Union soldiers; *The Independent*, Nov. 7, 1863; Sarah E. Deprieast to Gov., Jan. 8, 1865; Mary A. Belvin to Gov., Feb. 24, 1864. The following extract from a letter from Lucreesy Simmons to the Gov. July 17, 1862, is suggestive: "this same lady it was said last spring would receive 85 dollars now say she won't git but 40 and the fact is she don't git anything and she is on sufferance at this time."

[78] Selma *Reporter*, Apr. 25, 1864; *Gov.'s Letter Book*, May 8, 1863, p. 387; Apr. 25, 1864, p. 132. The regulations prescribed by the legislation of 1864 suggest abuses.

the number of indigent families and the rise in prices with depreciation of the currency. The aid which was given by the state to the indigent families of soldiers was a great contribution to the Confederate cause, but because it was not always evenly distributed among the counties and because it was on the whole inadequate to the needs, it was not an entirely effective method of preventing desertion.

CHAPTER VI

Efforts to Check Desertion: Effecting the Return of Deserters

THE problem of effecting the return of deserters was complicated by the collecting of deserters in certain sections of the state. In some places, deserters and their friends and relatives formed a majority of the population at home.[1] For the most part, the friends and relatives of deserters encouraged desertion and other persons condoned desertion which was induced by distressing circumstances.[2] Together they formed a sympathetic public opinion which was a powerful protection to deserters. From the beginning to the end of the war, deserters were harbored and protected by friends and relatives.[3] In some places in north Alabama, they went about their usual occupations with impunity, making no effort to hide. But in most cases, they hid quietly at home or in woods near their homes in dug-outs in level ground or in caves in hillsides, preferring neither to see nor to be seen. They were fed by members of their families. In constant communication with them, deserters

[1] *O. R.*, ser. iv, vol. iii, p. 1120; *Governor's Letter Book,* September 4, 1863, p. 67.

[2] *O. R.*, ser. iv, vol. iii, pp. 1119-1120; Saunders, *Early Settlers of North Alabama*, p. 171; Appleton, *Annual Cyclopedia*, 1863, p. 191; Selma *Reporter*, August 26, 1863; *Southwestern Baptist*, August 13, 1863; Montgomery *Daily Mail*, January 10, 1863; Richmond *Daily Examiner*, January 31, 1865.

[3] *O. R.*, ser. i, vol. xlvi, pt. ii, p. 1254; ser. iv, vol. iii, pp. 1064-1065, 1119-1120.

were warned of the approach of cavalry or of any other danger which threatened them. Forewarned, they could retreat to safer fastnesses or prepare to meet force with force.[4]

For the purpose of protection, deserters were usually more or less loosely organized. The opinion was current in the state that their organizations were very formidable.[5] It was reported, for example, that in Randolph county deserters, numbering several hundreds, had a military organization with company and regimental divisions and that on one occasion they had paroled twenty prisoners captured in a skirmish with government troops.[6] But popular fear exaggerated the size and strength of the organizations of deserters. The commanders of the larger expeditions sent from the provisional army against deserters in north Alabama concurred in the report of one of their number: " I have not been able to find any permanent organization among these wretches. In some particular places, they may be mobbed together." [7] Their organizations were too small to match large opposing forces. The usual squad consisted of fifteen to twenty deserters and tories, acting in concert under a leader. Often several squads combined for more

---

[4] *O. R.*, ser. iv, vol. iii, p. 1065; ser. i, vol. xxxii, pt. iii, p. 800; Memphis *Appeal*, September 28, 1864; John G. Moore to Governor Watts, March 4, 1864; B. W. Starke to Governor Shorter, July 30, 1863; Unwritten reminiscences of persons from north Alabama; Lonn, *Desertion*, p. 66. Some deserters in north Alabama hid in the day and farmed at night.—Unwritten reminiscences.

[5] *O. R.*, ser. i, vol. xxxii, pt. iii, pp. 855-856; ser. iv, vol. ii, pp. 741-743, pp. 819-820; *Clarke County Journal*, February 5, 1863; Montgomery *Weekly Advertiser*, September 2, 1863; Nelson Fennel to Governor Shorter, June 28, 1863; John P. West to Governor Watts, September 9 (1864); M. N. Brooks to Governor Watts, March 29, 1864.

[6] Montgomery *Weekly Mail*, October 21, 1863.

[7] *O. R.*, ser. i, vol. xxxviii, pt. iv, pp. 666-667; vol. xxxii, pt. iii, pp. 812, 859, 860, 858-860, 853.

effective action.[8]   They were well armed with guns and
ammunition which they had brought from the army or in
some cases taken from civilians or secured from the enemy.[9]
There were in the state some more formal military organizations, each composed of about a hundred men.   One such
company had its rendezvous at Pikeville in Marion county
and was under the command of John Stout, who was characterized by a military officer sent to take him as " a desperate and bad, though bold and not unskillful man." [10]
Another company had its rendezvous on the boundary line
between Dale and Henry counties and was under the command of Joseph Saunders, who had held the office of captain in the Confederate army and then in the Federal and
had deserted from both armies.[11]   Such organizations sometimes entrenched themselves in camps behind fortifications
and to some extent observed military discipline.[12]   One
organization of deserters in southeast Alabama had a formal, written constitution which pledged the members to
strict obedience to a leader who was himself liable to be
cashiered for assumption of too much authority; prescribed

[8] *Letter Book of the Commandant of Conscripts of Alabama*, p. 314;
O. R., ser. i, vol. xxxii, pt. iii, p. 860; Montgomery *Weekly Advertiser*,
September 2, 1863; Montgomery *Weekly Mail*, September 23, 1863; John
P. West to Governor Watts, September 9 (1864); J. N. Lightfoot to
Governor Watts, October 18, 1864; Joseph Hough to Governor Watts,
March 25, 1865; J. P. Cannon, *The Twenty-seventh Alabama*, p. 84.

[9] *O. R.*, ser. iv, vol. ii, pp. 607-608; ser. i, vol. lii, pt. ii, p. 496; Thomas
E. Barr to Governor Shorter, January 10, 1863; L. D. Cabaniss to Governor Watts, August 18, 1864; *Letter Book of the Commandant*, p. 334.
In some cases they may have manufactured powder.—Lonn, *Desertion*,
p. 70.

[10] *O. R.*, ser. i, vol. xxxii, pt. iii, p. 747.

[11] Oates, *The War between the Union and the Confederacy*, p. 428;
Brewer, *Alabama*, pp. 205-206; Ozark *Southern Star*, April 12, 1899.

[12] Joseph Hough to Governor Watts, March 22, 1865; Mobile *Register*,
June 4, 1863.

good moral character and abstinence from drinking and gambling as qualifications for membership; regulated depredations upon property, requiring the consent of the leader and the majority of members for the taking of property which was necessary to their safety and prohibiting the taking of all other property; and defined the absence from the company on the part of any member who was under charges from the judiciary committee as desertion meriting the usual punishment.[13]   In order to protect themselves, many groups of deserters and tories assumed the role of regular military organizations.   Some pretended to be details from the cavalry seeking to supply themselves with horses; others pretended to be impressment parties collecting supplies for the army.   Some posed as Union troops; others, as Confederate partisan rangers or independent scouts.   But the two favorite military roles assumed by deserters were that of companies in the process of formation—a never-ending process—and that of detachments to capture deserters.[14]

Deserters and tories made depredations upon the communities in which they collected.   The status of deserters was that of outlaws.   After they had repudiated the law of compulsory military service they could not invoke the aid of other laws.   As a result, they generally acted upon the principle that as every man's hand was against them, their hand was against every man.   The special motives which induced deserters to make depredations varied from need

[13] Montgomery *Daily Mail*, December 10, 1864.   This constitution was captured in a skirmish with deserters.

[14] Memphis *Appeal*, October 4, 1864; W. T. Walthall to Major (D. E. Huger), March 8, 1864; Mobile *Register*, February 15, 1863, quoting the Charleston *Courier*; J. T. Askew to Governor Watts, June 16, 1864; Mobile *Register*, September 26, 1862; A. A. Wall to Governor Watts (1864 ?); *O. R.*, ser. iv, vol. ii, p. 694; *Letter Book of the Commandant of Conscripts*, p. 371; Thomas C. Dunlap to Governor Watts, April 19, 1864.

for subsistence and protection to desire for plunder and revenge. For subsistence and protection, food and ammunition were necessities which often were not to be procured in lawful ways, and in self-defence, even murder seemed justifiable. From subsistence and protection the step to plunder of secessionists' property and revenge upon one's enemies was easy for the lawlessly inclined among deserters.[15] The number of tories and deserters in active depredation was probably a minority of the deserters in the state but it seemed larger because of the notoriety which their outrages brought and because of the imputation to them of some crimes committed by others. Estimates made by Professor Fleming of the number of deserters and tories in active depredation in north Alabama are 4000 to 5000, and in southeast Alabama, 1000.[16] Whether the number was larger or not, the charges laid to their account were serious. Deserters committed many crimes. They went from house to house compelling the occupants to give them keys to trunks and smoke-houses and taking whatever they pleased, especially provisions, clothing and ammunition. They shot live-stock in the woods and in the open; they robbed travelers and plundered commissary trains. They burned the property of staunch secessionists, such as corn-cribs, mills and dwelling houses. They burned court-houses and other depositories of public records in order to destroy statements of their liability to military service. Deserters committed acts of violence against the persons of men who were active in opposing them. They exiled some secessionists from their native county; they threatened others with punishment of various sorts. They kidnapped some men who were

[15] Mobile *Register and Advertiser*, April 22, 1864.

[16] H. V. Howard to H. P. Watson, Apr. 22, 1864; Montgomery *Advertiser*, September 23, 1863; Fleming, *Civil War and Reconstruction in Alabama*, p. 128.

objects of dislike because of their political affiliations or objects of envy because of their wealth, and in order to secure revenge or to elicit information about their money tortured them by hanging or by other ingenious devices. Finally, they murdered a good many peaceable citizens at work in the fields and a number of civil and military officers who had been active in trying to take deserters.[17] Since they were often protected by public sympathy and since they were organized, deserters successfully defied the civil authorities. In those counties in which they were numerous, they intimidated the officers, sometimes driving the sheriff out of the county and sometimes preventing the tax collector from

[17] *O. R.*, ser. i, vol. xxxii, pt. iii, pp. 745-748; ser. ii, vol. ii, p. 496; ser. iv, vol. ii, pp. 636-639, 680, 782-786; vol. iii, pp. 1042-1043; Petition of B. W. Starke and other citizens of Coffee county to Governor Watts (January, 1865); T. E. Barr to Governor Shorter, January 10, 1863; Nancy M. Twilbey to Governor Watts, November 9, 1864; J. M. Carmichael to Governor Watts, October 17, 1864; C. D. Lasseter and Wilie Duffee to Governor Watts, February 27, 1865; W. J. Peddy to General H. P. Watson, March 20, 1865; Josiah Jones to Governor Watts, March 20, 1865; Jacksonville *Republican*, October 10, 1863; Montgomery *Daily Mail*, March 29, 1865; Montgomery *Weekly Advertiser*, May 18, 1864, quoting the Clayton *Banner*; Montgomery *Daily Advertiser*, July 11, 1864, quoting the Tuscaloosa *Observer*; Fleming, *Civil War and Reconstruction*, pp. 119-122; William Polk, *Leonidas Polk*, vol. ii, p. 318. The following extract from a petition to Governor Watts by some citizens of Henry county, March 23 (1864) is typical: ". . . these bands now number in both counties upward of 300 men and are generally well armed and stand in bold defiance to all law and authority and are fast becoming a terror to all peaceable men and women. They have murdered within the last 12 months 4 good and loyal citizens; they have stripped several plantations of mules and horses and burnt to the ground several cribs of corn. They have plundered a great many houses and stole there from guns, ammunition, clothing, provisions and other property and appropriated the same to their own use and they constantly lay in ambush on our public roads with the avowed intentions of assassinating all who may endeavor in the execution of the law to thwart their plans or arrest them." See also *Letter Book of the Commandant of Conscripts*, pp. 314, 327.

collecting taxes and the circuit judge from holding court.[18] They rescued deserters from jail, forcing jailors to give them keys and riding rapidly with the prisoners out of town.[19] The opportunity for depredations attracted the criminal not only from the deserters of the Confederate army but also from the deserters of the Federal army and from men who belonged to neither army. One particularly vicious group of such men in north Alabama styled themselves " Destroying Angels." [20]

Deserters did not confine their anti-social activities to committing crimes and defying civil authorities. They waged war, both defensive and offensive. They were well armed. Their reliance upon arms is illustrated by the reply often made by deserters on their way home to demands for their passports—a reply made as they patted their guns— " This is my passport." [21] The spirit which animated the resistance of Alabama deserters to capture is accurately described in a defiant communication from twenty-five deserters of North Carolina, ". . . we are going home. We are all well armed and all hell can't take us." [22] In north Ala-

[18] *The Governor's Letter Book*, July 28, 1863, pp. 53-54; C. J. Rotenberry to Governor Shorter, September 3, 1863; J. M. Carmichael to Governor Watts, October 17, 1864; Angus Vaughn to Governor Watts, September 21, 1864; *O. R.*, ser. iv, vol. iii, p. 1043 (no court was held in southeast Alabama for two years).

[19] *O. R.*, ser. iv, vol. ii, p. 258; Montgomery *Daily Advertiser*, November 11, 1863; Mobile *Register*, Oct. 13, 1863, quoting the Talladega *Reporter;* *Clarke County Journal*, April 14, 1864; Montgomery *Daily Mail*, January 4, 1865; Montgomery *Weekly Mail*, September 23, 1863; B. W. Starke to Governor Watts, March 26, 1864.

[20] Fleming, *Civil War and Reconstruction*, pp. 120-121; Freemantle, *Three Months in the Southern States*, p. 141; Montgomery *Weekly Mail*, September 23, 1863.

[21] *Letter Book of the Commandant of Conscripts*, p. 334; *O. R.*, ser. iv, vol. ii, p. 731.

[22] Mobile *Register*, November 8, 1863, quoting the Richmond *Examiner*.

bama and in southeast Alabama, deserters waged guerilla warfare against officers of the Conscription Bureau and repeatedly defeated companies of cavalry sent to take them.[23] During 1864 it was useless to send small forces against deserters in those sections of the state.[24] Sometimes deserters and tories made raids upon the country near their woods. The raid through the southern part of Dale county in March, 1865, the third raid which the county had suffered in as many months, illustrates the method. About forty deserters, coming up from the swamp of the Choctawhatchee river, plundered the southern part of the county and about an hour before day on the 14th, fell upon the county-seat, Newton, with a yell described by an auditor as "demoniac." They attacked the court-house, in which some citizens of the county had encamped in order to protect themselves and their property. But the deserters were repulsed by county militia with the loss of one killed and two mortally wounded, and were forced to retreat to the swamp of the Choctawhatchee river.[25] Several times deserters and tories destroyed the saltworks which were located on the coast of west Florida and which were sponsored by the government of Alabama.[26] Sometimes they joined Federal

[23] *O. R.*, ser. iv, vol. ii, pp. 636-639; vol. iii, p. 251; *Letter Book of the Commandant of Conscripts*, pp. 314, 334; *Governor's Letter Book*, July 7, 1863, p. 45.

[24] *O. R.*, ser. iv, vol. ii, pp. 636-639; vol. iii, pp. 251-253; *Letter Book of the Commandant of Conscripts*, p. 334; *Governor's Letter Book*, September 4, 1863, p. 67; Wm. Wood to Governor Shorter, September 16, 1863; John Clisby to Governor Shorter, July 22, 1863.

[25] Petition of B. W. Starke and others of Coffee county to Governor Watts (January, 1865); Joseph Hough to Governor Watts, January 9, March 17, March 25, 1865; Montgomery *Daily Advertiser*, September 14, 1864. For accounts of other raids, see: *Southwestern Baptist*, March 2, 1865; Montgomery *Daily Mail*, March 29, 1865; Memphis *Appeal*, October 10, 1864; L. D. Cabaniss to Governor Watts, August 18, 1864.

[26] *O. R.*, ser. i, vol. xiv, pp. 716-717; *Governor's Letter Book*, Septem-

troops on raids and so inspired unusual fear in the loyal population.[27] The result of the depredations of deserters and their defiance of civil and military authorities was a reign of terror in certain counties of the state, especially in Franklin, Marion, Winston, St. Clair, Marshall and Walker in north Alabama and in Dale, Henry and Coffee in southeast Alabama.[28] A veteran who had lost an arm in service stated that he had never experienced as much uneasiness when he followed Stonewall Jackson as he did at his home in Dale county in 1864.[29] Several soldiers who on furlough to their homes in north Alabama in 1864 had been compelled to lie out in the woods by day and night expressed relief at reaching the battlefront again.[30]

At the beginning of the war, these conditions were not foreseen by Confederate authorities. If deserters entered into their calculations at all, they seemed a negligible factor—a small number of men, hiding, single and unarmed, from their disapproving fellowmen.[31] Provisions for apprehending and punishing deserters were correspondingly simple; deserters should be arrested by military officers and tried by military courts.[32] As deserters became more numerous and so more defiant, new machinery and methods had to be adopted for effecting their return. Under the

ber 22, 1862, p. 219; December 31, 1862, p. 294; January 10, 1863, p. 303; John G. Hartman to Governor Watts, May 3, 1864; N. W. Murphey to Governor Watts, June 12, 1864; J. T. Askew to Governor Watts, June 16, 1864.

[27] Montgomery *Daily Mail*, October 8, 1864; December 28, 1864; *Governor's Letter Book,* January 6, 1863, p. 299; Telegrams to Governor Shorter, from Governor Milton, December 30, 1862.

[28] *O. R.,* ser. iv, vol. ii, p. 638; vol. iii, p. 1042.

[29] J. M. Carmichael to Governor Watts, October 17, 1864.

[30] J. P. Cannon, *The Twenty-seventh Alabama,* pp. 84-92.

[31] *O. R.,* ser. iv, vol. ii, pp. 999-1000.

[32] *Rules and Articles of War,* arts. xviii and xx.

pressure of the war, machinery and methods were developed with difficulty and were never adequate.

The machinery for effecting the return of deserters represented a combination of civil and military machinery of both Confederate and state governments. During the first period of desertion, from about February, 1862 to February, 1863, the Governor of Alabama, upon his own initiative, employed state officers and state militia in the arrest of deserters. By a proclamation of July 5, 1862, all sheriffs and constables were directed to arrest deserters from the Confederate army and to deliver them to military officers or to jailors, and all jailors were directed to receive them.[33] A week later, by general orders of July 14, the War Department assigned the function of arresting deserters and returning them to their commands to the newly organized Bureau of Conscription. All persons engaged in enrolling conscripts were required to arrest deserters and deliver them either to jailors or to commandants of camps of instruction for conscripts. Jailors were requested to receive deserters for temporary confinement for the same compensation allowed by the state for prisoners. Commandants of camps of instruction were required to receive all deserters and to forward them to their respective commands.[34] It was soon evident that sheriffs and enrolling officers needed not only authority but also force to arrest deserters. The Governor of Alabama, assuming that the necessary force might be supplied by state militia, made efforts, unaided by the Assembly, to organize a militia. Since the militia which had existed—largely on paper—at the beginning of the war had been absorbed into the Confederate armies by the summer of 1862, the Gov-

---

[33] *Proclamation Book A*, p. 46.

[34] *General Orders* no. 49, 1862, Adjutant and Inspector General's Office. Camps of instruction in Alabama were located at Talladega, Notasulga and Montgomery.—*Letter Book of the Commandant of Conscripts*, p. 27.

ernor called upon men not subject to conscription to volunteer for state service. In response to his calls of May 12 and December 22, he received only a few companies, attributing the failure chiefly to the scarcity of military material in the state.[35] In the absence of adequate militia, the Governor requested the use of conscripts in arresting deserters in southeast Alabama where a loyal population had sent a large part of its men to the army. Early in January, 1863, five companies of conscripts who were shut out of Camp Watts by quarantine were detailed for thirty days to this work. Promptly, the Governor petitioned Richmond for exemption from Confederate service of all conscripts from six southeastern counties and for assignment of them to the brigade of General Clanton which was being raised for the protection of southeast Alabama. This petition was granted. Later, a similar one in regard to conscripts in certain central counties was granted also.[36]

During the second period, from about January 1, 1863 to March, 1864, when desertion became, in the words of President Davis "a frightful evil," the machinery for effecting the return of deserters was extended and strengthened by legislative enactments and additional executive orders with the object of increasing pressure upon deserters indirectly by judicial process against their harborers and directly by military force against deserters themselves. By an act of the General Assembly approved August 29, 1863, the state made provisions for effecting the return of deserters. Sheriffs and commandants of militia were ordered to arrest deserters and to deliver them to the proper military author-

---

[35] *Proclamation Book A*, pp. 42-43, 52-55; *Governor's Letter Book,* June 11, 1863, pp. 27-29; *O. R.*, ser. iv, vol. ii, p. 143; *Military Code of the State of Alabama*, 1861, p. 20.

[36] *Governor's Letter Book*, January 6, 1863, pp. 299-300, 301; January 8, 1863, pp. 301-302; January 14, 1863, pp. 307-308; February 5, 1863, p. 314.

ities, and all persons were directed to give any information
in their possession which might lead to the arrest of deserters. Wilful neglect of either of these duties was declared
a misdemeanor. Any person who should "knowingly and
wilfully feed, harbor, secrete or aid to escape any deserter
or straggler" from the army was declared guilty of a
felony.[37] By an act of Congress approved January 22,
1864, the Confederate Government made similar provisions
for reaching the harborers of deserters. Any person not
subject to the *Rules and Articles of War* who should entice
a soldier or person enrolled for service in the army to desert
or assist him to desert or to evade arrest after desertion was
liable to a maximum penalty of a fine of $1000 and im-
prisonment for two years.[38] A few days later, February 15,
a more drastic measure was passed by Congress. Upon
President Davis' request, made in view of serious difficulties in prosecuting the war, including the use by some judges
of the writ of *habeas corpus* to release deserters and the
efforts of secret societies to encourage desertion, the President was given authority for three months, subject to the
limitation of a military board of appeals, to suspend the
writ of *habeas corpus* in certain cases threatening the public
safety, two of which were desertion and aiding desertion.[39]

To aid in the apprehension of deserters, the duties of

[37] *Acts of the Called and the Third Regular Annual Session of the
General Assembly of Alabama*, 1863, pp. 13-15. The act carried an appropriation of $100,000.

[38] *O. R.*, ser. i, vol. xlviii, pt. i, p. 1323. This act was a modification
of an act of Congress, approved January 1, 1812.

[39] *Report of the Committee on the Judiciary*, May 21, 1864; *O. R.*,
ser. iv, vol. iii, pp. 68-69, 203-204. This act aroused a storm of criticism
but in the opinion of President Davis and of the Committee on the Judiciary, it was effective in checking desertion.—Selma *Reporter*, March 8,
1864 ("the strong odor of the Stuarts"); Montgomery *Daily Mail*, May
6, 1864 ("a very great error"); Selma *Reporter*, June 1, 1864; *Report of
the Committee on the Judiciary*, May 21, 1864.

army officers were more clearly defined and the conscription service was reorganized. April 16, 1863 army officers were instructed to withhold the pay of soldiers absent without leave, to offer rewards for the arrest of deserters, and to employ responsible persons to assist in arresting deserters.[40] Before that date, the conscription service was reported by both General Bragg and General Johnston to be highly inefficient.[41] In an effort to improve it, General Bragg organized a conscription bureau for the Army of Tennessee under Brigadier-General Pillow but was informed that its activities interfered with those of the regular organization for conscription.[42] But in July, by orders from the War Department the organization for conscription in Alabama, Mississippi and Tennessee was detached from the Bureau of Conscription and placed under control of General Johnston.[43] Brigadier-General Pillow was appointed by General Johnston superintendent of conscription in the three states.[44] He organized the Volunteer and Conscript Bureau like a network over Alabama, Mississippi and Tennessee, consisting of two branches — the conscription branch which was the permanent organization embracing officers and camps of instruction already formed by the Richmond Bureau of Conscription, and the supernumerary branch which was a temporary organization of officers and cavalry detailed from the Army of Tennessee and the Army of Mississippi. The two branches were distinct in organization but cooperated

[40] *Statutes at Large of the Congress of the C. S. of A.,* 1st Cong. 3rd Sess., p. 109; *Journal of the Congress of the C. S. of A.,* House, vol. vi, p. 115.

[41] *O. R.,* ser. i, vol. xx, pt. ii, p. 386; vol. xxiii, pt. ii, p. 637; ser. iv, pt. ii, p. 445.

[42] *O. R.,* ser. i, vol. xx, pt. ii, pp. 498-499; ser. iv, vol. ii, pp. 362, 374, 416, 430-441, 456, 482-483.

[43] *O. R.,* ser. i, vol. xxiii, pt. ii, pp. 912-913.

[44] *O. R.,* ser. iv, vol. ii, p. 680.

under the same superintendent in the work of recruiting volunteers and collecting conscripts, stragglers and deserters. In Alabama, General Pillow raised as a supporting force for the Volunteer and Conscript Bureau about twenty-five companies of cavalry composed of conscripts and non-conscripts and organized twenty-three rendezvous with six outposts each manned by a field officer with subordinate officers and by one company of infantry and by one company of cavalry.[45] The Volunteer and Conscript Bureau operated in Alabama from September, 1863 till January, 1864.[46] During the first month, General Pillow reported the collection of about 15,000 volunteers, conscripts, stragglers and deserters in his department.[47] For the other months, reports are not available and opinions about the success of the Bureau are conflicting. General Pillow himself considered his work a success although he reported that his field was limited to north Alabama because the population of central and south Alabama which were liable to service were already in the army and that part of the work in north Alabama was repetition, because some deserters had to be put in the army two, three, and even four times. General Bragg, General Johnston and Governor Shorter commended the energy and zeal of General Pillow and advised the extension of his Bureau over other states, and the Assembly of Alabama passed resolutions of appreciation of his effective work.[48] On the other hand, officials of the Bureau of Conscription complained that General Pillow exceeded his authority and wished to supplant the Bureau of Conscription, that by failure to keep records and by abuse

---

[45] *O. R.*, ser. iv, vol. ii, pp. 819-820, 675-676.

[46] *O. R.*, ser. iv, vol. ii, pp. 859, 1063-1064.

[47] *O. R.*, ser. iv, vol. ii, pp. 859, 862.

[48] *O. R.*, ser. iv, vol. ii, pp. 680-681, 444-445, 754; *Acts of Called and Third Regular Annual Session*, 1863, p. 218.

in granting exemptions and details he brought the conscription service into almost inextricable confusion and, finally, that by his methods, which were described in scores of indignant letters from citizens as those of a press gang, he made conscription odious and yet failed to put men into the field.[49]   After the Volunteer and Conscript Bureau was abolished in January, 1864, the Bureau of Conscription was again extended over Alabama, Mississippi and Tennessee.

In March and April, 1864, General Polk waged a vigorous campaign against tories, conscripts and deserters in the Department of Alabama, Mississippi and East Louisiana of which he was commander.   He sent detachments of troops to all of the disaffected sections, including south Mississippi, southeast Alabama and west Florida, and north Alabama. Colonel Lowry with the Sixth and Twentieth Mississippi Regiments conducted such a successful expedition against deserters collected in Jones and Smith counties, Mississippi, that General Polk recommended his promotion.[50]   Colonel Holland with a detachment of Mississippi troops arrested a number of deserters and tories in Conecuh and Covington counties, Alabama, and along Boggy Bayou, Florida.[51] The largest expedition was directed against north Alabama. Colonel Roddey was ordered to picket the Tennessee river to prevent the escape of deserters to the enemy.   Major-General Ferguson with the Third Brigade of Major-General S. D. Lee's corps of cavalry including the Ninth Texas

[49] *O. R.*, ser. iv, vol. iii, pp. 95-103; *Letter Book of the Commandant of Conscripts*, pp. 138, 376; Rowland, *Jefferson Davis, Constitutionalist*, vol. vi, pp. 372-379; *O. R.*, ser. i, vol. xxxii, pt. iii, pp. 644-646; ser. iv, vol. ii, p. 432; vol. iii, pp. 224-225; vol. ii, p. 749.

[50] *O. R.*, ser. i, vol. xxxii, pt. iii, p. 633; vol. lii, pt. ii, p. 657; Mobile *Register*, March 19, April 10, 16 and 19, May 6 and 15, 1864.

[51] *O. R.*, ser. i, vol. xxxv, pt. ii, p. 12; O. S. Holland to Col. G. G. Garner, March 21, 1864 (copy in the files of Governor Watts), Mobile *Register*, April 17, 1864.

Regiment under Colonel Jones and detachments of the First and Second Mississippi cavalry under Major J. J. Perry, and Brigadier-General Cockrell with the Second Brigade of Missouri infantry under General French's command together with other smaller detachments operated from headquarters in Tuscaloosa in the counties of northwest and north-central Alabama. Although the commanders of the expedition reported difficulty in getting deserters out of inaccessible hiding places in the mountains, they arrested a good many.[52] On the whole, General Polk considered the campaign against deserters very successful.[53]

The militia which had been organized since the beginning of the war was disrupted by Confederate requirements of June 16 and July 22, leaving, as the Governor said, only " a few scattering companies." [54] During the latter part of 1863 and the first half of 1864, the militia was reorganized under an act of the General Assembly approved August 29, 1863 and an act of Congress approved February 17, 1864.[55] Under the act of the General Assembly, an enumeration and classification was made of all the males of the state from 16 to 60 years of age except those in the Confederate army. Certain of these between 18 and 45 years composed the second class or state reserves. They were assembled into camps and organized for state defense. They were few in number and were absorbed into Confederate service by the process of the volunteering of individuals and by the opera-

[52] *O. R.*, ser. i, vol. xxxii, pt. iii, pp. 668-669, 683-684, 785, 824-825, 825-826, 827, 853, 855-856, 858-860, 863-864; vol. xxxviii, pt. iv, pp. 657-658.

[53] William Polk, *Leonidas Polk,* vol. ii, p. 339, quoting a letter dated June 11, 1864.

[54] *Governor's Letter Book,* July 21, 1863, p. 51; July 23, 1863, pp. 53-54.

[55] *Acts of the Called and the Third Regular Annual Session of the Assembly of Alabama,* 1863, pp. 3-11; *O. R.*, ser. iv, vol. iii, pp. 178-181; *Governor's Letter Book,* December 14, 1863, p. 101; *O. R.*, ser. iv, vol. iii, p. 463.

tion of the Confederate act of February 17, 1864.[56] Under
that act men between 18 and 45 who were incapacitated for
active field service were made liable to light service as state
reserves and men from 45 to 50 and boys from 17 to 18
were ordered to enroll themselves or else be conscripted as
if they were 18 to 45, and were allowed until May 1 to
volunteer in local companies or to form companies of state
reserves. The state reserves were assembled into camps
under the supervision of officers of conscription and were
organized under command of veteran officers who were incapacitated for active field service. On April 30, an active
army officer, Jones M. Withers, was appointed General of
Reserves of Alabama. By July, twenty-one companies had
been organized, nearly all of which were composed of men 45
to 50. These with the addition of some regular conscripts
and other scattering material were formed into four small
regiments, for state defense. They were usually employed
in provost guard duty, but were frequently called out to
repel invasion or detailed to arrest deserters.[57] However,
the reserves themselves, a large part of whom were originally assembled under guard, became notorious for absenteeism and desertion. The return of one company January
1, 1865 gave 37 present and 61 absent without leave; that
of one regiment November 30, 1864, 351 absent without
leave. The return of one company stated that a definite

[56] Miller, *Alabama*, p. 369; Memphis *Appeal*, October 6, 1864; Mont-
gomery *Weekly Advertiser,* July 27, 1864; N. D. Guerny to H. P. Watson,
January 1, 1865. Jefferson and Blount and probably other counties re-
ported that they had no men liable to service under the act.—Frank
Prince to Governor Watts, August 29, 1864; A. M. Gibson to Governor
Watts, August 29, 1864.

[57] *O. R.,* ser. iv, vol. iii, pp. 178-181, pp. 212, 257, 294; *The Independent,*
May 28, 1864; *O. R.,* ser. i, vol. xxxix, pt. ii, p. 711; *Letter Book of the
Commandant of Conscripts,* p. 271; Rowland, *Jefferson Davis, Constitutionalist,* vol. vi, pp. 362-365; Fleming, *Civil War and Reconstruction,* p.
83. See also *O. R.,* ser. i, vol. lii, pt. ii, p. 679.

record was impossible because of so much coming and going; the return of one regiment was not made at all November 30 because there were no officers present to make it.[58] The state reserves probably did more to encourage desertion than to check it.

Under the state act of August 29, 1863, the boys 16 to 17 years of age and the men 45 to 60 years composed the first class or county reserves. According to the enumeration, which was said to be neither complete nor accurate, they numbered nearly 29,000, but they were not all organized.[59] Before the organization of county reserves was completed, the organization of state reserves was ordered by the Confederate government February 17. A clash between the conscription officers and the Governor followed. Each side accused the other of taking its material. The commandant of conscripts said that the Governor refused to allow the conscription of certain men in organizations previously formed under his proclamations and the Governor called the policy of the Conscription Bureau in taking old men and boys from the farms and putting them into camps " egregious folly " and declared his intention to maintain the right of the state to have some troops of its own. The clash with the confusion attending it caused delay in organization during which deserters continued their depredations.[60] In the final division, the Confederate government

[58] *Governor's Letter Book*, August 19, 1864, p. 170; D. Compton to Governor Watts, December 20, 1864; W. R. Rush to Governor Watts, August 17, 1864; N. D. Guerny to H. P. Watson, January 1, 1865; *O. R.*, ser. iv, vol. iii, pp. 880-883; Third Alabama Reserves, Company K.

[59] *Adjutant and Inspector-General's Report of the enumeration of the Alabama militia under the act of the General Assembly approved August 29, 1863 to the General Assembly*, September, 1864. No enumeration was made in Winston county and in five counties under occupation by the enemy. The enumeration did not remain accurate because of changes by volunteering.

[60] *Letter Book of the Commandant of Conscripts*, pp. 42-43; 60-61,

took the men from 17 to 50 and the state, the boys of 16
and the men from 50 to 60. The county reserves were not
organized in the first, second and third congressional districts, composed of the eighteen counties of north Alabama
lying above Calhoun, Talladega, Jefferson, Bibb, Greene
and Pickens, which districts were exempted under the act
of August 29, nor in the black-belt counties and the counties
of southwest Alabama, which evidently had no need of
them. The reserves were organized and functioned in the
hill counties of north Alabama and in seven of the counties
of southeast Alabama.[61] The officers, including the county
commandant and beat commandants, were elected by the
members of the first class in each county and, in cases of
failure to elect, were appointed by the Governor. The reserves were mounted. They were supposed to drill weekly
and to be ready at any time to assemble for service in their
respective counties. The functions of the county reserves as
officially stated were suppressing insurrections, executing the
laws and repelling sudden invasions, or as popularly stated,
catching deserters. They rode out every now and then in
small squads and, as they said, " scoured the country " for
deserters.[62] By a later act, they were required to do regular patrol duty.[63]

100-102, 282; L. D. Browne to Governor Watts, December 14, 1864;
O. R., ser. iv, vol. iii, pp. 463-464.

   [61] *Acts of the Called and the Third Regular Annual Session of the
Assembly*, 1863, pp. 3-11; Letters to the Governor from the county commandants and other officers. The titles and the number of officers depended upon the size of the organization. The reserves were organized
in Monroe and Macon counties, which thus presented exceptions in south
Alabama.

   [62] *The Governor's Letter Book*, 1864, p. 154; E. B. Smith (colonel
and commandant, Randolph) to Governor Watts, April 18, 1864; R. G.
Young (captain, Tallapoosa) to Governor Watts, March 5, 1864.

   [63] *Acts of the Called and the Third Regular Annual Session*, 1863,
pp. 60-61.

Some companies of county reserves had zeal as the following extracts from officers' reports indicate: from Talladega, August 20, 1864, " When the militia was organized in this county, the woods was full of deserters & outliers. In some beats as many as 30. We have got them nearly all off to the army"; from Dale, March 20, 1865, " the Times was So warm the Tories made no Resistance but fled to the Swamp. Cild Captured & lost 11. no Hurt on our Side "; and from Shelby March 4, 1865, " We have within the last three weeks got in from the woods over 100 deserters." [64] Most of the companies were so worthless that the system was a farce. Equipment was inadequate. All the old pistols, squirrel guns, and other antiquated weapons were collected but would not go around. Sufficient guns and ammunition could not be bought in the counties nor supplied by the Governor. The lack of guns and ammunition was a serious handicap to the reserves, which two extracts from reports illustrate: (1) " we Had a fight with them a few Knights ago & for the like of arms we failed to capture them "; (2) " Some few weeks ago there was a raid come up Pea river near us. We all turned out from this beat (Monticello) but had few guns & no ammunition." [65] Discipline was extremely lax. Some members refused at pleasure to respond to calls to go upon scouting expeditions and others carried furloughs good for an in-

[64] Joseph D. McCain to Governor Watts; Joseph Hough to Governor Watts; John P. West to Governor Watts.

[65] James G. L. Henry to Governor Watts, March 10, 1865; John T. Heflin to Governor Watts, March 9, 1865; Thomas A. Davis to Governor Watts, September 4, 1864; Joseph Hough to Governor Watts, March 20, 1865; G. W. Culver to Governor Watts, December 11 and December 19, 1864; E. B. Wilkerson to Governor Watts, January 11, 1865; John Henderson to Governor Watts, August 8, 1864; Joseph D. McCain to Governor Watts, January 6, 1865; W. J. Peddy to Governor Watts, March 20, 1865; N. W. Murphey to Governor Watts, January 9, 1865.

definite period.[66]   Again, the personnel was not such as to ensure efficiency.   Men between 45 and 60 and boys between 16 and 17 were compelled to form these organizations.   Moreover, some of the companies were composed largely of tories and deserters.   For example, it was said that two-thirds of the reserves of Bibb county were men who had sons in the woods and who sent out runners to warn them in advance of every expedition.[67]   Again, it was said that the reserves of Calhoun county offered a fine refuge for deserters, that the safest way to keep from being returned to the army was to join the reserves.[68]   The system was rendered more ineffective by the provisions of the law which limited the operation of reserves to their respective counties, thus causing their work sometimes to amount to no more than chasing deserters across a line, and which excluded reserves from the counties of north Alabama where tories and deserters were most numerous and audacious.[69]

During the third period of desertion from August, 1864 to April, 1865, the organization which was depended upon to effect the return of deserters was entirely military.   The Confederate organization officially charged with this business was the Bureau of Conscription with a supporting

[66] W. S. Jackson to Governor Watts, August 30, 1864; February 10, 1865; Meade H. Jackson to Governor Watts, March 24, 1865.

[67] J. M. Shelton to Governor Watts, Dec. 28, 1864.

[68] Meade H. Jackson to Governor Watts, March 24, 1865. See also: Andrew Jay to Governor Watts, December 29, 1864; J. W. Suttle to Governor Watts, April 14 and May 23, 1864; John Smith to Governor Watts, March, 1865.

[69] Thomas P. Randle to Governor Watts, January 22, 1865. See also William Bush to Governor Shorter, January 23, 1863. Evidently the legislature expected the second class reserves to replace the Confederate cavalry in north Alabama, which was unpopular.—*Governor's Letter Book*, December 14, 1863, pp. 120-121; *Acts of the Called and the Third Regular Annual Session*, 1863, pp. 60-61.

force and with the state reserves. When the Volunteer and Conscript Bureau was abolished, conscription officials, believing that the supporting force of 25 companies raised by General Pillow was too large, cut it down to 8 or 9 companies. But the commandant of conscripts very soon perceived that this force was entirely too small to deal with the deserters collected in the state. To increase the force, he was authorized to form in each congressional district one company composed of 100 men of 18 to 45 years of age who were unfit for active Confederate service and, if necessary to bring the number to 100, of men 45 to 50 taken by special permission from the state reserves. He found the task difficult, especially in north Alabama, and as late as October was still prodding his officers to hurry up the organization.[70] On November 30 he and the general of reserves made a gloomy report to Richmond of the condition of the supporting force of the Bureau of Conscription in Alabama. On the average, 12 or 15 men commanded by disabled officers were stationed in each county when the average number of deserters to each county was about 300. The supporting forces were only partially armed, and some of them had ammunition that did not fit their guns. They were discontented, homesick, disobedient, and generally unreliable. The general of reserves asked for permission to raise a force of boys 16 years old.[71] A senator from Mississippi pronounced the supporting forces in that state and in Alabama " a nuisance to the people and a deception to the government." [72]

[70] *O. R.*, ser. iv, vol. iii, pp. 251-253, 294; *Letter Book of the Commandant of Conscripts*, pp. 235, 334, 13, 279, 286, 289, 290, 336, 341, 354-355, 358-359, 361, 362, 396.

[71] *O. R.*, ser. iv, vol. iii, pp. 880-883. For desertion from the supporting force, the penalty was conscription in active Confederate service.— *Letter Book of the Commandant of Conscripts*, p. 362.

[72] *O. R.*, ser. iv, vol. iii, p. 707.

The Bureau of Conscription in Alabama, which as a whole was considered by several competent observers as unsatisfactory as its supporting force, was placed in the fall of 1864 under command of the general of reserves and on March 17, 1865, was officially discontinued.[73] In February, the entire force of reserves was put on the duty of apprehending deserters and returning them to their respective commands.[74] But the reserves were composed of the same material as the supporting force and were quite as inefficient. They were described by the general of reserves as indifferent, sluggish, and selfish.[75] Besides, over half of them were absentees without leave and deserters.

The state organization which was charged with the arrest and return of deserters was the county reserves. The legislature of 1864 made no effort to create a new state militia but passed a few acts to regulate the county reserves. These acts show forcibly the inefficiency of the system. One of them, arising out of the fear that the county reserves would be taken over by the Confederate government as the state reserves had been, fixed inefficiency upon the county reserves by prohibiting any Confederate officer from commanding them.[76] To the functions already assigned, regular patrol duty was added, but in two months, fines from $5 to $20 were fixed for failure to perform this duty. A more drastic penalty was imposed upon officers and members for failure to perform other duties—transfer to the state re-

[73] *O. R.*, ser. iv, vol. iii, pp. 675-676, 707, 976-979; *Letter Book of Henry Bryan*, February 9, 1865; Rowland, *Jefferson Davis, Constitutionalist*, vol. vi, pp. 362-365; *O. R.*, ser. iv, vol. iii, p. 1183.

[74] *O. R.*, ser. iv, vol. iii, p. 1113.

[75] *O. R.*, ser. i, vol. xxxix, pt. ii, p. 711.

[76] *Governor's Letter Book*, October 7, 1864, p. 175; Nancy Twilbey to Governor Watts, November 9, 1864, endorsement by Governor Watts; *Acts of the Called and Fourth Regular Annual Session*, 1864, pp. 7-9.

serves.[77]   Upon petition, the counties of Dale, Henry and Coffee, which had reserves, and the counties of Fayette and Marion, which had been exempted from the organization of reserves, were authorized to form home guards for protection against deserters.[78]   A good indication of the worthlessness of the system of county reserves was the Governor's call March 3, 1865 upon the boys to defend the state from invasion.[79]

Methods of persuasion and methods of force in dealing with deserters were tried alternately and conjointly.   Frequent appeals to public opinion to compel deserters to return were made by political leaders and by the press.   The governors were requested by the Secretary of War in a confidential circular in July, 1862 to bring to the assistance of his department in returning absentees and deserters to their colors the powerful influence of public opinion in their respective states.[80]   Governor Shorter and his successor, Governor Watts, attempted to give such assistance by pointing out in their public addresses this duty to the people.[81]   President Davis made eloquent appeals to the people at home, especially the women, not to tolerate desertion.   He

[77] *Acts of the Called and Fourth Regular Annual Session*, 1864, pp. 70-71, 7-9.

[78] *Acts of the Called and Fourth Regular Annual Session*, 1864, pp. 31-32, 30, 153.

[79] *Clarke County Journal*, March 23, 1865, Proclamation by Governor Watts, March 3.   A conference of southern governors was held at Augusta, Georgia, in October, 1864, for consideration of several problems, one of which was returning deserters, but the results seem to have been unimportant.—*Journal of the Congress of the Confederate States of America*, vol. vii, pp. 257-258.

[80] *O. R.*, ser. iv, vol. ii, p. 7.

[81] *Governor's Letter Book*, July 23, 1862, p. 174; *Proclamation Book A*, p. 52; Papers of General W. W. Allen, addresses of Governor Watts at Talladega and Columbiana, clippings from the Talladega *Reporter*, 1863.

relied, he said in a speech at Jackson, Mississippi, December, 1862, upon the women of the land to return deserters to the ranks.[82] In a proclamation of amnesty to deserters issued in August, 1863, he said:

I conjure my countrywomen — mothers, wives, sisters, and daughters of the Confederacy—to use their all powerful influence in aid of this call, to add one crowning sacrifice to those which their patriotism has so freely and constantly offered on their country's altar and to take care that none who owe service in the field shall be sheltered at home from the disgrace of having deserted their duty to their families, to their country, and to their God.[83]

In the fall of 1864, he made a tour of the states of the Confederacy with the object of arousing public opinion to force the absentees back to the army.   In numerous speeches, including one to the legislature of Alabama, he urged upon the people the duty of returning absentees and deserters, asking the women to frown upon them and advising, " Young ladies, marry none but a soldier." [84]   In 1865, Congress issued an address to all good citizens asking them to discountenance indignantly all evasions of military duty: •

Let no skulker, deserter, or absentee without leave be tolerated in the community.   Let the reproachful glance of our women between whose honor and the brutal foe our noble army stands as a flaming sword, drive him back to the field.   With proper effort, strict discipline and an elevated tone of public opinion throughout the country, desertion and absenteeism in the army can be arrested and all men liable to military duty put into and kept in the ranks of our army.[85]

[82] Mobile *Register,* January 11, 1863.

[83] *O. R.,* ser. iv, vol. ii, pp. 687-688.

[84] Memphis *Daily Appeal,* September 30, 1864; Montgomery *Daily Mail,* October 4, 1864; Rowland, *Jefferson Davis, Constitutionalist,* vol. vi, pp. 354-356, 356-361, 358, 359, 360.

[85] Appleton, *Annual Cyclopedia,* 1865, p. 195.

The press made frequent and sometimes picturesque appeals. There should be no resting place for the feet of these creatures. Smoke them out of their holes and drive them with scorn or sneers or stronger inducements to their places. The withering scorn of the world would follow them from the day of desertion to their graves. Let the women unite in ostracizing absentees and deserters and returning them to the army and thus save themselves from a fate worse than death.[86]

In response to these and similar appeals some women of Mobile at a large meeting held in March, 1865 unanimously adopted resolutions pledging themselves to discourage in all practicable ways unauthorized and improper absenteeism from the army:

And to this end we mutually and solemnly pledge our truth:

1. To recognize no man socially who is either a deserter, a loafer from his post, or a skulker from service.

2. To hold all such persons marked as of leprous soul and as unworthy the respect of woman, whom they have not the manhood to defend, and

3. To disseminate these views and as far as in us lies to create thus a public opinion and a social law, which, we trust, may endure for generations.[87]

Several offers of amnesty were made to deserters who

---

[86] Appleton, *Annual Cyclopedia*, 1862, p. 246; Mobile *Register*, February 3, 1864, quoting the Charleston *Courier*; Mobile *Register*, December 13, 1863; Montgomery *Daily Advertiser*, March 5, 1865, quoting the *Army Argus and Crisis*. See also: Richmond *Examiner*, January 31, 1865; February 4, 1865; Mobile *Register*, September 23, 1862; Montgomery *Daily Mail*, January 10, 1863; Jacksonville *Republican*, December 19, 1863; Mobile *Register*, March 1, January 5, 7, 24, 1864; Memphis *Appeal*, October 7, 1864. For quotations of appeals by military authorities see: Montgomery *Daily Mail*, November 4, 1864; *Southwestern Baptist*, June 4, 1863; Jacksonville *Republican*, December 19, 1863.

[87] Montgomery *Daily Advertiser*, March 12, 1865, quoting the Mobile *Tribune*, March 2.

would return voluntarily. During the first period of desertion, two offers were made by General Bragg to absentees from the Army of Tennessee. A proclamation, issued November 28, 1862 upon the occasion of the close of " an arduous and brilliant campaign," offered amnesty to all absentees except commissioned officers who would return within a reasonable time and stated that the period of amnesty would be followed by a rigorous execution of the law. Another proclamation, issued April 23, 1863 as the result of information that absentees were anxious to return but afraid of punishment, offered amnesty to absentees who would return within twenty to forty days.[88]

During the second period of desertion, two offers of amnesty were made. On August 1, 1863, a proclamation was issued by President Davis, offering amnesty to all absentees from the Confederate army — except those who had been twice convicted of desertion — who would return within twenty days after the date of publication of the proclamation and granting immediate pardon to all soldiers awaiting trial or undergoing punishment for desertion. The proclamation made an appeal to the absentees, who, in the opinion of the President, had never intended to abandon the cause of the Confederacy, to return to its service and thus aid in winning victory, to which the alternative was subjugation, slavery and ruin.[89] The proclamation had been proposed by General Lee.[90] The results, however, were disappointing. Comparatively few soldiers returned and others deserted in order to enjoy a visit home and get the benefit of the proclamation. The news of the proclamation was not well spread in spite of the efforts of newspapers and conscrip-

[88] *O. R.*, ser. i, vol. xx, pt. ii, p. 429; *G. O.* no. 84, April 23, 1863, Hdqrs. of the Army of Tenn.

[89] *O. R.*, ser. iv, vol. ii, pp. 687-688.

[90] *O. R.*, ser. i, vol. xlii, pt. ii, p. 1167.

tion officials; "elegant appeals," said a sharp critic of the President, failed to move the very ignorant and thoughtless men who formed the majority of the army;[91] and, above all, popular depression following the fall of Vicksburg was still deep.

On April 16, 1864, a proclamation was issued by General Polk, offering amnesty to all absentees in the Department of Alabama, Mississippi and East Louisiana, including exchanged and paroled men but excluding deserters to the enemy and commissioned officers, who would return by May 20. The proclamation was issued reluctantly by General Polk in response to a petition from the legislature of Mississippi, which stated that many men regretted leaving the army but feared to return because of punishment and that they had not heard of the President's proclamation of amnesty. Absentees were informed that this was the last opportunity of pardon, and were assured that after May 20 General Polk would continue his policy of the vigorous use of force.[92] The results were gratifying. A thousand absentees were said to have reported at Meridian and a thousand at Macon, Mississippi, representing all the states of the Confederacy. Many had been staying securely since the fall of Vicksburg in the western counties of Alabama where there were no railroads—or conscription officials. Absentees, it was said, returned to General Johnston's army by car-loads.[93] General Polk reported as the combined result

[91] *O. R.*, ser. i, vol. xxix, pt. ii, p. 650; New York *Times*, September 6, 1863; *Governor's Letter Book*, October 28, 1863, p. 88; Jacksonville *Republican*, August 15, 1863; Selma *Morning Reporter*, September 22, 1863; Mobile *Register*, October 15, 1863; Montgomery *Daily Mail*, August 26, 1863; Richmond *Examiner*, August 15, 1863 ("elegant appeals"). See also Richmond *Examiner*, August 7, 1863.

[92] *O. R.*, ser. i, vol. xxxii, pt. iii, pp. 785-786. For distribution of the proclamation, see p. 824.

[93] *Clarke County Journal*, June 2, 1864, quoting the Meridian *Clarion*

of his military campaign against deserters in his department and his offer of amnesty to them a net gain to the army of 5000 men.[94] He attributed the success of the offer of amnesty to the alternative which he proposed—force.[95] However, at this time, popular depression was lifting with a desperate hope of winning the war.

During the third period of desertion, two offers of amnesty were made by General Lee and one was made by the Governor and the legislature of Alabama. August 10, 1864, in accord with a suggestion of the Secretary of War, an appeal to absentees was made by General Lee, shaming them for leaving their comrades to fight alone and for bringing disgrace upon their families and stating that " prompt and voluntary return of deserters alone can palliate their offense and entitle them to expect any clemency."[96] October 2, 1864, a proclamation was issued by Governor Watts, promising the deserters of Alabama who would return within forty days that no penalty of death would be inflicted. The proclamation was issued because it was believed that very few of the deserters had left the army with the intention of abandoning the cause of the South and because it was certain they were now all needed to fight for that cause.[97] Five days later an address was published by the legislature urging absentees to return to duty in order to aid in averting the threatened doom of enslavement and to prevent the draft of old men and boys to

and the Macon *Beacon*; Mobile *Register*, May 7, 10, 15, 26, 1864; Montgomery *Daily Advertiser*, May 15, 1864.

[94] William Polk, *Leonidas Polk*, vol. ii, p. 339.

[95] *O. R.*, ser. i, vol. xxxii, pt. iii, pp. 855-856.

[96] *O. R.*, ser. i, vol. xl, pt. iii, pp. 817-818; vol. xlii, pt. ii, p. 1169.

[97] *Clarke County Journal*, October 13, 1864. For a similar proclamation issued by the Governor of Mississippi, see the Memphis *Appeal*, November 5, 1864.

fill their places.[98]　On February 11, 1865, a proclamation
was made by General Lee under the authority of the President, offering amnesty to absentees and deserters who would
return within twenty days after the date of the proclamation.　Deserters who had gone to the enemy, deserters who
had been once pardoned, and deserters who had left the
army after the proclamation were excluded from the benefit
of amnesty.　The proclamation made an appeal to absentees
and deserters to fight for freedom, with the expectation that
" He who gave freedom to our fathers will bless the efforts
of their children to preserve it."　It stated that this offer
was the last opportunity for pardon and that failure to
accept it would be treated with the utmost penalty of the
law.[99]　A similar proclamation was issued on the same day
to transfers without a proper discharge from their former
company.[100]　In Alabama, three rendezvous camps, Montgomery, Selma and Mobile, were organized to receive those
who should return.[101]　It was said in Alabama that they
came in droves, crowding cars and boats.[102]　This response
was in accord with a final spurt of energy arising out of
indignation at the failure of the peace commissioners and
hope because of the restoration of General Johnston to command of his shattered army.

In addition to formal offers of amnesty, a general policy
of leniency toward deserters who returned to the army voluntarily was followed.　The policy was stated July 30, 1864
by the Secretary of War thus: " It is believed to be now

[98] *Acts of the Called and the Fourth Regular Annual Session,* 1864,
p. 44.

[99] *O. R.,* ser. i, vol. xlvi, pt. ii, p. 1229.　See also *O. R.,* ser. i, vol. li,
pt. ii, pp. 1082 and 1083.

[100] *O. R.,* ser. i, vol. xlvi, pt. ii, pp. 1230-1231.

[101] *Clarke County Journal,* March 30, 1865.

[102] *Clarke County Journal,* March 16, 23, 30, 1865.

generally understood that any deserter voluntarily returning is leniently dealt with "; and by General Lee, November 4, 1863, thus: " Courts-martial invariably take into account in their decisions the voluntary return of a prisoner and I have never known one who so returned to be sentenced to death." [103]

Methods of force in dealing with deserters were more varied than methods of persuasion. Methods to facilitate the use of force were reports of absence without leave and desertion, orders to absentees to return, and inspection of passes, furloughs and orders. November 27, 1862, a special report of absentees from all departments was called for by the War Department, and January 18, 1863 a special report of absentees from the Army of Tennessee was called for by General Bragg.[104] Records of absence without leave were kept by company commanders.[105] Reports of absentees were returned monthly from September, 1863, bi-monthly from June, 1864, and tri-monthly in 1865 by commanding officers of regiments and battalions to the chief of the Bureau of Conscription. Lists of absentees, arranged by residence in congressional districts were made from these reports and sent to the commandants of conscripts of the states to be distributed among the enrolling officers of the congressional districts.[106] In reverse order, reports of absentees in the states were made by enrolling officers and commandants to the Adjutant and Inspector-General's Office

[103] *O. R.,* ser. i, vol. xl, pt. iii, p. 817; vol. xxix, pt. ii, p. 820. See also *O. R.,* ser. i, vol. xxxix, pt. iii, p. 806; vol. li, pt. ii, pp. 781-782.

[104] *General Orders from the Adjutant and Inspector-General's Office,* 1862 (Columbia, 1864), no. 96; *O. R.,* ser. i, vol. xx, pt. ii, p. 501.

[105] *Journal of Congress of C. S. A.,* vol. vi, p. 115.

[106] *O. R.,* ser. iv, vol. ii, p. 801; vol. iii, p. 518; *Returns of Allen's Division of Wheeler's Cavalry Corps,* 1865; *Returns of General Johnston's Army,* 1865; *O. R.,* ser. i, vol. xxv, pt. i, p. 647; vol. xxix, pt. ii, p. 654.

in Richmond. During the period of General Pillow's operations, few records were kept in Alabama, but an elaborate system of records was prescribed by his successor.[107] From May 2, 1864, field returns of troops before and after a march were made by commanding officers to the Adjutant and Inspector-General's Office.[108] Orders to absentees from a certain command to return within a given time or be accounted deserters were frequently issued. They were accompanied by a threat, stated or implied, that failure to return would be followed by the use of force. They were a kind of storm warning.[109] Inspection of passes, furloughs, and orders was made by sentries on railroad trains and by enrolling officers, provost-marshals and guards in town and country. To aid in making records, all soldiers on furlough immediately upon arrival in their respective districts were required to report to a provost-marshal or enrolling officer.[110] To detect imposters, in 1865 inspection of orders of scouting parties of cavalry was required.[111] To detect frauds in substitution, in the summer of 1863, a special detective was employed by the Bureau of Conscription and, in the fall of that year, commandants of conscripts were ordered to secure from subordinate officers the papers of all substitutes and forward them to Richmond for examination.[112] By order of General Hood, September 13, 1864,

[107] *O. R.*, ser. iv, vol. ii, pp. 5-6; *Letter Book of the Commandant of Conscripts*, pp. 27, 5, 13, 147-148, 144-145.

[108] *G. O. from A. and I. G. O.*, 1864, no. 45; Selma *Reporter*, May 2, 1864.

[109] *Cf. supra*, pp. 16-17.

[110] *O. R.*, ser. iv, vol. ii, p. 14; Freemantle, *Three Months in the Southern States*, pp. 127, 134; Mobile *Register*, October 16, 1863; *O. R.*, ser. iv, vol. ii, p. 913; Montgomery *Daily Mail*, February 7, 1863; *Democratic Watchtower*, May 18, 1864.

[111] *Clarke County Journal*, January 26, 1865.

[112] *O. R.*, ser. iv, vol. ii, pp. 582-583; Mobile *Register*, June 26, 1863, quoting the Richmond *Examiner*.

the roll was called every hour on retreat and picked bodies of cavalry were kept ready to pursue deserters.[113] These methods were not always effective. Reports were often incomplete and sometimes never made; orders to absentees were frequently ignored; and inspection of papers called forth ingenuity in forgery and aroused angry protests from citizens that the system was a nuisance.[114]

Arrests of deserters were made usually by civil officials or by military officers; occasionally by private citizens or by private soldiers.[115] Frequently field officers were detailed from the army to the work of collecting absentees from their commands in the counties where the commands had been recruited.[116] " Responsible persons " might be employed by commanders of brigades to arrest deserters.[117] To encourage arrests, advertisements for deserters were published often during 1862 and 1863 in the newspapers of

[113] *General Field Orders*, no. 18, September 13, 1864, Hdqrs. of the Army of Tenn. in the Field; *Mississippi Historical Society Publications*, Centenary Series IV, p. 261, Wm. A. Love, " Reminiscences of the closing days of the War of Secession."

[114] *Letter Book of the Commandant of Conscripts*, pp. 147-148; Mobile *Register*, December 2, 1863; Eggleston, *A Rebel's Recollections*, p. 194, pp. 218-219; Jacksonville *Republican*, January 9, 1864; *Southern Historical Society Papers*, vol. viii, p. 80, " Proceedings of Congress " (September 10, 1862 Mr. Dargan of Alabama offered resolutions to investigate the abuses of provost-marshals).

[115] *O. R.*, ser. iv, vol. ii, pp. 5-6; Mobile *Register*, February 13, 1863; October 15, 1863; John Hall to his sister, June 1, 1863; W. A. McClendon, *Recollections of War Times*, p. 186; Goodloe, *Confederate Echoes*, p. 121.

[116] For examples, see: *Alabama Beacon*, February 27, 1863; *Special Orders from the Adjutant and Inspector-General's Office* (Richmond, 1861-1863), no. 13, January 16, 1863; Mobile *Register*, January 28, 1863; Montgomery *Daily Mail*, February 7, 1863; E. D. Willett, *Company B of the Fortieth Alabama*, pp. 42-43; *Democratic Watchtower*, September 30, 1863; John A. Hall to his father, March 7, 1865.

[117] *Journal of the Congress of the Confederate States of America, House*, vol. vi, p. 115.

Alabama.   These advertisements gave the name and command and sometimes residence, date of desertion and a description of the personal appearance of the deserter and offered a reward of $30 for his arrest.[118]   The following advertisement is typical:

Deserted $30 Reward
Camp near Fredericksburg, Va.

Jan. 5, 1863.

The above reward will be paid for each of the following named men who have deserted from Company I, 5th Alabama Regiment.
. . . . (1 omitted)
Private ————— —————, aged 18 years, 5 ft. 9 in. high, light complexion, light hair, blue eyes.

S. T. Woodward, Capt.
Grove Hill Guards [119]

Occasionally private citizens, tired of depredations, employed a man to hunt down deserters with a pack of dogs such as were used for hunting runaway negroes.   Occasionally they formed a party themselves, sometimes acting with soldiers, and hunted deserters with or without dogs.[120]

[118] *Cf. supra,* p. 30; *Rules and Articles of War,* art. xviii.   The reward for delivery of a deserter at a jail was $15.—*Proclamation Book A,* p. 46; *Journal of the Congress of the C. S. of A., House,* vol. vi, p. 115.

[119] *Clarke County Journal,* February 5, 1863.   This deserter walked home from Virginia.   Claiming that he had rheumatism in his right hand, he bound his fingers down so long that he was never able to straighten them.—Unwritten reminiscences.   This advertisement ran for weeks along with another advertisement offering a reward of $225 for a runaway horse.   Advertisements for deserters seldom appeared in 1864, probably because of former errors in names, longer and so more expensive lists, and disappointing results.

[120] Montgomery *Weekly Advertiser,* May 4, 1863; Montgomery *Daily Advertiser,* October 28, 1863; Petition of certain citizens of Hamden Beat, Marengo county, to Governor Watts, August 31, 1864; W. S. Jackson to Governor Watts, May 27, 1864; Joseph Silver to Governor Watts, August 18, 1864; Montgomery *Daily Mail,* April 8, 1865;

Military expeditions against deserters varied in size from a squad of a dozen or so to a force of two or three thousand, but they were usually small. They varied in composition with reserves, forces of the conscription bureau, detachments from the army of men from Alabama or from other states, and combinations of these forces, but they were usually mounted. Methods varied with size and composition of the expedition but usually involved fighting deserters in ambush in swamps or mountains, killing a few and capturing a few.[121] Whether deserters were arrested with a small show of force or captured by a military expedition, they were disposed of in much the same way. They were turned over to sheriffs, provost-marshals or commandants of posts or camps—a few of which were established especially for the reception of deserters — and were sent under guard to their respective commands for trial by courts-martial.[122]

Punishments for desertion, which were awarded by courts-martial at their discretion, were varied. The extreme punishment, which could be awarded only by concurrence of two-thirds of the court, was death.[123] The method

Register of Applications for Amnesty and Pardon, vol. i, pp. 22, 46, 94; vol. ii, p. 335; N. Y. *Times*, October 20, 1863. For the suggestion of a military officer that dogs be used to catch deserters, see *O. R.*, ser. i, vol. xxxii, pt. iii, p. 853.

[121] *Letter Book of the Commandant of Conscripts*, pp. 78, 295, 314, 323, 372, 381; D. M. Robison to Governor Watts, June 5, 1864; *O. R.*, ser. i, vol. xxx, pt. iv, p. 502; vol. xlv, pt. ii, pp. 694-695; Mobile *Register*, May 14, 1864. For reports of General Polk's campaign against deserters, *cf. supra*, pp. 202-203.

[122] *O. R.*, ser. iv, vol. ii, pp. 777, 828; *Letter Book of the Commandant of Conscripts*, pp. 191, 344, 398; *Circular*, August 23, 1864, Hdqrs. of Dept. of Tenn. and Ga., by General Hood (Papers of General Allen); *Southwestern Baptist*, April 13, 1865; *Clarke County Journal*, March 30, 1865.

[123] *Rules and Articles of War*, arts. 20 and 87; C. H. Lee, *The Judge Advocate's Vade Mecum* (Richmond, 1864), p. 121.

of execution was prescribed by sentence of the court: to be shot to death with musketry at such time and place as the commanding general may direct.[124] The ceremony of execution was designed to deter other soldiers from desertion. The brigade to which the deserter belonged was marched out to the field of execution and drawn up to form three sides of a hollow square, facing inward. The band played a dead march. The deserter rode on a wagon, seated on his coffin. A heavy guard followed. The deserter was brought to the open side of the square and made to kneel between his coffin and his grave. His arms were tied to a stake behind him and his eyes were blindfolded with a handkerchief. An officer read the specifications, charges and sentence of the court and the special orders by the commanding general for the execution. The firing-squad of about a dozen soldiers, whose muskets had been loaded at headquarters, half of them with powder only, half of them with buck and ball, took their station a few paces in front of the deserter. At the order, " Ready, aim, fire!" they discharged their muskets. The body of the deserter was buried immediately during a death-like silence.[125] Soldiers dreaded to go

[124] For example, see *G. O.* no. 41, 1863, Dept. and Army of Northern Virginia; *G. O.* no. 28, 1864, Hdqrs. of the Army of Tennessee.

[125] Details varied a little. Sometimes the deserter, accompanied by a spiritual adviser, walked to execution behind or in front of those who carried his coffin; sometimes he was shot while seated on his coffin. Occasionally, prisoners were brought and visitors admitted to see the execution. If the first discharge did not kill the deserter, a second was made. *Clarke County Journal*, March 24, 1864; *Confederate Veteran*, vol. ii, p. 235, H. J. Cheney, " Penalties for Desertion"; Montgomery *Daily Advertiser*, November 25, 1863; Mobile *Register*, October 4, 1863; *Democratic Watchtower*, September 23, 1863; Montgomery *Daily Mail*, April 19, 1863; Selma *Reporter*, November 9, 1864; *Confederate Veteran*, vol. x, pp. 67-68, B. L. Ridley, " Camp Scenes around Dalton"; A. H. Noll, *Dr. Quintard, Chaplain* (Sewanee, 1905), pp. 83-86; J. E. Hall to his father, October 6, 1864.

through the ordeal of witnessing an execution. Many of them said that they preferred going into battle.[126] However, the death penalty was not frequently inflicted upon deserters. According to the records of Colonel Fowler, of all the " permanent " deserters from Alabama troops in the Army of Northern Virginia from 1861 to January 1, 1865, including deserters to the enemy, less than one-half of one per cent were executed.[127] The death penalty was inflicted more often upon deserters who went to the enemy than upon deserters who went home.

Other forms of punishment for desertion were usually awarded by courts-martial.[128] They were designed to inflict pain or discomfort, or to restrict liberty or to cause humiliation. During the early part of the war, whipping with a cowhide strap, " 39 lashes laid on the bare back," was an official punishment, but at the petition of an Alabama command was abolished by Congress, April 16, 1863.[129] A

[126] Hubbard, *Notes of a Private*, pp. 106-107; J. R. Maxwell, *Autobiography*, p. 156; Ford, *Life in the Confederate Army*, p. 14; J. E. Hall to his father, October 6, 1864; E. K. Flournoy to his wife, April 15, 1864.

[127] For figures upon which calculations are based see *Publications of the Alabama Historical Society Transactions*, vol. ii, pp. 190-191, " Recapitulation of Alabama Troops in the Army of Northern Virginia, February 1, 1865."

[128] The following paragraphs on punishments are based upon several hundred orders, relating with few exceptions to soldiers in Alabama commands. The orders, printed on loose leaflets, are now collected in the Office of the Adjutant-General at Washington. In the following paragraphs, at least one definite reference to the orders is given for each statement. For other references, see *General Orders from Headquarters of the Army of Tennessee, 1862-1865, passim* and *General Orders of the Department and Army of Northern Virginia, 1862-1865, passim.*

[129] Mobile *Register*, September 11, 1861; S. C. Kelly (30th Ala.) to his wife, June 8, 1862; Mobile *Register*, February 18, 1863; G. O. no. 41, 1863, Dept. and Army of Northern Virginia; Memorial of J. S. Harwell and Eugene McCaa, citizens from Alabama serving as volunteer soldiers, against punishment by lash imposed by courts-martial; O. R., ser. iv, vol. ii, p. 496 (April 16, 1863).

modified form of whipping was drumming out of the army, which was performed by allowing the deserter to run and every soldier who could catch him to hit him a lick, but after the conscription law, drumming out of the army meant drumming around camp or to the guard house.[130]   Bucking, thrusting the point of a bayonet wrapped in sacking into the mouth of a man whose arms were pinioned, and branding the letter " D " on some part of the body were punishments rarely used because commanding generals usually disapproved them.[131]   A substitute for branding, pricking with indelible ink the letter " D " in the cuticle on one hip, was used in both of the great armies.[132]   Confinement in stocks and pillory, punishments which had survived from colonial days in disciplining slaves in Georgia, was used a good deal in the Army of Tennessee during winter quarters at Dalton.[133]   Riding a wooden horse, a structure 6 to 12 feet high, a similar punishment, was used in both armies.[134] Two punishments which caused fatigue, walking a ring carrying a weight, and standing on the head of a barrel or on a block of wood marking time or holding a weight still, were used frequently.[135]   Confinement in a guard-house on bread

[130] S. C. Kelly to his wife, June 8, 1862; *G. O.* no. 98, 1862; *G. O.* no. 62, 1863, Dept. and Army of Nor. Va.

[131] *Confederate Veteran*, vol. x, p. 67, B. L. Ridley, " Camp Scenes around Dalton "; *G. O.* no. 7, 1862; nos. 22, 62, 7, 1863, Dept. and Army of Nor. Va.; *G. O.* no. 6, 1864, Hdqrs. of A. of Tenn.

[132] *G. O.* no. 32, 1864, Hdqrs. of A. of Tenn.; *G. O.* no. 98, 1862, Dept. and Army of Nor. Va.

[133] *Confederate Veteran*, vol. ii, p. 235, H. J. Cheney, " Penalties for Desertion " (The writer considered this punishment " more aggravating than shooting " and said it was the only act of General Johnston which was not thoroughly approved by his soldiers.)   *G. O.* no. 9, nos. 12, 16, 1864, Hdqrs. of A. of Tenn.

[134] *G. O.* no. 16, 1864, Dept. and Army of Nor. Va.; *G. O.* no. 83, 1863, Hdqrs. of A. of T.

[135] *G. O.* no. 7, 1863; no. 11, 1864, Dept. and Army of Nor. Va.

and water for a short time was used all during the war, but was said to be harder on the guards than on the deserters.[130] Confinement in a state penitentiary for a period as long as five years was authorized by act of Congress in 1863 but was usually limited by courts to a shorter period.[137] Hard labor in the penitentiary or in camp usually on fortifications was used during the latter part of the war.[138] Attaching a ball and chain to one leg of the deserter while he was working on fortifications or confined to camp was the common method of dispensing with guards.[139] Forfeiture of furlough and forfeiture of pay were prescribed as punishments for deserters although soldiers who did not desert rarely got pay or furloughs.[140] Common punishments which were designed to make deserters appear conspicuous or ludicrous were having half or all of the head shaved, wearing a barrel shirt, and wearing a placard with descriptive label such as " Deserter," " Straggled from a fight," "Double-quicked to the rear," "Cavalry."[141] By general orders, a special punishment for cavalrymen convicted of desertion was transfer to the infantry.[142] Punishments of

[136] G. O. no. 57, 1863, Dept. and Army of Nor. Va.; G. O. no. 32, 1864, Hdqrs. of A. of Tenn.; Mobile *Register*, January 26, 1864.

[137] General Lee thought that the maximum number of years, 5, allowed by the law should always be imposed by courts-martial, but Judge Campbell did not accept his interpretation.—G. O. no. 71, 1863, Dept. and Army of Nor. Va.; *Endorsements, Courts-martial*, pp. 10-11, December 19, 1864; O. R., ser. iv, vol. ii, p. 496.

[138] G. O. no. 3, 1864, Dept. and Army of Nor. Va.; G. O. no. 119, 1863, Hdqrs. of Army of Tenn.

[139] G. O. no. 87, 1862, Dept. and Army of Nor. Va.; G. O. no. 71, 1863, Hdqrs. of Army of Tenn.

[140] G. O. no. 55, 1863, Dept. and Army of Nor. Va.; G. O. no. 7, 1864, Hdqrs. of Army of Tenn.

[141] G. O. no. 22, 1863; no. 63, 1864, Dept. and Army of Nor. Va.; G. O. no. 6, 1864, Hdqrs. of Army of Tenn.

[142] *Public Statutes of the Confederate States of America*, 2nd Cong., 1st Sess., p. 260, January 7, 1864; O. R., ser. i, vol. xlv, pt. ii, pp. 658-659.

officers were public reprimand, suspension from rank and pay, and dismissal from the service of the Confederate States (to be conscripted into it).[143] Milder punishments did not excuse deserters from drills and fights.[144] The typical punishment was a combination of three or more of these forms, for example:

———— ———— Co. H, 33rd Alabama. Charge: Desertion. . . . Sentence: To have one-half of his head shaved, to have the letter *D* marked with indelible ink on the left hip, to be marched before the regiment with the word *Deserter* on a placard placed upon some conspicuous part of his body and to be placed in a pillory for 4 hours a day for 60 days.[145]

———— ———— Co. D, 44th Alabama. Charge: Desertion. . . . Sentence: To forfeit 2 months' pay, to walk a ring 50 ft. in diameter every alternate hour from reveille to retreat for 30 successive days, carrying a weight of 50 lbs., and to be confined to regimental quarters during the intervals.[146]

Sentences regularly provided that so much of the punishment as practicable should be administered in view of the regiment.

The number of Alabama soldiers tried for desertion in the Army of Tennessee from 1862 to 1865 was greater than the number tried for desertion in the Army of Northern Virginia during the same period. The number of Alabama soldiers convicted of desertion in the Army of Tennessee was less than half of the number tried for desertion; the number convicted of desertion in the Army of Northern Virginia was a little over half of the number tried for de-

[143] *G. O.* no. 66, 1863, Dept. and Army of Nor. Va.; *G. O.* no. 6, 1864, Hdqrs. of A. of Tenn.

[144] *G. O.* no. 57, 1863, Dept. and Army of Nor. Va.

[145] *G. O.* no. 27, 1864, Hdqrs. of Army of Tenn.

[146] *G. O.* no. 7, 1863, Dept. and Army of Nor. Va.

sertion. The periods of greatest strictness of the courts in trials for desertion were August and December, 1862; January, February and April, 1864; and January, February and March, 1865.[147]

On the whole, the courts-martial of the Army of Tennessee and the Army of Northern Virginia showed great leniency to deserters both in punishments and in acquittals. In the sentences they passed they frequently stated that leniency was due to a certain cause, like the youth of the accused, his good character, his previous good conduct, his falling under the influence of evil-minded persons, or most often to " mitigating circumstances developed at the trial." [148] The generals of the two great armies frequently protested that the punishments awarded by courts-martial were inadequate to the crime of desertion. General Bragg pronounced some of the sentences " a burlesque upon justice," " a farce " calculated to bring all discipline into contempt.[149] General Lee protested that the paltry punishments frequently awarded by courts-martial were an encouragement to the infamous crime of desertion and would prove subversive of all efficiency in the army.[150]

[147] G. O., 1862-1865, Dept. and Army of Nor. Va., passim; G. O., 1862-1865, Hdqrs. of Army of Tennessee, passim. See also O. R., ser. iv, vol. ii, p. 7, and Freeman, Lee's Dispatches, no. 84, pp. 154-158.

[148] For example, see G. O. no. 62 and no. 68, 1863, Dept. and Army of Nor. Va.; G. O. no. 75 and no. 94, 1863, Hdqrs. of Army of Tenn. For a statement that leniency was due to the fact that discipline in a certain Alabama Regiment was "criminally lax," see G. O. no. 26, 1863, Dept. and Army of Nor. Va.

[149] G. O. nos. 50, 63, 1863, Hdqrs. of Army of Tenn.

[150] G. O. nos. 6, 8, 33, 41, 48, 101, 1863, Dept. and Army of Nor. Va. Gen. Lee stated that good soldiers were dissatisfied at the impunity of deserters.—O. R., ser. i, vol. xxix, pp. 649-650. General Beauregard protested that " the trifling sentences awarded by this court . . . (are) a precedent ruinous to discipline."—G. O. no. 44, 1863, Dept. of S. C., Ga. and Fla. The sentences awarded by Gen. Johnston's courts-martial were somewhat more severe.

Moreover, sentences of courts-martial might be lightened or altogether lifted. In minor cases, remission of all or part of the penalty could be made by the reviewing officer, the general who called the court-martial; in case of sentence of death, appeal for reprieve or pardon could be made by the reviewing officer or other persons in petition through the Secretary of War to the President. The usual grounds for remission of sentences by the reviewing officer or pardon by the President were unanimous recommendation by the court, extreme youth or imbecility of the deserter, " mitigating circumstances " inducing desertion or voluntary return of the deserter, previous good conduct of the private himself or meritorious conduct of some member of his family.[151] Since these grounds were common, remission and pardon were common, and thus increased leniency in treatment of deserters. Errors in procedure sometimes made a travesty of justice; for example, one deserter who had been con- demned to be shot was released because the presiding officer of the court failed to sign the proceedings.[152] It was said that President Davis was very skillful in finding technical errors in procedure, and that if he could not find an error, he pardoned the deserter anyhow.[153] It is true that General Longstreet made a vigorous protest against the frequent

[151] *Rules and Articles of War,* art. 65; *Special Orders* no. 61, 1863, A. and I. G. O.; *General Orders* nos. 52, 140, 1863, A. and I. G. O.; Freeman, *Lee's Dispatches,* no. 82, pp. 149-154; *G. O.* no. 97, 1862, Dept. and Army of Nor. Va.; *G. O.* nos. 16, 19, 1863, Dept. and Army of Nor. Va.; *G. O.* nos. 5, 16, 1864, Dept. and Army of Nor. Va.; *G. O.* no. 19, 1862, Hdqrs. of A. of Tenn.; *G. O.* no. 33, 1864, Hdqrs. of A. of Tenn.

[152] *G. O.* no. 90, 1863, Dept. and Army of Nor. Va. For similar cases, see: *G. O.* no. 98, 1862, Dept. and Army of Nor. Va.; *G. O.* no. 112, 1863, Hdqrs. of Army of Tenn.

[153] Reagan, *Memoirs,* pp. 164-165. For authority of the President to pardon, see *Statutes at Large of the Confederate States,* vol. ii, pp. 61-62. President Davis's *Endorsements* on sentences of courts-martial seem not to justify the charge of extreme leniency.

pardons to deserters which was endorsed by General Lee and submitted to the War Department, but the protest was endorsed by President Davis with these words: " When deserters are arrested they should be tried, and if the sentences are reviewed and remitted that is not a proper subject for the criticism of a military commander." [154]   It is also true that on April 13, 1864 General Lee wrote to President Davis that failure of courts-martial to convict deserters and " indulgence of your Excellency " had relaxed discipline and increased desertions.[155]

Three proposals toward solving the problem of desertion were not tried. Of these the most persistent and frequent was recruiting new organizations from deserters. This policy was advocated by men who held prominent positions and who were acquainted with conditions in the state, including General Pillow, General Morgan, General Roddey and Judge Arrington, and was endorsed in 1863 by so high an authority as Judge Campbell. The expediency of recruiting new organizations from deserters was urged upon the grounds that the practice existed and, if legalized, could be regulated and that it was the only way to return deserters within the country occupied by the enemy and deserters in other parts of the state who had too much pride to re-enter their old commands. But the proposal was consistently opposed by General Lee, General Johnston and President Davis. They acknowledged that recruiting new organizations from deserters might have a temporary beneficial effect in certain localities but insisted that it would have a dis-

---

[154] *O. R.*, ser. i, vol. xlii, pt. iii, p. 1213. See also: *O. R.*, ser. i, vol. li, pt. ii, pp. 781-782; Pollard, *Lost Cause*, p. 652. Senator Phelan of Mississippi charged that the courts and pardoning authorities showed favoritism to absentees and deserters who had social or political influence. —*O. R.*, ser. iv, vol. iii, p. 709.

[155] Freeman, *Lee's Dispatches*, no. 84, pp. 154-158.

astrous effect upon the army as a whole, tempting soldiers to desert.[156] It would have been amnesty plus reward. A proposal, made in February, 1865 by General Preston, Superintendent of the Bureau of Conscription, was concurrent legislation by the states declaring desertion a crime to be proceeded against in special state courts, but the difficulty of securing such legislation and the ineffectiveness of civil courts in trials for desertion were objections to this method. A proposal, made at the same time by General Lee, was the imposition of civil disabilities upon deserters, but General Preston pointed out that in the states where this method had been tried, it had had not the slightest effect upon desertion.[157] Various proposals were made for improving the organization and methods already in use, but none of them seemed practicable. The press called for discipline in the army and infliction of the death penalty upon offenders; civil authorities, for disapproval of desertion by public opinion; and conscription authorities, for more military force.[158]

[156] *O. R.*, ser. iv, vol. iii, pp. 964-965; vol. ii, p. 636; ser. i, vol. xxxix, pt. ii, pp. 698-699; vol. lii, pt. i, p. 73; vol. xlix, pt. ii, p. 1134; ser. iv, vol. iii, pp. 1042-1043; vol. ii, p. 674; ser. i, vol. ii, pp. 669-670; vol. xxix, pt. ii, pp. 844-845; vol. li, pt. ii, pp. 669-670; vol. xxxii, pt. iii, pp. 644-646; ser. iv, vol. iii, p. 294; vol. iii, pp. 1177-1178; *Letter Book of the Commandant of Conscripts*, pp. 367, 371, 292, 217-218. The proposal to grant amnesty to deserters and to allow them to volunteer in new organizations of the same branch was a slight modification of the proposal to recruit them in new organizations.—*Journal of Congress of C. S. A.*, vol. vii, p. 783. A correspondent of the Mobile *Register* suggested confiscation of the property of deserters as suitable punishment.—Mobile *Register*, January 22, 1864.

[157] *O. R.*, ser. iv, vol. iii, pp. 1119-1123.

[158] *The Alabama Beacon*, January 22, 1864; Montgomery *Daily Advertiser*, October 3, 1864; Richmond *Examiner*, February 13, August 7, August 13, 1863; March 10, 1865; Mobile *Register*, January 9, January 26, May 3, 1864; *The Independent*, August 15, 1863. "The consequence (of light punishment) has been that the South has not yet had any real army

It was generally recognized that the system for effecting the return of deserters was a failure.[159] The organization was inadequate. The supporting forces of the Bureau of Conscription and the militia were not a match in fighting material nor in number for the deserters. Composed of men who were unfit for active military service, poorly armed, and indifferent to the performance of duty, they were inferior to deserters, who were trained in military service, well armed, and fighting for their lives. Usually, they were far inferior in number to deserters. The failure of the state legislature to provide militia seemed to be criminal negligence but the unwillingness of men to do state service, the regular absorption of state troops by Confederate levies, and the scarcity of men discouraged efforts to organize militia. The most successful force used against deserters was detachments from the army, like those under General Pillow and General Polk. However, since the Confederate army was usually largely outnumbered by the Federal army, detachments could not be spared often enough to get the better of deserters. These detachments were like a thumb occasionally applied to the hole where the leak was. Moreover, the methods were inconsistent. Occasional severity punctuated leniency. The threats of severity made by Confederate authorities must have sounded to deserters like the cry of " Wolf, wolf !" And appeals to return were unheard or unheeded.[160] The chances of escape were too good

at all, but only some voluntary associations kept together by the spirit of the few and the coaxing of the many."—Richmond *Examiner*, September 11, 1863.

[159] For an acknowledgement by officers of the Bureau of Conscription, see *O. R.*, ser. iv, vol. ii, pp. 722-723.

[160] An incident which happened in the Twenty-sixth Alabama Regiment May 15, 1863 illustrates the ineffectiveness of persuasion. On that day while officers were presenting to the regiment, which had been called together by the long roll, arguments and entreaties against desertion,

not to be taken. Deserters could count upon the protection of public opinion at home. Public opinion made the legislation on harboring deserters a dead letter. For example, in the southern part of Barbour county in the winter of 1864-65 a dinner was given in honor of fifty-seven deserters who had recently come to that neighborhood and the constable declined to execute the subpœnas issued to the hosts.[161] Public opinion, said the Superintendent of the Bureau of Conscription in 1865, attached no stigma of disgrace to desertion and shielded 100,000 criminals from justice.[162] If public opinion should fail as a protection, deserters could count upon the weakness of the means of arrest. With their organizations, they could defy such forces as were usually sent against them. If they wished to return to the army, they could count upon amnesty proclamations, one of which was issued every few months, or upon the regular policy of military authorities of imposing mild penalties upon deserters who voluntarily returned. But if the worst should come to the worst, deserters might count upon the general leniency of military courts, founded upon "mitigating circumstances," which, in the words of General Lee, "deserters know so well how to invent and which in fact do often exist."[163] Effecting the return of deserters was a problem which Confederate authorities never solved.

four members of the regiment deserted.—Selma *Reporter*, July 4, 1864, letter from an officer.

[161] D. M. Seales to Governor Watts, January 5, 1865.

[162] *O. R.*, ser. iv, vol. iii, pp. 1119, 1112. See also *O. R.*, ser. i, vol. xlvi, vol. ii, p. 1254.

[163] *O. R.*, ser. iv, vol. iii, p. 1121.

CHAPTER VII

DESERTION TO THE ENEMY

CONFEDERATE soldiers who took, or applied to take, the oath of allegiance or of amnesty, prescribed by the Federal government were deserters. They bound themselves under the oath of allegiance to protect, support and defend the constitution and government of the United States against domestic and foreign enemies, to be loyal to them and to perform all duties required by their laws, or under the oath of amnesty, prescribed by President Lincoln, December 8, 1863, to protect, support and defend the constitution of the United States and the union under it and to abide by all acts of Congress and proclamations of the President relating to slavery.[1] They were divided into two classes,—rebel soldiers who, after they had been captured as prisoners of war, took the oath, and rebel soldiers who gave themselves up to the enemy. The latter class was larger. Each of these classes was divided into two classes,—those who wished to enter the service of the United States and those who wished to be released. The latter class was larger.[2] Some rebel soldiers took the oath of allegiance or of amnesty under pressure of persuasion by Federal authorities or of hardships

---

[1] *Prison Roll* no. 611, Louisville, Ky., November, 1863; *O. R.,* ser. ii, vol. vi, pp. 680-682.

[2] *Register of Confederate Deserters,* vol. i and vol. ii, *passim; Rolls* and *Registers of Federal Prisons,* especially Camp Chase, Camp Douglas, Chattanooga, Elmira, Knoxville, Louisville, Rock Island, Army of the Potomac and Nashville, *passim.* Fourteen of the forty-eight Federal prisons contained few or no prisoners from Alabama. As it is not always easy or even possible to tell whether the soldiers named on rolls and in registers came into prison by capture or by surrender, the definite number in each class cannot be given.

of imprisonment.³ Consequently, they did not consider the oath morally binding and broke it as soon as circumstances allowed.⁴ Doubtless some deserters who broke their oath were quite free from moral scruples. General Grant said that many rebel soldiers took the oath and enlisted in United States service only to get the bounty and desert at the first opportunity and the judge advocate-general of the United States directed the military courts to deal severely with those rebel deserters captured in arms with amnesty oaths in their pockets.⁵ Federal authorities refused to allow many of the rebel applicants to take the oath.⁶ Prisoners of war who took the oath with a mental reservation may not have been actuated by the motive of desertion, but it is not possible to make a distinction between them and the soldiers who took the oath in good faith.

³ Joe Barbiere, *Scraps from the Prison Table at Camp Chase and Johnson's Island* (Doylestown, 1868), p. 253; E. Y. McMorries, *History of the First Regiment of Alabama Volunteer Infantry* (Montgomery, 1904), pp. 46, 67; *General Orders* no. 50, 1863, Hdqrs. of Army of Tenn.; W. G. Delony to Governor Shorter, January 10, 1863. For an extreme case, see M. B. Toney, *Privations of a Private* (Dallas, 1907), p. 118. In June, 1865, certain prisoners at Elmira, New York, were threatened with deportation to the Dry Tortugas where they would die of yellow fever.

⁴ One of the leading ministers of the South, Dr. B. M. Palmer, said, in discussing the oath taken by citizens, that no faith was to be placed upon an oath exacted under compulsion and accordingly it might be taken with a mental reservation to break it as soon as opportunity should be afforded of doing it with safety.—B. M. Palmer, *The Oath of Allegiance to the United States Discussed in Its Moral and Political Bearings* (Richmond, 1863), published by the Soldiers' Tract Association of the M. E. Church South, 22 pages. The Commissary-General of Prisoners of the United States said that many deserters were willing to represent themselves as anything and swear to anything in order to secure their release. —*O. R.*, ser. ii, vol. vi, p. 943.

⁵ *O. R.*, ser. ii, vol. vi, ɪp. 614, vol. vii, ɪpp. 144-148. See also *O. R.*, ser. ii, vol. vii, p. 155.

⁶ *Prison Rolls, passim.*

The distribution of Alabama soldiers who deserted to the enemy may be studied by number, by time, and by residence. Over 800 Alabama soldiers enlisted in the six infantry regiments of the United States Volunteers, which with the exception of two companies of the Fifth Regiment were organized before General Lee's surrender;[7] over 150 joined the United States navy before April 9, 1865;[8] and at least 2,800 took the oath or applied to take it before that date.[9]   The total

[7] Card index of United States Volunteers, giving name, former Confederate command, and place of enlistment in the United States Army; *Official Army Register of the Volunteer Force of the United States Army* (Washington, 1867), pp. 135-139; *O. R.,* ser. i, vol. xlviii, pt. ii, p. 77.

[8] *Exit Roll,* Transferred to the United States Navy, January 25, 1864, Rock Island, Ill.

[9] This number was obtained by counting the names of Alabama soldiers listed in the *Register of Confederate Deserters* and listed on prison rolls and registers.   Nearly half of the number are listed in the two volumes of the *Register of Confederate Deserters* together with place and date of release.   The others are listed in several hundred rolls and registers of Federal prisons and prison camps.   In view of the overlapping periods of time represented and of the several places and the varied requests involved, care was taken to eliminate duplicate names on rolls and registers, but as the process of counting and checking was tedious and liable to error, the smallest round number has been given.   In case of one register of the Army of the Potomac, an estimate involving about fifty deserters was made by using the percentage which Alabama deserters formed of the whole number of Confederate deserters listed in the other registers of the Army of the Potomac (with the same percentage of duplicates).   With some exceptions, including those of the Army of the Potomac, the rolls and registers form complete records of the disposition of prisoners.   As a whole, they form, in the personal opinion of Mr. Winfred Beck, Supervisor of Confederate Records, Office of the Adjutant-General, Washington, records which are about 95% complete. Accordingly, the number of Alabama deserters which was obtained by the count was increased by 5%.   The deserters who enlisted as volunteers in the regular army organizations were not included in the total number of Alabama deserters to the Union.   Compare these numbers with the number of deserters from Alabama reported in *House Executive Document,* 39th Cong., 1st Sess., no. 1, vol. iv, pt. i, p. 141, 5 officers and 1,578 men.—Lonn, *Desertion during the Civil War,* p. 231.

number of Alabama soldiers who deserted to the enemy was between 3,600 and 4,000. The periods of desertion to the enemy were the same as those of desertion home. The peaks of desertion to the enemy were: (1) February and March, 1862; (2) October, 1863-February, 1864; and (3) July, 1864-April, 1865. A high peak, comparatively and absolutely, was reached in March, 1862. During the last period, desertions averaged over 100 each month and steadily increased, mounting to the greatest height reached during the war in March and April, 1865.[10] An incident which throws light on the large number of deserters during this period was a successful assault made on Grant's lines at Petersburg in March, 1865 by Confederate troops under General Gordon under the pretense that they were deserters to the enemy.[11] Among the deserters of this period there were some old men and young boys who had been recently enlisted but there were many veteran soldiers who had served three years.[12] Distribution by residence of deserters who went to the enemy is shown on Map E. The chief differences between the distribution by residence of deserters who went to the enemy and of deserters who went to their homes were (1) the large number of deserters to the enemy from Mobile

---

[10] From the same records, a chart was made of the number of desertions which occurred each month but it is not complete because some rolls are missing, some are undated, and some bear the date of the officer's report instead of the date of the deserter's application or release. However, the chart corresponds exactly to references to desertion in the writings of contemporaries. See: *O. R.*, ser. i, vol. xxxii, pt. iii, p. 287; vol. xl, pt. iii, p. 529; vol. xlii, pt. iii, p. 1249; Grant, *Memoirs*, vol. i, p. 561; Grant, *Letters to a Friend*, p. 38; New York *Times*, August 14, November 27, 1864; January 6, January 22, March 5, 1865; *O. R.*, ser. i, vol. xlv, p. 47. For examples of reports of Union officers of desertion from the Confederate army, see *O. R.*, ser. i, vol. xlii, pt. iii, pp. 680, 687, 696, 700, 726, 807, 820, 833, 868, 883.

[11] Grant, *Memoirs*, vol. ii, pp. 431-432.

[12] New York *Times*, March 6, 1865; *O. R.*, ser. ii, vol. vi, pp. 614-615.

county, (2) the small number from the southeastern counties, and (3) the large number in the Tennessee valley counties, especially the four counties north of the river. The number of deserters to the enemy shaded gradually from the heaviest concentration in the Tennessee valley counties through the hill counties into south Alabama and included soldiers from every county in the state.[13]

The treatment of rebel deserters by Union authorities was based upon the principle that desertion from the enemy should be encouraged. From 1862 to the fall of 1863, a policy was followed by which desertion was encouraged passively; from that time to the end of the war a policy was followed by which desertion was encouraged actively. The first policy, which was clearly defined by December, 1863, was that of paroling or imprisoning deserters at the discretion of the officer commanding the department in which they were found. A deserter who reported to the headquarters of the department or to some more convenient place, was held in confinement and, as soon as practicable, examined by officers to ascertain his character and his motives in giving himself up. If he appeared to be a bona-fide deserter he was released upon conditions which varied slightly among departments but which were generally the same. He sur-

---

[13] *Register of Confederate Deserters*, vols. i-ii, *passim*; *Prison Rolls, Prison Registers, passim*. In cases where command instead of residence was recorded (e. g., the card index of the United States Volunteers), the deserter was assigned to the county from which his command had been recruited. In some cases, it was not possible to determine residence. In a few cases, it is probable that deserters made false statements about their residence. It is difficult to account for the small number of deserters from Marion county. It is probable that conscripts of that county were unusually successful in evading service because of the large tory element at home. It is also difficult to account for the large number of deserters from Montgomery county. It is probable that the foreign element from the city of Montgomery increased the number as it did in Mobile. The number from Macon and Perry was surprisingly large.

DESERTERS TO THE ENEMY....▨

(The 19 counties marked ▨ furnished the
largest number of deserters to the enemy in
comparison with their white populations and
with the exception of Morgan and Winston the
highest number absolutely The counties marked x
furnished the next highest number absolutely.)

rendered his arms and was forbidden to possess others; he took the oath of allegiance and gave parole; and, as security, he made bond to an amount fixed by the commanding officer. Then he was allowed to go wherever he pleased and to follow whatever occupation he could. The penalty for violation of oath or parole was death. If, upon examination, the deserter appeared to be a spy or other suspicious character, he was confined in a military prison, preferably Camp Chase, and was considered a political prisoner, not a prisoner of war.[14] This policy was not entirely satisfactory. After release, many of the deserters who lived in Confederate states or who lived in Kentucky and other northern states—the majority of early deserters—did not go to their homes because of danger or because of lack of money or inclination. Without occupation, they were drawn into bushwhacking in the states where they had been released. Citizens of Kentucky petitioned the military authorities not to release more deserters, calling them a curse to the state.[15]

The increase of deserters from the rebel army after Gettysburg and Vicksburg caused a change in policy. The chief feature of the new policy was making provisions for the disposition of deserters after their release. The immediate object was to relieve citizens from the menace of idle deserters and the army from the danger of spies;[16] the ultimate object was to offer such inducements to deserters that the army of the enemy would be weakened as much by desertion as by military operations.

In the summer of 1863 Confederate deserters were

[14] O. R., ser. ii, vol. iv, pp. 150, 286, 745-746; vol. v, pp. 19, 21-23, 27-29, 32, 34-36, 51-52; ser. i, vol. xxii, pt. ii, pp. 122-123; ser. ii, vol. v, pp. 85-86, 101, 160, 173, 176, 263, 299-300, 361, 390-391, 593, 465, 533, 554; ser. i, vol. xxiii, pt. ii, pp. 184, 328; ser. ii, vol. vi, pp. 91, 227-228, 319-320.

[15] O. R., ser. ii, vol. vi, pp. 197-198. Larger prison space was needed.

[16] O. R., ser. i, vol. xxxix, pt. ii, p. 161.

admitted to the military service of the United States both by volunteering and by draft. It seemed only fair that they should be under the same obligations to defend their country as other loyal citizens. In response to applications from deserters, permission was given to military officers in August, 1863 to receive them as volunteers and in response to requests from such volunteers, discretionary authority was given to General Grant in December, 1864 to transfer them to lines where they did not face their former friends.[17] Under the draft of June, 1863, deserters were enumerated but since they were liable to execution if captured by the Confederate army, they were assigned to supply service behind the lines or were enlisted in military service against the Indians in the Department of the Northwest.[18]

After deserters were exempted from draft in December, 1863, the practice of recruiting them as volunteers in United States service was begun and liberal bounties were offered to those who would enter for the war.[19] Six regiments of infantry, called The United States Volunteers, were recruited from deserters from the Confederate army. The First Regiment was organized from January to April, 1864; the Second, Third and Fourth, in October, 1864; the Fifth from March 22 to May 2, 1865; and the Sixth, April 2, 1865.[20] Since these volunteers would be liable to execution as deserters if captured by the Confederate army, they were all placed in military service against the Indians in the

[17] *O. R.*, ser. ii, vol. vi, p. 228; ser. i, vol. xxx, pt. iii, p. 529; vol. xlii, pt. iii, pp. 842, 863.

[18] *O. R.*, ser. iii, vol. iii, pp. 353, 791.

[19] *O. R.*, ser. i, vol. xl, pt. iii, p. 783; vol. xxxi, p. 396; vol. xlii, pt. iii, p. 842; Address to Loyal Alabamians, February 1, 1864, by command of Major-General Logan.

[20] *Official Army Register of the Volunteer Force of the United States Army*, pp. 135-139.

Department of the Northwest.[21] Of these, the First Regiment rendered the longest and most satisfactory service. However, it was necessary to subject it to special treatment, which was used as a model for the other regiments. After its arrival in the Northwest in August, 1864 the companies were divided among four forts in Minnesota Territory and Dakota Territory and were stationed with other troops because they could not be trusted in large numbers alone. They were placed under regular army officers, who were instructed to use stringent discipline.[22] The reports of these officers indicated difficulties. For example, the First Regiment of Volunteers could be managed only with a strong hand because it contained many desperate characters who were given to open boasting of their secession proclivities; the members should not be mounted because horses would be an inducement to desertion, the tendency to which seemed to be incurable in rebel deserters; and they committed such depredations on the naked frontier as to cause wonder about what they would do in an inhabited portion of the world.[23] But after a winter of special treatment during which they suffered from cold and scurvy and were thinned by death, the First Regiment of the United States Volunteers was reported to be well disciplined.[24] The Second Regiment was sent to the Northwest in March, 1864, and divided among four forts on the frontier of Kansas. After the war, they were stationed

[21] *O. R.*, ser. i, vol. xli, pt. ii, p. 619.

[22] *O. R.*, ser. i, vol. xli, pt. ii, p. 737; pt. iv, pp. 261, 397, 398; vol. xlviii, pt. ii, pp. 262-263. The First Regiment was sent in August on an expedition into North Carolina for the purpose of capturing contraband and later on the way to the Northwest was detained to aid in enforcement of the draft in Wisconsin.—*O. R.*, ser. i, vol. xl, pt. i, p. 820; vol. xli, pt. iii, p. 73.

[23] *O. R.*, ser. i, vol. xli, pt. iv, p. 261; pt. iii, p. 598; pt. iv, p. 292. See also *O. R.*, ser. i, vol. xli, pt. iv, p. 337.

[24] *O. R.*, ser. i, vol. xlviii, pt. ii, pp. 1228, 1109.

along the Santa Fé road to protect travelers. The Fifth Regiment was sent to Kansas in May, 1865 and was stationed with the Second Regiment along the Santa Fé road.[25] The Third Regiment, which reached the Northwest also in March, was divided among forts in Nebraska Territory and Colorado Territory and after the war, was stationed at eight points along the Overland stage line.[26] The Fourth Regiment was small and was composed chiefly of boys. They deserted in large number on the way out to Dakota Territory and continued to desert after their arrival.[27] In August, 1865, the Sixth Regiment was stationed at points along the Powder river.[28] In the summer of 1865, the six regiments of United States Volunteers were scattered along overland roads and at remote forts in the Indian country from Kansas to the Rocky mountains, from the Cimarron crossing of the Arkansas river to Ft. Rice, North Dakota. At that time according to a report made to General Grant by General Pope, commanding officer of the Department of the Northwest, they were discontented, mutinous, and rapidly deserting.[29]

Concurrent with the practice of recruiting deserters in the Federal army, the practice of offering deserters exemption from military service and other privileges was followed for the purpose of encouraging desertion. In December, 1863, orders by General Grant and in February, 1864, orders by the War Department were issued stating that rebel deserters were not subject to draft.[30] In August, 1864 orders by the

[25] *O. R.,* ser. i, vol. xlviii, pt. i, p. 131; pt. iv, pp. 1205-1206, 1212; pt. ii, pp. 454, 1044.

[26] *O. R.,* ser. i, vol. xlviii, pt. ii, pp. 274-276, 709.

[27] *O. R.,* ser. i, vol. xlviii, pt. ii, pp. 647, 766.

[28] *O. R.,* ser. i, vol. xlviii, pt. iv, p. 354.

[29] *O. R.,* ser. i, vol. xlviii, pt. ii, pp. 751, 1239. See also *O. R.,* ser. i, vol. xlviii, pt. i, p. 353.

[30] *O. R.,* ser. i, vol. xxxi, p. 396; vol. xl, pt. iii, p. 783.

War Department were issued stating that they were not subject to draft nor acceptable as substitutes or recruits.[31] As it was said that Confederate authorities cultivated the belief that all deserters would be drafted into the Federal army and that most Confederate deserters objected to further military service, these orders were issued over and over during 1864.[32]   Other privileges were offered by President Lincoln's amnesty proclamation of December, 1863, by General Orders no. 64, February, 1864, from the War Department and by Special Orders no. 82, August, 1864, and no. 44, March, 1865, by General Grant.   By President Lincoln's proclamation, pardon with restoration of property rights except in cases of slaves and in cases involving a third party was offered to those who had participated in the rebellion (with few exceptions) who would take the oath of amnesty.[33]   The procedure in disposing of deserters who offered to take the oath of amnesty was the same as that in case of deserters who offered to take the oath of allegiance.[34] By general orders from the War Department, employment for regular wages in government workshops and permission to go to their homes if within Federal lines or to some point in the North were offered to deserters from the Confederate

[31] *O. R.,* ser. iii, vol. iv, p. 648.

[32] *O. R.,* ser. i, vol. xlvi, pt. ii, p. 587; ser. iii, vol. iv, pp. 90-91; New York *Times,* November 22, 1864; *O. R.,* ser. i, vol. xxxv, pt. ii, pp. 38-39; ser. iii, vol. iv, pp. 53, 419-420; ser. i, vol. xlii, pt. ii, pp. 555-556; vol. xli, pt. iv, pp. 128; vol. xlvi, pt. ii, pp. 829, 31; pt. iii, p. 396.

[33] *O. R.,* ser. ii, vol. vi, pp. 680-681.   The press in Alabama considered the proclamation an invitation to slaves to revolt.

[34] *O. R.,* ser. ii, vol. vii, p. 131; ser. i, vol. xxxi, pt. iii, p. 396; ser. iii, vol. iv, p. 118; ser. i, vol. xlix, pt. i, p. 721.   Abuses by deserters caused somewhat stricter regulations to be made later.   See: *O. R.,* ser. i, vol. xlv, pt. ii, pp. 506-507; ser. ii, vol. vii, p. 1158; vol. vi, pp. 225-227.   The deserter was given a copy of the oath.—Lonn, *Desertion during the Civil War,* p. 95.

army.[35] By special orders of General Grant in 1864, subsistence and transportation to their homes if within Federal lines or to some point in the North and employment at regular wages in the quartermaster's or some similar department were offered to deserters.[36] By special orders in March, 1865, purchase at the highest current prices of arms, horses or other property which deserters should bring was promised. These offers were extended to deserters not only from military service but from any civilian employment in connection with the Confederate army.[37] To bring these offers to the attention of Confederate soldiers, the proclamation and the orders were printed in the form of hand bills in large quantities and were distributed by officers appointed for the purpose.[38] They were distributed on scout and cavalry expeditions and in other ways, including some ingenious devices like placing piles of them at springs of water and picket posts, wrapping them in newspapers, music or other papers passed in surreptitious exchange, and letting them down from elevated places near Confederate camps during a high wind.[39] They were also circulated by officials in prison camps.[40] In addition, they were explained by Federal soldiers whenever opportunities to fraternize with

[35] *O. R.*, ser. i, vol. xl, pt. iii, p. 783 (*G. O.* no. 64).

[36] *O. R.*, ser. i, vol. xlii, pt. ii, pp. 555-556 (*Sp. Or.* no. 82).

[37] *O. R.*, ser. i, vol. xlvi, pt. ii, pp. 828-829.

[38] *O. R.*, ser. iii, vol. iv, pp. 50-53, 703; ser. i, vol. xxxv, pt. ii, p. 80; vol. xxxiii, pp. 795-796.

[39] Mobile *Register*, April 3, 1864; Mrs. Pickett, *Pickett and His Men*, pp. 364-365; Stiles, *Four Years under Marse Robert*, pp 312-313; *Clarke County Journal*, November 24, 1864; *O. R.*, ser. i, vol. xlii, pt. ii, p. 1083; Lonn, *Desertion during the Civil War*, p. 99. Once during the siege of Petersburg, proclamations were let down into Confederate lines in the form of the tail of a kite.—Clayton *Banner*, August 2, 1864, quoting the Petersburg *Express*.

[40] *O. R.*, ser. ii, vol. viii, p. 1083.

Confederate soldiers were offered. For example, on one occasion in February, 1865 at the request of a group of Confederate pickets in the Army of Northern Virginia, a Federal soldier who was a Mason was appointed to go out to explain the privileges for deserters.[41]   Moreover, secret agents were sent into the South to cultivate disaffection and to encourage desertion.[42]

The most common way of reaching the Union lines was deserting at the front singly or in squads from picket duty or by eluding pickets.[43]   Deserters preferred rainy or foggy weather and dark nights, but during the last few weeks of the war sometimes went over in broad daylight.[44]   Another way of reaching Union lines was using the services of individuals or companies which did a regular business in piloting deserters, maintaining a kind of underground railroad and making liberal use of forged papers.[45]   This business was said to be lucrative as well as precarious.   A unique example was that of an embalming surgeon of Richmond who, being allowed under cover of his profession to pass with assistants back and forth into the Union lines, took deserters as his assistants and occasionally as corpses.[46]   Under

[41] *O. R.*, ser. i, vol. xlvi, pt. ii, p. 587.

[42] Lonn, *Desertion during the Civil War*, p. 100.

[43] New York *Times*, March 2, 1865; October 17, 1864 (by the correspondent from the Army of the Potomac); Mobile *Register*, December 1, 1863; *O. R.*, ser. ii, vol. viii, p. 441; vol. vi, p. 994; ser. i, vol. xlii, pt. iii, p. 1179. Sometimes whole picket posts deserted at the same time and sometimes pickets greeted each other unexpectedly at the headquarters of the Army of the Potomac.—New York *Times*, November 19, October 17, 1864.

[44] New York *Times*, March 9, March 11, February 26, 1865.

[45] Richmond *Examiner*, February 22, 1865; Montgomery *Daily Mail*, April 12, 1864; Mobile *Register*, January 14, 1864; December 20, 1863.

[46] Mobile *Register*, February 13, 1864, quoting the Richmond *Enquirer*; Mobile *Register*, February 20, 1864, quoting the Richmond *Sentinel*; Jones, *Diary*, vol. ii, p. 149. Occasionally a prisoner of war exchanged

the orders of the United States government offering transportation and employment, many deserters were sent to
Washington, Philadelphia, " north of the Ohio river " or to
their homes if under Federal occupation.[47]

Confederate authorities were alarmed by the Federal
policy to encourage desertion. They attempted to counteract
it by offering privileges to Federal deserters and to neutralize
it by suppressing information about proffered privileges.[48]
They insisted that the Confederate army had not suffered
as much from desertion as the Federal army.[49] They adopted
stricter regulations to stop fraternization with Union soldiers
and to improve picket duty, and punished with death the
deserters to the enemy and the pilots who were caught.[50]

places with a fellow prisoner, assuming his name, and was transferred to
a Northern prison where he applied for release under oath.—*Prison
Rolls, passim.*

[47] *Exit Rolls of Prisons, passim.* General Dix of New York requested
that no more of these prisoners be sent North until after the election
of 1864 as they were all in favor of a cessation of hostilities.—*O. R.,*
ser. ii, vol. vi, p. 989. A black list of prisoners of war who took the oath
was published by other prisoners of war at Cairo, Illinois, November
20, 1862.—Montgomery *Daily Mail,* November 20, 1862.

[48] *O. R.,* ser. i, vol. xl, pt. iii, pp. 781-783; vol. xlix, pt. i, p. 750;
ser. iv, vol. iii, pp. 591, 863; ser. i, vol. xlii, pt. ii, p. 1200.

[49] Appleton, *Annual Cyclopedia,* 1864, p. 218. The number of desertions from the Union army during 1864 was 28% of the enrollment and
during 1865, 45% of the enrollment.—E. N. Woodbury, *A Study of
Desertion,* chap. i, chart 1.

[50] *O. R.,* ser. i, vol. xlii, pt. iii, p. 1179; New York *Times,* March 2,
1865; Mrs. Pickett, *Pickett and His Men,* p. 365; *General Field Orders*
no. 8, June 25, 1864, by Hood; Selma *Reporter,* February 23, 1864;
Mobile *Register,* November 8, December 20, December 23, 1863; February 14, 1864. Men who took the oath of allegiance to the United States
were not exempted from conscription in the Confederate army.—*General
Orders from the Adjutant and Inspector-General's Office,* 1862, no. 62.
Deserters to the enemy were excluded from the benefits of amnesty
proclamations.—*O. R.,* ser. i, vol. xxx, pt. iv, p. 489; vol. xxxii, pt. iii,
pp. 785-786; vol. xlviii, pt. ii, pp. 1287-1288.

According to statements made by deserters to Union authorities, desertion from the Confederate army was very difficult.[51]

However, in spite of the efforts of Confederate authorities, the policy of the Federal authorities to encourage desertion was on the whole successful. It is true that false representations were made by many deserters to secure their release and that bushwhacking in Tennessee, Kentucky and north Alabama and other violations of oaths of amnesty were common,—conduct which was attributed by General Thomas chiefly to natural rebel depravity.[52] But in spite of abuses the main object was achieved, increase of desertion with the inevitable result of lessening the number and impairing the morale of the Confederate army.[53] There were several factors, of course, in the increase of desertion, but in the opinion of both General Grant and General Lee, the

[51] *Rolls of Prisons, passim.*

[52] *O. R.*, ser. ii, vol. vi, p. 943; ser. i, vol. xlix, pt. i, pp. 720-721; ser. ii, vol. vii, pp. 155, 144-145, 33, 865-869; *O. R.*, ser. i, vol. xxxii, pt. iii, pp. 287-288. General Thomas proposed in order "to remove these poor wretches from the temptations of secessionism" to send as many of them as possible to the wheat fields of the Northwest where they might be reformed at useful labor. He said April 7, 1864, "I believe many of them return to the enemy after recruiting their health and strength, because they are rebels by nature; others because of family influence and others like the drunkard to his bottle, because they have not sufficient moral firmness to resist the natural depravity of their hearts." The increased caution of Federal authorities which was made necessary by these abuses by deserters caused complaints from north Alabama that desertion was being discouraged.—*O. R.*, ser. i, vol. xlix, pt. i, pp. 720-721.

[53] In an indirect way, desertion helped to weaken the Confederate army. Deserters were encouraged to give any information which they could about conditions in the Confederacy. Although much of the information given by deserters was discounted as unreliable, some of it was doubtless valuable to Union authorities.—George H. Gordon, *A War Diary of Events in the War of the Great Rebellion* (New York, 1885), pp. 272-275; *O. R.*, ser. i, vol. xxxvi, pt. ii, p. 912; vol. xxxii, pt. iii, p. 795; Lonn, *Desertion during the Civil War*, pp. 101-105.

privileges offered by Union authorities were one of the important factors.[54]   It seems that Union authorities diagnosed the chief cause for the desertion of Confederate soldiers to their homes as economic need and offered a remedy in the form of service in the army for regular pay and bounties, purchase of equipment at the highest current prices and employment for good wages in non-military occupations.[55]

Various reasons for desertion were assigned by deserters to Union officials.   One of the reasons which was most frequently assigned was compulsory military service.   Many had been conscripted into the Confederate army, forced to serve against their will.   Some had tried to leave the Confederate States but had been prevented; others had hid in the woods for months until they had been captured or had given themselves up to save their families from getting into trouble.   Some had been brought into the army under guard.   Many had volunteered in order to avoid conscription.   By this action they had been able to choose their command or to escape arrest or to save themselves from disgrace.   Many had volunteered under the force of public opinion.   This public opinion was a " universal sentiment " which it was impossible to resist.[56]   It tolerated no difference and allowed no choice.   It was especially suspicious of Union men and foreigners.   Under it, all were compelled to conform through policy or through fear.   Those who did not volunteer were subjected to jeers and insults or to threats of confiscation of

[54] Grant, *Memoirs*, vol. ii, pp. 426-427; *O. R.*, ser. i, vol. xlii, pt. ii, pp. 1175-1176.

[55] A northern journalist was quoted by the Richmond *Examiner,* March 15, 1865, as saying that deserters were bringing over the whole Confederacy and selling it at a bargain. Pollard expressed the opinion that the Yankees encouraged desertion to an extent never known before.— *Southern History,* vol. ii, p. 432.

[56] *Prison Rolls, Johnson's Island,* September 15, December 31, 1864; *Ft. Warren,* July 13, July 16, 1864; *Elmira,* July, August 15, 1864.

property or of violence to themselves or their families. A few had been threatened with the alternative of hanging.[57] Under this force, some had entered the Confederate army with the intention of deserting as soon as possible. Many had volunteered under misapprehension. As they frequently said but did not explain, they had volunteered under " false representation." [58] They had been " over-persuaded " by prominent citizens or by their crowd. They had volunteered " under excitement " or the influence of liquor, had had " no time to think," and had not understood at the time what they were doing.[59] They had " enrolled for defense " only. They had expected a short war or no actual hostilities. To explain the fact that they had served in the Confederate army for months or years, some said they had deserted at the first opportunity, or that they had tried several times to desert, or that they had thought it not honorable to desert.[60]

Another reason which was frequently assigned was loyalty to the Union. Some had always thought the Union right, had always been Union men, had always been loyal. They had voted the Union ticket and opposed secession and the rebellion. Others, more cautious, had always felt friendly to the United States government, or been " inclined toward it " or had been " inclined toward the South but not radical." Still others had thought at the beginning of the war that the South was right but had changed their minds and now wished to see the Union reestablished. Usually, deserters wished to demonstrate their loyalty to the Union by taking

[57] For example, see *Prison Roll, Ft. Warren,* July 13, 1864.

[58] *Prison Rolls, Camp Douglas,* October, December, 1864; February, 1865.

[59] *Prison Rolls, Elmira,* August, September 15, October 31, 1864; *Johnson's Island, undated* (after March, 1864).

[60] One deserter had a little difficulty explaining why on one occasion he had " hollered " for Jeff Davis and Vallandgham and drunk a glass of whiskey to Jeff Davis.—*Ft. Warren,* July 16, 1864.

the oath of amnesty, but occasionally, by fighting for it, especially in the navy. A reason which was sometimes the obverse of loyalty to the Union was lack of interest in the South. The deserters who assigned this reason were men of foreign or Northern nativity. The deserters of foreign nativity were usually French, German and Irish, and those among Alabama troops had been recruited chiefly from Mobile. Deserters of Northern nativity usually had friends or relatives in the North, especially in Kentucky, Ohio, Pennsylvania and New York. They stated that they had "no interests" in the South, by which they seem to have meant business and property investments and social relations. A very few deserters said that they had no negroes, over which the war was being fought. A reason which was closely related to these two was dissatisfaction with the policies of the Confederacy. Many deserters said that they had "had enough of the Confederacy," were "tired of C. S. A." They expressed themselves as "disgusted with their manner of doing things," and as unwilling to fight for "southern despotism." They made objection to the "tyranny of Confederate service," an objection which was probably specifically stated in these two cases: (1) "The colonel was mad at me before I left, said the company was playing off" and (2) "I and the captain fell out. I shot him." [61] However, the dissatisfaction was as a rule very generally stated without details. One did "not like the way they was going on"; another was tired of "the wicked way" they were carrying on this war.[62]

One of the chief reasons assigned by deserters was weariness with the war. Many wished "to be neutral." Some had relatives in both armies. One said that he did not know

[61] *Ft. Warren*, July 14-15 and October 11, 1864; *Johnson's Island*, undated (after March, 1864).

[62] *Ft. Warren*, July 16, 1864; *Camp Douglas*, November 1-16, 1863.

which side was right; another said that he "thought both sides wrong and think so yet." [63] Some wished to go home to be neutral; others wished to go to California, or even to Nicaragua or Ireland to get clear away from the war. Many were "tired of the war," "weary of rebellion." They did not want to fight any more, did not approve of the war. One said that the war was not as successful as he thought it would be and another said that it was too unnatural for him. [64] Many were sure "the South is gone up," "the rebellion has played out," and consequently, saw no use in "standing out" any longer. They wished not only to stop fighting, but "to get out of prison" and "to go home," whenever their homes were within Federal lines. One deserter said that he was willing to submit to anything and do anything within the bounds of reason to go home. [65] However, many of those whose homes were not within Federal lines stipulated that they would not be sent South under any circumstances. [66]

Another reason was economic dependence of their families. Some stated that they had entered the Confederate army in order to get employment; others stated that they deserted it in order to get employment offered by Union authorities. Several, in a petition, praying for their release, declared, "We all have families to care for." [67] One said, "My wife is suffering and I think more of her than I do of the Confederacy." [68]

[63] *Ft. Warren*, July 16, 1864; *Johnson's Island*, undated (after March, 1864).

[64] *Ft. Warren*, July 16, 1864.

[65] *Johnson's Island*, undated (after March, 1864).

[66] *Camp Douglas*, Applications not to be sent South for exchange, November 1-16, 1863.

[67] *Camp Douglas*, Applications to take the oath of allegiance, July 7, 1862 (5 signatures).

[68] *Johnson's Island*, undated (after March, 1864).

In cases where a brief answer was given, the reasons which appeared most frequently were " Conscripted," " Loyal," and " To go home." [69]   In cases where full answers were given a variety of reasons was assigned. The following full answers are typical:

Loyal. Enlisted in Rebel Army through false representation and desires to take oath of Allegiance and become a loyal citizen.

Rather Union in sentiment but the surrounding influence was such that he could not help going into Confederate army. That the reason he deserted was that he got tired and disgusted with the manner in which (they) done things. Never had an opportunity to desert before.

Volunteered October 13, 1861 for 1 yr. Was conscripted at end of time. Native N. Y. but was in Mobile at outbreak and could not get away. Was forced to enlist from mere force of public opinion. His father lives at Rochester. Brother in U. S. navy. Desires to go to his father.[70]

[69] For example, see: *Camp Douglas*, August 9, December, 1864; *Rock Island*, March, 1864; *Camp Morton*, December, 1863; *Elmira*, August 15, 1864. A few prisoners of war from north Alabama said that if they were allowed to go home, they would take the oath; if not, they preferred to be held for exchange. Their cases were considered doubtful. —*Camp Morton*, December, 1863.

[70] *Camp Douglas*, October, 1864 (a deserter from the Twenty-sixth Alabama Regiment) ; *Johnson's Island*, February 1, 1865 (a deserter from the Sixty-third Georgia Regiment) ; *Elmira*, October 31, 1864 (a deserter from the Twenty-first Alabama Regiment). For references for the preceding statement of reasons assigned by deserters for desertion, see *Prison Rolls*, applications to take the oath, *passim*. Some rolls did not state reasons why deserters applied for release, for example, Ft. Delaware, undated. Others stated reasons which told little, for example, Roll of Prisoners of War at Camp Chase who desire to take oath, November, 1863. The following *Prison Rolls* are quoted most frequently: *Alton*, December 4, 1863; June 30, July 15, 1864; *Camp Chase*, August, 1862; December 15, 1863; June 10, September 1-15, October 1-15, October 16-31, November 1-15, November 16-30, December 16-31, 1864; January 1-15, January 16-31, April 1-15, 1865; *Camp Douglas*, June 10, August

The reasons assigned by deserters should be taken *salis cum grano*. No doubt, they were given often without reflection, suggested by the questions of examining officers or the answers of fellow deserters, or by some other chance influence,[71] and false statements were made sometimes with deliberation. No doubt, the reasons assigned were often partial, selected by deserters with a natural desire to justify themselves or to please Union authorities. However, on the whole, the reasons assigned by deserters correspond well to the causes of desertion given by their contemporaries, Confederate and Federal. The chief causes for desertion given by Confederate newspapers were cowardice and foreign and Northern nativity; by private soldiers, cowardice, privations, and despair of winning the war; by officers, hardships due to the scarcity of food and prolonged military service, and especially want in the families of soldiers.[72]

9, July, August 3, 9, September 24, October 27, November, December, 1864; January, February, March, 1865; *Camp Morton*, October, 1862; December 5, 8, 9, 10, 11, 15, 16, 21, 1863; *Elmira*, July, August (Rolls 79, 82, 83, 84); September (Rolls 85-86); October (Rolls 88-89); November (Rolls 91-96), December 16 (Roll 94), 1864; January 31, March 15, 31, April 15, 1865; *Ft. Delaware*, August 30, November 1, 1863; March 6, 15, 1864; *Ft. Warren*, July 13, 14-15, 16, October, 1864; *Rock Island*, March, May, 1864; *Hart's Island*, April, 1865; *Johnson's Island*, November 20, 1863, undated (after March, 1864); January 15, September 15, 30, December 31, 1864; January 16, 1865; *Pt. Lookout*, 1864.

[71] For example, see *Prison Rolls of Camp Douglas*, December, 1864–February, 1865 and *Prison Rolls of Camp Chase*, October–December, 1864.

[72] Mobile *Register*, March 20, 1863; December 19, 1863, quoting the Savannah *Republican*; December 21, 1863, quoting the Savannah *News*; *Clarke County Journal*, October 15, 1863; Richmond *Examiner*, July 8, 1864; Crenshaw Hall to Bolling Hall, February 22, 1865; Crenshaw Hall to Laura Hall, March 12, 1865; W. A. Ramey to Governor Watts, March 20, 1864; *Confederate Veteran*, vol. xxiv, p. 556, John C. Stiles, "The Disintegration of Lee's Army"; Unwritten reminiscences; Colonel J. L. Sheffield (Forty-eighth Alabama) to Governor Watts, April 15, 1864 ("I saw on yesterday 18 grown women, one old man and 7 children crossing the Sand Mt. in the direction of Larkin's Crossing on the

The chief causes for desertion given by the New York *Times* were scarcity of food and clothing and military defeat, and by General Grant, the peace feeling and especially desire for employment.[73]

The reasons for desertion assigned by deserters to Union authorities were based on complete indifference or ignorance of the issues for which they had been fighting and an earnest desire to return to the business and family life of peace times.

Tennessee River for the purpose of going in the enemy's lines. They told me they were going to where they could get *Bread*. Some of them had husbands in our army, the consequence will be that when they get in the enemy's lines—*Desertion* by their Husbands—who will go also into the enemy's lines.") ; Stiles, *Four Years under Marse Robert*, p. 341; Oates, *War between the Union and the Confederacy*, p. 492 (southeast Alabama) ; *O. R.*, ser. i, vol. xlii, pt. iii, p. 1249 (by General Lee, December 1, 1864, privations) ; p. 1179 (by G. W. C. Lee, desertions from "that class which has no interest in our cause"). See also Governor Milton to Secretary Mallory, May 23, 1864.

[73] New York *Times*, November 23, December 20, 1863; July 21, October 14, October 17, November 7, November 19, November 22, November 27, 1864; Grant, *Memoirs*, vol. i, pp. 580-581 (after Vicksburg) ; *O. R.*, ser. i, vol. xlii, pt. iii, p. 842 ("Every day I get letters from rebel deserters who in the absence of employment have enlisted."—December 7, 1864) ; Grant, *Memoirs*, vol. ii, pp. 426-427. ("Then too I knew from the great number of desertions that the men who had fought so bravely, so gallantly and so long for the cause which they believed in as earnestly, I take it, as our men believed in the cause for which they were fighting —had lost hope and become despondent. Many of them were making application to be sent North where they might get employment until the war was over, when they could return to their Southern homes.") See also: R. U. Johnson and C. C. Bull, *Battles and Leaders of the Civil War* (New York, 1884-1887), vol. iv, p. 580, G. L. Kilmer, "Company I, Fourteenth New York Heavy Artillery"; *O. R.*, ser. i, vol. xlviii, pt. ii, p. 207 (by Brigadier-General Powell Clayton).

CHAPTER VIII

Conclusion: Consequences of Desertion

CONFEDERATE leaders considered desertion the chief cause of serious military defeats. In 1862, General Lee reported to the War Department that desertion was the cause of his retreat from Maryland.[1] In 1863, the press suggested that desertion was the cause of the surrender of Vicksburg and the failure at Gettysburg.[2] In 1864, civil and military leaders stated that desertion was the cause of the defeats at Mission Ridge and Chattanooga by which Tennessee was lost and of the fall of Atlanta by which Georgia was lost.[3] Confederate leaders based their statements on the assumption that defeat was due to inferior numbers. " When," asked President Davis, " with anything approaching numer-

[1] *O. R.*, ser. i, vol. xix, pt. ii, pp. 622-623. Colonel James W. Jackson of the Forty-seventh Alabama Regiment wrote to his wife September 21, 1861 that there were double as many stragglers as men in line and expressed the opinion that if the stragglers were in line, " we would be in the heart of the enemy's country in three weeks."

[2] *The Alabama Beacon*, July 31, 1863, quoting the Columbus *Sun*; January 22, 1864, quoting the Savannah *Republican*; Mobile *Register*, January 7, 1864; Montgomery *Weekly Mail*, September, 2, 1863, quoting the Richmond *Whig* (" We should have conquered a peace twelve months ago if our army could have been maintained at anything like the strength on the roll.")

[3] Jacksonville *Republican*, January 9, 1864; Mobile *Register*, December 2, 1863; December 9, 1863 (Senator B. H. Hill said desertion was the only reason Chattanooga was lost) ; January 26, 1864 (" For these creatures was lost the battle of Missionary Ridge."—" One Who has Suffered ") ; Richmond *Examiner*, February 4, 1865. See also *O. R.*, ser. i, vol. xxxii, pt. iii, p. 795. The Richmond *Examiner*, September 11, 1863, said that all the ills of the Confederacy, political, financial and social, both public and private, were caused by imperfect defense which was caused in turn by desertion.

256

ical equality have we failed to be victorious?"[4] In appeals
to absentees to return, he stated that all or half of the absentees would make the Confederate army large enough to
assure victory.[5] The Alabama Assembly and the Confederate Congress made similar statements.[6] They seemed to
have no fear that returned deserters would impair the
morale of the army. Confederate leaders believed not only
that desertion was the cause of defeats and thus prolonged
the war[7] but that it was a potential or actual cause of the
failure of the Confederacy. During the war, General Lee
called desertion " the great evil which threatens our cause,"
and Judge Campbell said of it, " The condition of things
in the mountain districts of Alabama, Georgia and North
Carolina menaces the Confederacy as fatally as the armies
of the enemy."[8] After the war, it was frequently said that
the failure of the Confederacy was due to desertion. A
private in an Alabama command wrote in April, 1865, " It
is a sad thought with me when I think of the many noble
soldiers that has been Slaine and for nothing, or that is the
way I consider it. and who was the cause of it. Skulkers, Cowards, extortioners and Deserters not the Yankees
that makes it worse."[9] Colonel W. H. Stewart called deserters " the assassins of the Confederate States."[10] Gen-

[4] *The Alabama Beacon*, January 22, 1864, quoting the Savannah
Republican.

[5] Richmond *Examiner*, August 7, 1863; *O. R.*, ser. iv, vol. ii, pp. 687-
688; Appleton, *Annual Cyclopedia*, 1863, p. 17; Rowland, *Jefferson Davis,
Constitutionalist*, vol. vi, pp. 341-344, pp. 345-347; Memphis *Daily Appeal*,
October 7, 1864.

[6] *Clarke County Journal*, November 17, 1864; Appleton, *Annual
Cyclopedia*, 1865, p. 195.

[7] *O. R.*, ser. i, vol. xxxix, pt. iii, p. 806.

[8] *O. R.*, ser. i, vol. xxix, pt. ii, p. 650; ser. iv, vol. ii, p. 786.

[9] J. M. J. Tolley (Twenty-fourth Alabama) to Captain James A. Hall.

[10] *Confederate Veteran*, vol. xviii, p. 334, W. H. Stewart, " The True
and the Traitors."

eral Johnston in an enumeration of the causes for the failure of the Confederacy named desertion as the chief cause, saying that during the last ten or twelve months of the war when men with dependent families were obliged to return to their homes, the Confederate armies were so heavily outnumbered that they were defeated.[11]

It is difficult to estimate the importance of desertion as a factor in the failure of the Confederacy. Desertion weakened the man power of the Confederacy. Deserters were withdrawn both from military service at the front and from productive labor at home. Deserters were neither soldiers nor laborers; they were outlaws. To deal with them, a good many men were withdrawn from the army and from civilian employment. Desertion lowered the morale of the people of the Confederacy. As both cause and result of popular depression, desertion moved in a vicious circle of lowered morale, a condition probably more disastrous to the Confederacy than inferiority of numbers.

The causes of desertion were a more far-reaching source of weakness than desertion itself. The causes of desertion were complex and related to many phases of life in the Confederacy, but the chief cause for desertion of Alabama troops, and probably of other troops, was poverty in the families of soldiers. This condition was baffling to Confederate authorities. Although causes for desertion in any war must be related to conditions which exist at that time, it is certain that whenever scarcity of money and men exists in any section, disaffection toward war will follow. Since that was the condition which obtained in north and in southeast Alabama from 1862 to 1865, desertion remained an unsolved problem in the state.

[11] J. E. Johnston, *Narrative*, pp. 423-424.

SELECTED BIBLIOGRAPHY

I. Manuscript Material

A. PRIMARY SOURCES

1. Records of the State Executive Office

The Governor's Letter Book, December 5, 1861–May 12, 1863; May 13, 1863—April 1, 1865.

Letters to Governor A. B. Moore, 1861; to Governor J. G. Shorter, 1862-1863; to Governor T. H. Watts, 1864.

Letters to Governor Watts and H. P. Watson, Adjutant-General, concerning the state militia, 1864.

Proclamation Book A, December 24, 1860 to December 26, 1881 (pp. 2-72, not a complete record).

Register of Applications for Amnesty and Pardon, vol. i, August 5–September 27, 1865, pp. 400; vol. ii, September 27, 1865–July 12, 1866, pp. 197. (Vol. i contains 1197 applications; vol. ii, 1787).

Reports of Commissioners' Courts to the State Comptroller under the Act to provide for the indigent families of soldiers, approved November 11, 1861. Made early in 1862.

Reports of Probate Judges to the Comptroller under the Act to provide for the indigent families of soldiers, approved November 12, 1862. Made January 1, 1863.

Reports of indigent families of soldiers made by the Probate Judges to the Comptroller, April, May, July, August, 1863.

Reports of indigent families of soldiers made by the Probate Judges of the several counties January, May, October, 1864.

Reports from Probate Judges and Sheriffs in response to Governor Shorter's Circular of March 15, 1862 of the number of companies from the counties in Confederate service (37 of the 52 counties reported).

Statements, accounts, vouchers of Duff Green, Quartermaster-general, arranged year by year, 1861-1865, of expense incurred for indigent families.

Telegrams of Governor Shorter, 1861-1862.

Telegrams to Governor Shorter, 1862-1863.

(State Archives, Montgomery, Alabama.)

2. County records

Record book of Blount County, January 6, 1862–April, 1880, pp. 472. Pp. 1-107, 1862-1865, indigent families of soldiers.

County records, Marshall, August, 1859–May, 1864.

Records of Commissioners' Court, Lowndes County, October 2, 1861-July, 1864; August, 1853–November 6, 1865 (contains lists of indigent families for 1862, 1863, 1864).

(State Archives.)

3. Records of the Confederate Executive Office

Endorsements, November 12, 1864 to March 31, 1865, pp. 1-39; Courts-martial, 1861 to 1865, pp. 40-518; Archive Office, chap. i, vol. 199.

Letter Book, Letters sent and received, Department of Mississippi, Alabama and East Louisiana, chap. ii, vol. xiii.

Letter book, Letters received at Headquarters of Polk's Corps.

Proceedings of the Board of Examiners and Report upon the case of Colonel Sam Henry, Ninth Alabama Regiment, respectfully forwarded for the decision of His Excellency the President and attention called to the within order suspending Colonel Henry until the action of the President is made known, February 12, 1863.

Proceedings of courts-martial in cases of a few privates.

(War Department, Adjutant-General's Office, Confederate Section of the Old Records Division, Washington, D. C.)

4. Military records

Adjutant-General of Alabama, 1861-1865, Register of Volunteer Corps.

Letter Book of the Commandant of Conscripts of the State of Alabama (H. C. Lockhart), May 5–October 15, 1864. Pp. 400.

(State Archives.)

Muster rolls, returns, military circulars, and miscellaneous loose manuscripts concerning the Confederate Army, 1861-1865.

(Library of Congress.)

Muster rolls of state guards organized under the Governor's proclamation, 1862-1863 and of militia for local defense, 1864-1865.

Muster rolls, pay rolls, morning reports, recapitulations, and miscellaneous records of various companies belonging to regiments of Alabama infantry 1-61, to a few cavalry and artillery organizations, partisan rangers, and reserves.

Records of Alabama commands from the date of organization to January, 1865, compiled by regimental and company officers under the direction of Colonel Fowler, Superintendent of Army Records for the State of Alabama. They include names of members, date of enlistment, term, birth-place, post-office, residence, age, occupation, and engagements participated in by each member. The records are complete for the Fourth, Ninth, Tenth, Eleventh, Thirteenth, Fifteenth, Forty-third, Forty-fourth, Forty-eighth, and Sixtieth regiments of infantry; and partial for the Eighth, Eighteenth, Forty-sixth, and Forty-seventh regiments of infantry, the First and Fifth battalions of infantry, and the Seventh cavalry. Cited as *Fowler Reports.*

(State Archives.)

Records of prisoners from the Confederate Army. Exit rolls, rolls of prisoners released on oath, rolls of prisoners who desired to take the oath, rolls of enlistments in the United States Army and Navy. Prisons: Alton, Ill., Camp Butler, Camp Chase, Camp Douglas, Chattanooga, Cincinnati, David's Island, Nashville (Dept. of the Cumberland), Elmira, Ft. Columbus, Ft. Delaware, Ft. McHenry, Ft. Monroe, Ft. Warren, Hart's Island, Johnson's Island, Knoxville, Little Rock, Louisville, Knoxville, Memphis, New Orleans, Newport News, Pt. Lookout, Rock Island, Ship Island, Washington, D. C., Wheeling, various Federal Army Corps.

Registers. Army of the Potomac, vol. 81, December 1, 1864–March 11, 1865; Army of the Potomac, Register 74, 1863, vol. 73 and vol. 74; Knoxville, Reg. no. 19; Louisville, Register no. 9 and no. 10, May, June, July, 1863; New Orleans, Register no. 879, April, 1863–April, 1864; Point Lookout, Book no. 6, August, 1863–January, 1864.

Register of Confederate Deserters, Book I, 423 double pages; Book II, labeled, *Record of Deserters Rebel Army, No. 2, 1864.* (Overflow of Book I. Contains names of some prisoners released in other years than 1864.) The Register gives rank, regiment, residence (town or county and state), when and where deserted, when and where released. Arrangement is partly chronological, partly alphabetical, and partly by places where release was granted.

(War Department, Office of the Adjutant General of the United States Army, Old Records Division, Confederate Section, Washington, D. C.)

Roster of Confederate soldiers enlisted in United States Service (card index), U. S. Volunteers.

(War Department, Office of the Adjutant General.)

Record books of companies, or orderly books. Company A, 41st Alabama Infantry, September 7, 1862–December 16, 1864 (Two books contain a record from March, 1862–February 24, 1865), H. H. Sartain, Captain; Company F, 41st Alabama Regiment of Infantry, April 1, 1862–March 25, 1865, B. F. Eddins, Captain; Company G, 41st Alabama Regiment of Infantry, James White, Captain, pp. 244; Company G, 32nd Alabama Regiment of Infantry, Captain R. A. Hardie, pp. 110; Company C, 45th Alabama Regiment of Infantry,

1862-1865, pp. 180; Company E, 60th Alabama Regiment of Infantry, D. A. Clark, Captain, pp. 133.

(State Archives.)

5. *Papers of public men*

Papers of Brigadier-General W. W. Allen.

(State Archives.)

Papers of P. G. T. Beauregard.

Letter Book, November 30, 1864–March 9, 1865, Major Henry Bryan, Assistant Inspector-General of the Military Division of the West.

Letter Book A, Military Division of the West from October 11, 1864 to December 31, 1864.

(Library of Congress.)

Papers of Colonel W. W. Jackson, 47th Alabama Regiment of Infantry.

Letter Book of Colin J. McRae, Agent of the Ordnance Department of Confederate Government, 1862.

(State Archives.)

6. *Letters and diaries*

General Braxton Bragg, Letters to His Wife, 1861-1865. (Photostatic copies of the originals.)

(Library of Congress.)

Captain P. D. Costello, Co. I, 25th Alabama Regiment, Coffee County, Letters to his wife, 1862.

Bolling Hall Manuscripts. Correspondence of Bolling Hall, Sr., of Ellerslie (plantation near Montgomery); Bolling Hall, Jr., Lt-Col., 2nd Battalion Hilliard's Legion; J. Elmore Hall, Capt. Co. B, 59th Alabama; John E. Hall, Lt., Co. E, 2nd Battalion, Hilliard's Legion; James A. Hall, Capt. Co. K, 24th Alabama; Tom B. Hall, Co. M, 6th Alabama; Crenshaw Hall and other members of the Hall family.

Captain Samuel Camp Kelly, Co. E, 30th Alabama Regiment, Letters to his wife, March 19, 1862–April 17, 1865.

Colonel Newton N. Davis, 24th Alabama Infantry, Letters to his wife at Columbus, Miss., June, 1862-January, 1865. (Residence, Pickens Co., Alabama.)

Dr. Phillips Fitzpatrick, Letters to his wife and others, 1862-1864.

E. K. Flournoy, private in Co. H, 46th Alabama, Letters to his wife, Brundidge, Ala., 1863-1864.

(State Archives.)

B. SECONDARY SOURCES

1. Regimental histories

Cannon, J. P., *History of the Twenty-seventh Regiment of Alabama Infantry C. S. A.*

DuBose, John Witherspoon, *Eighth Confederate Cavalry, 1862-1865.*

Miller, George Knox, *History of the Eighth Confederate Cavalry, 1861-1865.*

Oates, William C., *History of the Fifteenth Alabama Infantry Regiment.* (Manuscripts in the Alabama State Archives. Prepared under the direction of Thomas P. Owen, Director.)

2. Special history

Woodbury, E N., *A Study of Desertion.* Morale Branch, War Plans Division, General Staff. August, 1920.

(War Department, Office of the Adjutant-General of the U. S. Army. War Plans Division.)

II. PRINTED MATERIAL

A. PRIMARY SOURCES

1. Public records

Acts of the Thirty-fifth General Assembly of the State of Alabama, held in the city of Montgomery, 1861-1864. (Beginning with acts of the first called session, commencing on the second Monday of January, 1861, and ending with acts of the fourth regular annual session, commencing on the second Monday in November, 1864.) Montgomery, 1861-1865. 5 vols.

Army Regulations, adopted for the use of the Army of the Confederate States in accordance with the late acts of Congress. Revised from the Army Regulations of the United States Army, 1857, retaining all that is essential for officers of the Line, to which is added An Act for the establishment and Organization of the Army of the Confederate States of America. Also Articles of War for the Government of the Army of the Confederate States of America. Atlanta, 1861. Pp. 203. Revised editions for 1862, 1863 and 1864 were published under the title *Regulations for the Army of the Confederate States . . . published by the direction of the President for the government of all concern*ed . . . J. W. Randolph. Richmond, 1862-1864.

Court-martial Orders from Headquarters of the Department of S. C., Ga. and Fla., 1863.

Confederate States of America. Congress:

Memorial of J. S. Harwell and Eugene McCaa, citizens of Alabama serving as volunteer soldiers, protesting against punishment by the lash imposed by courts-martial. Richmond, January 23, 1863. Pp. 2.

Minority Report of the Committee on Military Affairs on the bill to increase the military force of the Confederate States. January 5, 1864. Pp. 5.

Mr. Rogers' Minority Report in relation to Army absentees, deserters, etc. February 15, 1865. P. 1.

Report of the Committee on the Judiciary upon the suspension of the Writ of Habeas Corpus, by Mr. Russell. May 21, 1864. Pp. 10.

Report of the Minority of the Committee on the Judiciary. . . . Pp. 17.

Speech of the Hon. Thos. S. Gholson of Virginia on the policy of employing negro troops and the duty of all classes to aid in the prosecution of the War. Delivered in the House of Representatives of the Congress of the Confederate States on the 1st day of February, 1865. Richmond. Pp. 20.

(Pamphlets in the Library of Congress.)

General Orders from the Adjutant and Inspector-General's Office, Confederate States Army, from January, 1862 to December, 1863 (both inclusive) in two series, prepared from files of Headquarters, Department of South Carolina, Georgia and Florida. With full indexes. Columbia, 1864. Pp. 159 for 1862. Pp. 276 for 1863 and Appendix.

General Orders . . . .from January 1 to June 3, 1864 . . . . by R. C. Gilchrist, Acting-Judge-Advocate General. With full index. Columbia, 1864. Pp. 161.

General Orders from the Army and Department of Tennessee, 1862-1865.

General Orders from the Army and Department of Northern Virginia, 1862-1865.

(Printed loose leaflets filed in the Office of the Adjutant-General, Old Records Division.)

Hill, Benjamin Harvey, *Speech of the Hon. Benj. Harvey Hill, delivered before the Georgia Legislature in Milledgeville, on the evening of the 11th of November, 1862.* Printed by request of members. Milledgeville, January, 1863. Pp. 20.

Journal of the Congress of the Confederate States of America, 1861-1865. Fifty-eighth Congress of the United States, Second Session, Senate Document no. 234. Washington, 1904-1905. 7 vols.

Journal of the Called and Regular Annual Sessions of the Senate and of the House of Representatives of the State of Alabama, held in the city of Montgomery, 1861-1863. Montgomery, 1862-1864. 6 vols.

Military Code of the State of Alabama. Revised and digested with all amendments and additions to the end of the regular session of 1861. By H. P. Brittan, Sec. of State. Montgomery, 1861. Pp. 95.

Minutes of the Fortieth Annual Session of the Alabama Baptist State Convention. Held at Selma, Nov. 7, 8, 9, 10, 1862. Tuskegee, 1862.

Minutes of the Forty-fourth Session of the Alabama Baptist Association held with the Bethany Baptist Church, Lowndes County, from the 9th to the 12th of October, inclusive, 1863. Montgomery, 1863.

Official Army Register of the Volunteer Force of the United States Army for the years 1861, 1862, 1863, 1864, 1865. Published by order of the Secretary of War in compliance with the joint resolution of the Senate and the H. of R. Approved March 2, 1865. Washington, July 16, 1867. Pp. 411.

Official Records of the War of the Rebellion:

    Series I, Vols. 7, 10, 16-20, 23, 25-27, 29-49, 51-53. Military Operations.

    Series II, Vols. 4-8. Prisoners.

    Series III, Vols. 1-5. Union correspondence.

    Series IV, Vols. 1-3. Confederate correspondence. Washington, 1880-1901.

Report of the Comptroller of Public Accounts to the General Assembly of Alabama, 1861-1865. Montgomery, 1861-1866. Pp. 94, 72, 67, 57, 30, 34.

Special Orders of the Adjutant and Inspector-General's Office, Confederate States, 1861. Richmond. Pp. 318 and index, 101.

Special Orders . . . 1863. Pp. 604 and index, 248.

Statistics of the United States in 1860, compiled from the original returns and being the final exhibit of the Eighth Census under the direction of the Secretary of the Interior. Washington, 1866, 4 vols. *Population, Agriculture, Manufacturing, Social Statistics.*

The Statutes at Large of the Provisional Government of the Confederate States of America from the institution of the Government, February 8, 1860 to its termination, February 18, 1862, inclusive, arranged in chronological order together with the constitution etc. Edited by M. Matthews. Richmond, 1864. Pp. 411.

The Statutes at Large of the Confederate States of America, commencing with the first session of the First Congress, 1862, carefully collated with the originals at Richmond (and ending with) *the first session of the Second Congress.* Richmond, 1862-1864. Pp. 306.

2. Newspapers

The Alabama Beacon. Greensboro, Greene County. Weekly. January 10–May, 1864.

    (State Archives.)

Clarke County Democrat (after Nov. 13, 1862, *Clarke County Journal*). Grove Hill. Weekly. March 21, 1861–April 13, 1865.

    (Office of the Probate Judge of Clarke County.)

The Democratic Watchtower. Talladega, Talledega County. Weekly. January–December, 1861; January 13, 1863–December 14, 1864.

The Independent. Gainesville, Sumter County. Weekly. January 5, 1861–November 26, 1864. (Missing, Jan., February, April, 1863.)

Jacksonville *Republican,* Jacksonville, Calhoun County. Weekly. October 17, 1861–March 16, 1865. (Missing, Dec., 1861; all of 1862 except Jan. and June; and Feb., 1865.)

(State Archives.)

Mobile *Advertiser and Register.* Mobile. Daily. January, 1861–May, 1864. (Missing, Dec. 5-20, 1861; July–Aug., 1863; June–Dec., 1864.) Cited as Mobile *Register.*

Mobile *Morning News.* Mobile. Daily. April 27–Dec. 30, 1865.

(Office of the Mobile *Register.*)

Montgomery *Daily Advertiser.* Montgomery. December 5, 1863–October, 1864.

Montgomery *Daily Mail.* Montgomery. October 14, 1862–July 26, 1863; January 2, 1864–June 1, 1865.

Montgomery *Weekly Advertiser.* Montgomery. Jan. 2–Sept. 18, 1861; Oct., 1862–Sept. 27, 1864.

Montgomery *Weekly Mail.* May 10, 1862–April 26, 1864.

(Office of the Montgomery *Advertiser.*)

New York *Herald.* New York. Daily. April 1, 1864–July 29, 1864.

(State Archives.)

New York *Times.* New York. Daily. 1863-1865.

(New York Public Library.)

Richmond *Daily Examiner.* Richmond, January, 1863–March, 1865. Cited as Richmond *Examiner.*

(Library of Congress.)

Selma *Daily Reporter.* Selma, Dallas County. April 4, 1861–December, 1864.

The Southwestern Baptist. Tuskegee, Macon County. Weekly. Jan. 3, 1861–April 13, 1865.

Miscellaneous numbers of:
Charleston (S. C.) *Tri-Weekly Courier.*
Clayton *Banner.*
Dadeville *Banner.*
Daily Dispatch (Richmond).
Memphis (Tenn.) *Daily Appeal.*
Southern Confederacy.
Southern Punch.
The Sunday Mississippian.

(State Archives.)

3. Unofficial collection of documentary material

The American Annual Cyclopedia and Register of Important Events of the year 1861 (1862, 1863, 1864, 1865) embracing political, civil, military, and social affairs; public documents, biography; statistics; commerce, finance, literature, science, agriculture and mechanical industry. D. Appleton and Company. New York, 1865-1868. 5 vols.

Daniel, Lizzie Cary, Confederate Scrap-Book. Richmond, 1893. Pp. 255.

Lee's Dispatches. Unpublished Letters of General Robert Edward Lee, C. S. A. to Jefferson Davis and the War Department of the Confederate States of America, 1862-1865 from the private collection of Wymberley Jones de Renne of Wormsloe, Ga. Edited with an introduction by Douglas Southall Freeman. New York and London, 1915. Pp. 400.

Moore, Frank, editor, Rebellion Record. New York, 1862-1868. 12 vols.

Moore, Frank, editor, The Civil War in Song and Story, 1860-1865. New York, 1889. Pp. 560.

Rowland, Dunbar, editor, Jefferson Davis, Constitutionalist, His Letters, Papers and Speeches, Vol. V (Jan. 10, 1861–Aug. 24, 1863); Vol. VI (Aug. 24, 1863-May 12, 1865). Jackson, 1923.

" Proceedings of the First Confederate Congress, First Session (in part)," Southern Historical Society Papers, new series, vol. vi, pp. 5-206. (Comprises full abstracts of the debates compiled from newspapers, chiefly the Richmond Examiner. Covers the period from Feb. 18, 1861–March 25, 1862.)

" Proceedings of the First Confederate Congress, Second Session through August 30, 1862," Southern Historical Society Papers, new series, vol. vii, pp. 279; " Proceedings of the First Confederate Congress, Second Session through September 26, 1862," ibid., vol. viii.

Smith, William R., The History and Debates of the Convention of the People of Alabama. Begun and held in the city of Montgomery on the 7th day of January, 1861, in which is preserved the speeches of the secret Session and many valuable state Papers. Montgomery, 1861.

Speeches of William L. Yancey, Esq., Senator from the State of Alabama. Made in the Senate of the Confederate States, during the session commencing on the 18th day of August, 1862. Montgomery, 1862. Pp. 54.

4. Diaries, Letters, Speeches

Chestnut, Mary Boykin, A Diary from Dixie. Edited by Isabella D. Martin and Myrta L. Avary. New York, 1905. Pp. 424.

Cumming, Kate, A Journal of Hospital Life in the Confederate Army of Tennessee from the Battle of Shiloh to the end of the War with sketches of Life and Character, and Brief Notices of Current Events during that Period. Louisville and New Orleans, 1866. Pp. 199.

DeLeon, T. Cooper, *Four Years in Rebel Capitals. An Inside View of Life in the Southern Confederacy from Birth to Death. From original notes, collated in the Years 1861 to 1865.* Mobile, 1890. Pp. 376.

Jones, John Beauchamp, *A Rebel War Clerk's Diary at the Confederate States Capital.* Philadelphia, 1866. 2 vols.

Palmer, Benjamin M., D.D. (late of New Orleans), *The Oath of Allegiance to the United States discussed in its moral and political bearings.* Published by the Soldiers' Tract Association, M. E. Church, South. Richmond, 1863. Pp. 22.

5. Travels and histories by contemporaries

Abrams, A. S., *President Davis and his administration, being a review of the "Rival Administrations," lately published in Richmond, and written by E. A. Pollard, author of the "First and Second Years of the War."* Atlanta, 1864. Pp. 20.

Freemantle, Sir Arthur James Lyon (Lieutenant-Colonel of the Coldstream Guards), *Three Months in the Southern States.* April–June, 1863. New York, 1864. Pp. 309.

Gilchrist, R. C. (captain and acting-judge-advocate general, Department of South Carolina, Georgia and Florida), *The duties of a Judge-Advocate in a trial before a general court-martial. Compiled from various works on military law. Published with the approbation of the Secretary of War.* Columbia, S. C., 1864. Pp. 47.

Lee, C. H., *The Judge-Advocate's Vade Mecum, embracing a general view of military law and the practice before courts-martial of the Army and the Navy, with an epitome of the law of evidence as applicable to military and naval trials.* Richmond, 1864. Pp. 251.

(Stevenson, William G.), *Thirteen Months in the Rebel Army, being a narrative of personal adventures in the infantry, ordnance, cavalry, courier, and hospital services, with an exhibition of the power, purposes, earnestness, military despotism and demoralization of the South by An Impressed New Yorker.* New York, 1864. Pp. 232.

Tansill, Robert (Colonel of the late Confederate States Army), *A free and impartial exhibition of the causes which led to the failure of the Confederate States to establish their independence.* Washington, 1865. Pp. 24.

Tharin, R. S., *Arbitrary arrests in the South, or scenes from the experience of an Alabama Unionist.* New York, 1863. Pp. 245.

Pollard, Edward A., *A Southern History of the War in Two Volumes.* New York, 1866.

———— ————, *The Lost Cause, A New Southern History of the War of the Confederates comprising a full and authentic account of the rise and progress of the late Southern Confederacy—the cam-*

paigns, battles, incidents, and adventures of the most gigantic struggle of the world's history—drawn from original sources, and approved by the most distinguished Confederate Leaders. New York, 1867. Pp. 762.

6. Memoirs

Barbiere, Joe (Lt-Col. in C. S. A.), *Scraps from the Prison Table at Camp Chase and Johnson's Island.* Doylestown, Pa., 1868. Pp. 397.

Beers, Mrs. Fannie A., *Memories. A Record of Personal Experiences and Adventures during four years of war.* Philadelphia, 1891. Pp. 336.

Cannon, J. P. (M. D., late of the 27th Alabama), *Inside of Rebeldom; the daily life of a private in the Confederate Army.* Washington, 1900. Pp. 288.

Campbell, John A., *Reminiscences and documents relating to the Civil War during the year 1865.* Edited by Peter Hamilton. Baltimore, 1887. Pp. 68.

Clayton, Mrs. Victoria V., *White and Black under the Old Regieme.* Milwaukee and London, 1899. Pp. 195.

Curry, J. L. M, *Civil History of the Government of the Confederate States with some personal reminiscences.* Richmond, 1901. Pp. 318.

Eggleston, George Cary, *A Rebel's Recollections.* New York, 1874. Pp. 260.

Ford, Arthur P., *Life in the Confederate Army, being some personal experiences of a private soldier in the Confederate Army by Arthur P. Ford and Marion Johnstone Ford.* New York and Washington, 1905. Pp. 136.

Goodloe, Albert T. (First lieutenant of Company D, 35th Alabama, *Confederate Echoes. A Voice from the South in the Days of Secession and of the Southern Confederacy.* (Based on a diary kept during the war.) Nashville, 1907. Pp. 452.

Gordon, John B., *Reminiscences of the Civil War.* New York, 1903. Pp. 465.

Grant, Ulysses S., *Personal Memoirs of U. S. Grant.* New York, 1885-1886. 2 vols.

Hagood, Johnson, *Memoirs of the War of Secession. From the original Manuscripts of Johnson Hagood, Brigadier-General C. S A.* Edited by U. R. Brooks. Columbia, S. C., 1910. Pp. 496.

Hague, Parthenia Antoinette, *A Blockaded Family. Life in Southern Alabama during the Civil War.* Boston and New York, 1888. Pp. 176.

Hood, John Bell, *Advance and Retreat, Personal Experiences in the United States and Confederate States Armies.* New Orleans, 1880. Pp. 358.

Johnston, Joseph E., *Narrative of Military Operations directed during the late war between the States by Joseph E. Johnston.* New York, 1874. Pp. 602.

McClendon, W. C. (Henry Pioneers, 15th Alabama), *Recollections of War Times by an Old Veteran while under Stonewall Jackson and Lt.-Gen. James Longstreet. How I got in and how I got out.* Montgomery, 1909. Pp. 238.

Mosby, John S., *Mosby's War Reminiscences; Stuart's Cavalry Campaigns.* New York, 1898. Pp. 256.

Oates, William C. (Colonel of the 15th Ala.), *The War between the Union and the Confederacy and its lost opportunities with a history of the Fifteenth Alabama Regiment and the forty-eight battles in which it was engaged, being an account of the author's war experiences in the greatest conflict of modern times.* New York and Washington, 1905. Pp. 808.

Pember, Phoebe Yates (Superintendent of a hospital in Richmond), *A Southern Woman's Story.* New York and London, 1899. Pp. 192.

Pickett, LaSalle Corbell, *Pickett and his men.* 2nd ed. Atlanta, 1900. Pp. 429.

Doctor Quintard, Chaplain C. S. A. and second Bishop of Tennessee, being his story of the War, 1861-1865, edited and extended by the Rev. Arthur Howard Noll. Sewanee, 1905. Pp. 183.

Reagan, John H., *Memoirs with special reference to secession and the Civil War.* New York and Washington, 1906. Pp. 351.

Stiles, Robert (Major of Artillery in Army of Northern Virginia), *Four Years under Marse Robert.* New York and Washington, 1903. Pp. 368.

" Our Women in the War. The lives they lived; the deaths they died," —from the *Weekly News and Courier,* Charleston, S. C. Charleston, 1885. Pp. 482.

Underwood, J. L., editor, *The Women of the Confederacy. In which is presented the heroism of the women of the Confederacy with accounts of their trials during the war and the period of Reconstruction, with the ultimate triumph over adversity. Their motives and their achievements as told by writers and orators now preserved in permanent form by Rev. J. L. Underwood.* New York and Washington, 1906. Pp. 313.

B. SECONDARY SOURCES

1. General histories

Channing, Edward, *A History of the United States.* Vol. VI, *The War for Southern Independence.* New York, 1925. Pp. 645.

Dodd, William E., *The Cotton Kingdom.* New Haven, 1921. Pp. 161.

Eggleston, George Cary, *The History of the Confederate War. Its*

Causes and Its Conduct. A narrative and Critical History. Vol. II. New York, 1910. Pp. 369.

Johnson, Robert Underwood, and Bull, Clarence Clough, editors, *Battles and Leaders of the Civil War, being for the most part contributions by Union and Confederate Officers based upon " The Century War Series."* New York, 1884-1887. 4 vols.

Rhodes, James Ford, *History of the United States from the Compromise of 1850 to the McKinley Bryan Campaign of 1896.* Vol. IV. 1862-1864. Vol. V. 1864-1865. New York, 1920-1928.

Stephenson, N. W., *The Day of the Confederacy.* New Haven, 1920. Pp. 214.

2. Local and special histories

Brewer, Willis, *Alabama, her history, resources, war record, and public men from 1850 to 1870.* Montgomery, 1872. Pp. 712.

Fleming, Walter Lynwood, *Civil War and Reconstruction in Alabama.* Cleveland, 1911. Pp. 815.

Hodgson, Joseph, *The Cradle of the Confederacy or the Times of Troup, Quitman and Yancey. A Sketch of Southwestern Political History from the Formation of the Federal Government to A. D. 1861.* Mobile, 1876. Pp. 528.

Gildersleeve, Basil L., *The Creed of the Old South, 1865-1915.* Baltimore, 1915. Pp. 126.

Jack, Theodore Henly, *Sectionalism and Party Politics in Alabama from 1819-1842.* Wenasha, Wis., 1919. Pp. 93.

Livermore, Thomas Leonard, *Numbers and Losses in the Civil War in America, 1861-1865.* Boston and New York, 1901. Pp. 150.

Lonn, Ella, *Desertion during the Civil War.* New York and London, 1928. Pp. 251.

Miller, L. D., *History of Alabama Adapted to the Use of Schools and for General Reading.* Birmingham, 1901. Pp. 409.

Moore, Albert Burton, *Conscription and Conflict in the Confederacy.* New York, 1924. Pp. 367.

Saunders, James Edmonds, *Early Settlers of Alabama, with notes and genealogies by his granddaughter, Elizabeth Saunders Blair Stubbs.* New Orleans, 1899. Pp. 530.

Kilpatrick, Emmett, *The Political History of Alabama during the War of Secession.* Paris, 1924. Pp. 161.

Wise, Jennings Cropper, *The Long Arm of Lee or the History of the Artillery of the Army of Northern Virginia with a brief account of the Confederate Bureau of Ordnance.* Vol. II. Lynchburg, Va., 1915. Pp. 995.

Regiments:

Jones, E. W., " History of the Eighteenth Alabama Infantry Regiment," *Jones Valley Times,* 1906. (Member of Co. G.)

McMorries, Edward Young, *History of the First Regiment of Alabama Volunteer Infantry,* C. S. A. State of Alabama, Department of Archives and History. Bulletin No. 2. Montgomery, 1904. Pp. 142.

Park, Robert Emory, *Sketch of the Twelfth Alabama Infantry of Battle's Brigade, Rhode's Division, Early's Corps, of the Army of Northern Virginia.* Reprinted from the *Southern Historical Society Papers,* vol. xxxiii. Richmond. (Captain of Co. F.)

Powell, R. H., "Third Alabama Infantry. Reminiscences of Army Life, Camp Scenes and Personal Sketches," Union Springs *Times,* March 14, 1866–April 10, 1877.

3. Biography

Bruce, Philip Alexander, *Robert E. Lee.* Philadelphia, 1907. Pp. 380.

Eckenrode, H. J., *Jefferson Davis, president of the South.* New York, 1923. Pp. 371.

Henderson, G. F. R., *Stonewall Jackson and the American Civil War, with an introduction by Field-Marshal, Right Honorable Viscount Wolsey, K. P., G. C. B., G. C. M. G., etc.* New York and Bombay, 1906. Vol. i, pp. 447; vol. ii, pp. 528.

Polk, William, *Leonidas Polk, Bishop and General.* Boston, 1915. 2 vols.

Pollard, Edward A., *Life of Jefferson Davis with a Secret History of the Southern Confederacy, gathered " Behind the Scenes" in Richmond, containing curious and extraordinary information of the principal southern characters in the late war, in connection with President Davis, and in relation to the various intrigues of this administration.* Philadelphia: Chicago: St. Louis: Atlanta, 1869. Pp. 536.

Taylor, Walter H., *Four Years with General Lee, being a summary of the more important events touching the career of General Robert E. Lee in the War between the States together with an authoritative statement of the strength of the army which he commanded in the field.* (Late Adjutant-General of the Army of Northern Virginia, of Lee's staff.) New York, 1878. Pp. 199.

DuBose, John Witherspoon, *The Life and Times of William Lowndes Yancey, A History of the Political Parties in the United States from 1834 to 1864; especially as to the origin of the Confederate States.* Birmingham, 1892. Pp. 752.

4. Periodicals

Andrews, W. L., "Early History of Southeast Alabama," *Ozark Southern Star,* May 3, 1899.

Bradwell, I. G., "Last Days of the Confederacy," *Confederate Veteran,* vol. xxix, pp. 56-58.

——, "Memories of 1860," *Confederate Veteran,* vol. xxxi, p. 382.

——, "Life in the Confederate Army," *Confederate Veteran*, vol. xxiv, pp. 20-25.

Brooks, R. P., "Conscription in the Confederate States of America, 1862-1865," *Bulletin of the University of Georgia*, March, 1917. Reprinted from the *Military Historian and Economist*, vol. i, no. 4, Harvard University Press, pp. 419-442.

"Carolina South," "In the 'Back Country' of South Carolina, 1862-1864," *Magazine of History*, vol. ix, pp. 33-44.

Cheney, H. J., "Reminiscences of War Incidents," *Confederate Veteran*, vol. xviii, pp. 517-519.

——, "Penalties for desertion," *Confederate Veteran*, vol. ii, p. 235.

Dodge, David, "Cave Dwellers of the Confederacy," *Atlantic Monthly*, vol. lxviii, pp. 514-521.

Fleming, Walter L., "The Peace Movement in Alabama during the Civil War," part I, "Party Politics, 1861-1864," *The South Atlantic Quarterly*, vol. ii, pp. 114-124, 246-260; part II, "The Peace Society, 1863-1865," *ibid.*, pp. 246-260.

Fisher, Clyde Olin, "The relief of soldiers' families in North Carolina during the Civil War," *South Atlantic Quarterly*, vol. xvi, pp. 60-72.

Foote, Frank H., "Recollections of Army Life with General Lee," *Southern Historical Society Papers*, vol. xxxi, pp. 237-247.

Gipson, Lawrence Henry, "The collapse of the Confederacy," *Mississippi Valley Historical Review*, vol. iv, pp. 437-458.

Hite, Cornelius Baldwin, "The Confederate Army," *Confederate Veteran*, vol. xxi, pp. 221-222.

Jones, Thomas G., "Last Days of the Army of Northern Virginia." An address delivered before the Virginia Division of the Association of the Army of Northern Virginia at the Annual Meeting, Richmond, Va. October 12, 1893. *Southern Historical Society Papers*, vol. xxi, pp. 57-103.

Love, Wm. A., "Reminiscences of the closing days of the War of Secession," *Mississippi Historical Society Publications*. Centenary series, vol. iv, pp. 258-267.

M'Neilly, J. H., editor, "Last Days of the Confederacy. Letters from Jefferson Davis during that period," *Confederate Veteran*, vol. ii, pp. 71-72.

McKim, Randolph Harrison, "Glimpses of the Confederate Army," *Review of Reviews*, vol. xliii, pp. 431-437.

Owsley, Frank L., "Defeatism in the Confederacy." Reprinted from the *North Carolina Historical Review*, July, 1926, pp. 13.

Pressley, John G. (Lt.-Col.), "Diary," *Southern Historical Society Papers*, vol. xiv, pp. 35-62.

Ridley, B. L., "Camp Scenes around Dalton," *Confederate Veteran*, vol. x, pp. 66-68.

Sellers, J. L., " Economic incidence of the Civil War in the South," *Mississippi Valley Historical Review,* vol. xiv, pp. 179-191.

Simmons, J. W., " Conscripting Atlanta Theatre in 1863," *Confederate Veteran,* vol. xi, p. 279.

——, " Sad realities of war," *Confederate Veteran,* Feb., 1901, pp. 86.

Stewart, W. H. (Col.), " The True and the Traitors." Address at the Mobile Reunion to the ladies and gentlemen of the United Confederate Choirs of America. *Confederate Veteran,* vol. xviii, pp. 332-333.

Stiles, John C., " The Disintegration of Lee's Army," *Confederate Veteran,* December, 1916, p. 556.

Woodbury, E. N., " Causes for military desertion; a study in criminal motive," *Journal of Criminal Law and Criminology,* vol. xii, pp. 213-222.

5. *Fiction*

Clemens, Jeremiah, *Tobias Wilson, a tale of the Great Rebellion.* Philadelphia, 1865. Pp. 328.

DeLeon, T. Cooper, *John Holden, Unionist. A Romance of the Days of Forrest's Ride with Emma Sansom.* New York, 1910. Pp. 338.

Herrington, W. D., *The Deserter's Daughter.* Southern Field and Fireside Novelette, no. 3, New Series. Raleigh, 1867. Pp. 27.

Peck, Samuel Mintern, *Alabama Sketches.* Chicago, 1902. Pp. 299.

INDEX